The Impact of Information Technology Governance on Business Performance

INFORMATIONSTECHNOLOGIE UND ÖKONOMIE

Herausgegeben von Christian Becker, Wolfgang Gaul, Armin Heinzl, Alexander Mädche und Martin Schader

Band 49

PL ACADEMIC RESEARCH

Miroslav Lazic

The Impact of Information Technology Governance on Business Performance

PL ACADEMIC RESEARCH

Bibliographic Information published by the Deutsche Nationalbibliothek
The Deutsche Nationalbibliothek lists this publication in the Deutsche Nationalbibliografie; detailed bibliographic data is available in the internet at http://dnb.d-nb.de.

Zugl.: Mannheim, Univ., Diss., 2012

Library of Congress Cataloging-in-Publication Data

Lazic, Miroslav, 1984-
The impact of information technology governance on business performance / Miroslav Lazic.
pages cm. — (Informationstechnologie und Ökonomie ; Band 49)
ISBN 978-3-631-62721-1
1. Information technology—Management. I. Title.
HD30.2.L398 2013
338'.064—dc23

2013006370

D 180
ISSN 1616-086X
ISBN 978-3-631-62721-1

PL Academic Research is an Imprint of Peter Lang GmbH.

Peter Lang – Frankfurt am Main · Berlin · Bruxelles · New York · Oxford · Warszawa · Wien

www.peterlang.de

Foreword

For a considerable amount of time, research and academia have been aiming at understanding and designing the organisational framework for the provision and usage of corporate information technology (IT). Against this background, IT governance (ITG) has become a central issue, as it determines the framework for decision rights and accountabilities in the use of IT.

The discussion of a contingent organisational framework for the deployment of corporate IT is not novel, with literature on this topic dating back to the 1960s. However, the enactment of the Sarbanes-Oxley Act and comparable legal regulations in other countries revived the question of responsibilities and accountabilities in relation to the provision and usage of information and related technologies. Regarding the design of a corporation's ITG, three major stakeholders have to be brought in line: top-management, which is primarily focused on efficiency goals, line management of the singular business units, aiming at effectivity goals and the IT management itself, being responsible for the provision and operation of the required IT infrastructure. Corporate IT can only be applied to its best use if the accountabilities and decision rights of these groups of stakeholders are clearly defined and well aligned. Publicly traded corporations that are not able to present a documented ITG framework run the risk of not passing annual audits, or passing only with additional requirements.

As a result, a number of organisations and associations initiated the development of so called ITG frameworks. These are aiming at structuring corporate IT tasks in order to allow for a distribution of decision rights among the respective stakeholders. In extraordinary cases, like e.g. the breakdown of an outsourcing provider, an ITG matrix would also be applied to clarify accountabilities. The threat of a personal liability for potential outages should provide incentives for the responsible managers to pursue their respective tasks proactively in order to deter possible damage of the corporation. Alongside with rising awareness among all managerial levels of a corporation, the altered legal framework has set the topic of ITG on the agenda of supervisory boards as well.

Meanwhile, a large body of scholarly literature on ITG has emerged. However, the majority of the published academic work is focused on distinguishing different forms of ITG, or empirically examining which type of ITG is most appropriate depending on the internal and external context of an organization. In doing so, these studies have strongly contributed to both, theory and practice. However, almost none of them enriches the theoretical understanding of the relationship between ITG and business performance and its causality. Yet, this question is vital for both, theory and practice because only if the theoretical link between ITG and business performance is fully revealed, research can confidently make suggestions on how to design and implement ITG.

Miroslav Lazic's dissertation has addressed this important and exciting research gap. It is among the first studies that are able to provide answers to the question of how ITG influences business performance. Doing so, this work makes several contributions to extant literature. Above all, the study adds to the broad body of knowledge on ITG by improving our theoretical understanding of the causal relationship between ITG and business performance. Moreover, the findings shed light on the interacting effects of complementarity and the diverging antecedents of sub-additive and super-additive value synergies. By applying and enhancing reference theories in the case of ITG, the study contributes, in addition, to theory development in adjacent disciplines, such as organisational theory and strategic management.

Translating the theoretical findings into to managerial guidelines, the results of this study provide decision makers with substantial insights on how to design and implement ITG. The outcomes not only shed light on the question of how to improve business performance with IT through efficiency gains but also of how to add value in terms of super-additive synergies that potentially result in sustainable competitive advantages. Altogether, Miroslav Lazic's dissertation is remarkable in terms of its contribution to theory and practice.

The study was part of a research project with Protiviti Germany and conducted in close cooperation with major German blue-chip corporations.

The book targets both practitioners and researchers. Managers obtain valuable knowledge on the impact of IT governance. In particular, managers are offered a clear guiding frame for planning and implementing ITG initiatives with insights on the effects and value contributions that can be expected from actively designed ITG. Academic readers are offered a systematic and profound contribution on IT governance and its impact as well as on theory building in the Information Systems discipline and beyond.

Mannheim, October 2012 Armin Heinzl

Acknowledgements

Looking back at the past three and a half years, working on my doctoral thesis was an exceptionally enriching and challenging experience. Without the support of the many individuals to whom I would like to express my deepest gratitude, I would not have been able to complete this work in comparable quality or time.

Above all, I would like to thank my supervisor Professor Dr. Armin Heinzl for the opportunity to do research in Information Systems at the University of Mannheim. Professor Heinzl not only was a great advisor in terms of research, but also he offered me support in any situation during my time at his chair. He gave me the freedom to pursue my ideas and do research on the topics I enjoyed. At the same time he ensured quality, guided my research efforts and encouraged me to present our work internationally.

With Paul Meyer and Thomas Kude I was fortunate to have two great friends as research colleagues. Discussing our ideas and reflecting on each other's work was always very motivating and valuable for my research. Working with and learning from Paul and Thomas was a great pleasure. I am very thankful for their support.

I would like to thank Professor Dr. Leslie Willcocks and Professor Dr. Jannis Kallinikos for inviting me to a research stay at the London School of Economics and Political Science. While working in London, I had the chance to gain new insights and see my own work from a new perspective. The conversations with Jannis, the PhD students and all members of the ISIG were extremely valuable to me. The warm welcome and the tremendous support of the entire department added up to a great and memorable time at LSE.

Moreover, I would like to thank Professor Dr. Dr. h.c. mult. Alfred Kieser, Professor Dr. Walter A. Oechsler, Professor Dr. Hans Peter Grüner, as well as Professor Dr. Alexander Mädche for serving as members of my committee.

This work is built upon a rich set of data which I was able to gather from numerous industry experts in insightful and inspiring conversations. I very much appreciated their time and effort. Furthermore, I would like to acknowledge the contribution of Martin Groth and Michael Klinger, who supported my research project and served as valuable discussion partners.

I would like to express my gratitude to Olivia Walker for the ongoing support during the process of writing my research articles. Also, I would like to thank Alexander Neff for his help in collecting data. Moreover, I would like to thank our administrative staff Luise Bühler and Ingrid Distelrath, as well as the student assistants Nina Jaeger, Melanie Marnet, Olga Oster, Lea Offermann, Santana Overath, and Bernd Folberth for their support.

My colleagues at the Chair of General Management and Information Systems are among the main reasons that I look back at wonderful years. Working and sharing my time with Sven Scheibmayr, Erik Hemmer, Lars Klimpke, Sebastian Stuckenberg, Tommi Kramer, Kai Spohrer, Marko Nöhren, Christoph Schmidt, Alexander Scheerer, and Tillmann Neben was professionally and personally very valuable and enriching for me. Therefore, I would like to express my sincere appreciation to them.

I would like to thank former colleagues and previous graduates from our chair, Thomas Butter, Jens Arndt, Michael Geisser, Jessica Winkler, Sina Deibert, Tobias Hildenbrandt, and Boris Quaing. In particular, I would like to thank Professor Dr. Jens Dibbern for his valuable comments on my research and his support in the course of my research semester abroad.

Finally, I wish to thank my closest friends and family for their unconditional support in the past years. My deepest gratitude goes to my partner Isabel, my sister Sandra, my dad Sretko, and my mum Vera.

Mannheim, October 2012 Miroslav Lazic

Contents

List of Figures xv

List of Tables xvii

List of Abbreviations xix

1. Introduction 1
   1.1 Problem Statement 1
   1.2 Research Objective 2
   1.3 Research Design 4
   1.4 Study Organisation 4

2. Theoretical Foundations 7
   2.1 Information Technology 7
      2.1.1 Terminology 7
      2.1.2 The Emergence and Management of Corporate IT 9
   2.2 IT and Business Performance 11
      2.2.1 The Notion of Value 11
      2.2.2 The Resource-Based View as a Theoretical Lens 12
      2.2.3 Extensions of the Resource-Based View 18
      2.2.4 IT Business Value 21
      2.2.5 Business Performance 31
      2.2.6 Summary 33
   2.3 Previous Work on IT Governance 34
      2.3.1 Corporate Governance 34
      2.3.2 Defining IT Governance 41
      2.3.3 IT Governance Structures 48
      2.3.4 IT Governance Contingency Analyses 50
      2.3.5 Contemporary IT Governance Frameworks 55
      2.3.6 IT Governance Impact Analyses 64
      2.3.7 Summary 66
   2.4 Preliminary Research Framework 66

3. Research Design ... 69
3.1 Ontological and Epistemological Stance ... 69
3.2 Research Strategy ... 71
3.3 Case Study Design ... 73
3.4 Case Sampling Procedure ... 75
3.5 Data Collection and Analysis ... 77
3.6 Summary ... 79

4. Empirical Exploration and Theory Building ... 81
4.1 Data Selection and Analysis ... 81
4.2 Proposed Explanatory Model ... 84
4.3 The Impact of IT Governance ... 86
4.3.1 Infrastructure and Applications ... 87
4.3.2 Business Processes ... 99
4.4 Performance Effects of Relatedness ... 112
4.4.1 IT Relatedness ... 113
4.4.2 Business Process Relatedness ... 117
4.4.3 Interacting Effects between IT Relatedness and Business Process Relatedness ... 121
4.5 Moderating Effect of Absorptive Capacity ... 124
4.6 Summary ... 127

5. Empirical Substantiation and Theory Corroboration ... 129
5.1 Data Selection and Analysis ... 129
5.2 Single-Case Analysis ... 133
5.2.1 OMEGA ... 133
5.2.2 PSI ... 134
5.2.3 CHI ... 136
5.2.4 PHI ... 138
5.2.5 YPSILON ... 139
5.2.6 TAU ... 140
5.2.7 SIGMA ... 142
5.2.8 RHO ... 144
5.2.9 PI ... 145
5.2.10 OMIKRON ... 146
5.2.11 Summary ... 148

5.3 Cross-Case Analysis 148
5.3.1 The Impact of IT Governance 148
5.3.2 Performance Effects of Relatedness 153
5.3.3 Interacting Effects between IT Relatedness and Business Process Relatedness 158
5.3.4 Moderating Role of Absorptive Capacity 159
5.3.5 Summary 161

6. Discussion of Findings 163
6.1 Theoretical Implications 164
6.2 Managerial Implications 171
6.3 Limitations and Future Research 174

7. Summary and Conclusion 179

Appendix 181
1. Attributes Used to Assess the Case Studies 181
2. Interview Guidelines 185
2.1 Exploratory Phase 185
2.2 Corroborative Phase 186
3. Coding Scheme for the Corroborative Phase 187
4. Assessment of Constructs for the Corroborative Phase 191
4.1 OMEGA 191
4.2 PSI 194
4.3 CHI 197
4.4 PHI 200
4.5 YPSILON 204
4.6 TAU 208
4.7 SIGMA 212
4.8 RHO 216
4.9 PI 218
4.10 OMIKRON 221

Bibliography 225

List of Figures

Figure 1: Research framework 3
Figure 2: IT business value model (Melville et al. 2004) 23
Figure 3: IT governance and management as illustrated by Peterson (2004b) 42
Figure 4: Streams of IT governance research 47
Figure 5: IT decision making patterns of firms (adapted from Weill 2004, p. 8) 58
Figure 6: Preliminary research framework 68
Figure 7: Explanatory model of the impact of IT governance on the business performance of a firm 85
Figure 8: Assessment of IT governance maturity and IT relatedness 149
Figure 9: Assessment of IT governance maturity and business process relatedness 151
Figure 10: Assessment of IT relatedness and business process relatedness 153
Figure 11: Assessment of IT relatedness and business performance impact 155
Figure 12: Assessment of business process relatedness and business performance impact 157
Figure 13: Revised model of the impact of IT governance on the business performance of a firm 162

List of Tables

Table 1: Relationship between ITG and CG (adapted from Van Grembergen et al. 2004) 41
Table 2: Prominent IT governance definitions 45
Table 3: IT governance capabilities (Peterson 2004b, p. 12) 60
Table 4: Conceptualisation of basic constructs 68
Table 5: Relevant dimensions for the selection of a research strategy (Yin 2009, p. 8) 72
Table 6: Case sample of the exploratory phase 82
Table 7: Interview partners in the exploratory phase 83
Table 8: Definition of employed constructs 86
Table 9: Case sample of the corroborative phase 130
Table 10: Interview partners in the corroborative phase 131
Table 11: Identified constructs and exemplary indicators 132

List of Abbreviations

AC	Absorptive capacity
BITA	Business/ IT alignment
BS	British standard
BU	Business unit
CEO	Chief Executive Officer
CFO	Chief Financial Officer
CG	Corporate governance
CIO	Chief Information Officer
CMS	Content management system
COBIT	Control Objectives for Information and Related Technology
COSO	Committee of Sponsoring Organizations of the Treadway Commission
CRM	Customer relationship management
DP	Data processing
EDI	Electronic data interchange
ERP	Enterprise resource planning
EUC	End-user computing
HIR	Human IT resource
HR	Human resources
IS	Information system
ISO	International Organization for Standardization
IT	Information technology
ITBV	IT business value

ITG	IT governance
ITIL	IT Infrastructure Library
KBV	Knowledge-based view
MIS	Management information systems
OEM	Original equipment manufacturer
PAT	Principal-agent theory
RBV	Resource-based view
SIS	Strategic information systems
SISP	Strategic information systems planning
SLA	Service level agreement
SOX	Sarbanes-Oxley Act
SRM	Supplier relationship management
TCO	Total cost of ownership
TIR	Technical IT resource
US	United States of America

1. Introduction

1.1 Problem Statement

The fundamental importance of information technology (IT) in today's business operations can hardly be refuted. Following a recent article in the Wall Street Journal, 87% of business leaders believe that information technology is critical to strategic success (Chen 2010; Worthen 2007). In a consequence, IT spending is constantly rising, with IT costs in average representing more than 4% of revenue within corporations, which is a significant fraction of the total expenditures (Gartner 2011). Gartner (2012) further expects that worldwide IT spending will exceed $3.6 trillion in 2012, which accounts for a 3% increase from 2011, where an increase of 7.9% was observed.

The pervasive and growing willingness to invest excessive amounts in information technology eventually demonstrates that IT has become crucial for the support, sustainability and growth of businesses (De Haes and Van Grembergen 2009). Therefore, a strong focus on the governance of IT and its related resources, called *IT governance* (ITG), is inevitable. Regarding empirical studies which posit that *"above-average IT governance"* (Weill 2004, p. 1) can account for more than 20% higher profitability, actively designed and documented ITG is critical.

Consequently, IT governance is increasingly attracting attention in practice and research (De Haes and Van Grembergen 2009). Boosted by the passage of the Sarbanes-Oxley Act (SOX) in 2002, many organisations started with an implementation of ITG, but academic research within this area is still in an early stage.

Nowadays, a diverse range of topics is collected under the umbrella term ITG, such as strategic alignment, control and accountability, delivery of business value through IT, performance management or risk management, with some of these research streams going back to the 1960s, as shown by Brown and Grant (2005). Bearing this wide field in mind, it is not surprising that several definitions and conceptualisations of the term IT governance are in use; hence, it is crucial to define the concept more precisely.

Within this study, IT governance is regarded in line with Weill (2004, p. 3) as *"the framework for decision rights and accountabilities to encourage desirable behavior in the use of IT"*. Following Brown and Grant (2005), this is the most contemporary concept of IT governance. Van Grembergen et al. (2004) describe ITG as being embedded within several layers of the firm, from board level to operational IT. However, according to Peterson (2004b), a clear distinction between ITG, which is based at the top-management level, and IT management, which is concerned with decisions on the operational level, is crucial.

This is very much in line with Weill (2004, p. 2 f.): *"IT governance is not about what specific decisions are made. That is management. [...] Good IT governance draws on corporate governance principles to manage and use IT to achieve corporate performance goals"*, as well as the definition by the ITGI (2003, p. 10): *"IT governance is the responsibility of the board of directors and executive management. It is an integral part of enterprise governance and consists of the leadership and organisational structures and processes that ensure that the organisation's IT sustains and extends the organisation's strategies and objectives."*

Although contemporary literature acknowledges that good IT governance has a positive impact on the performance of a firm, the outcomes and models developed in preceding research endeavours on ITG are descriptive and prescriptive, while mostly lacking a theoretical foundation (De Haes and Van Grembergen 2009). In other words, the available literature shows empirically that ITG can create value and offers recommendations on how to establish good IT governance, but there is to date no explanation of how the assumed value is exactly created. Theoretical models explicitly dealing with ITG are generally scarcely available (De Haes and Van Grembergen 2009). Recent exceptions, like e.g. Liang et al. (2011), consider ITG mainly in relation to business/ IT alignment (BITA), which in turn is understood in relation to business performance. Although this is an important first step, it is still unsatisfying as many questions are left unanswered, as shown in this study.

To sum up, despite the diverse body of literature on ITG, a theoretically grounded explanation of the positive impact of IT governance on business performance is not available today.

1.2 Research Objective

In face of this significant lack of research, this project attempts to open the black box of the relationship between IT governance and business performance, which leads to the first research question:

- *How are IT governance and business performance related?*

As this research project aims at building a mid-range theory that not only analyses but that as well explains (Gregor 2006) the relationship between IT governance and business performance, the second research question is:

- *How can the assumed positive impact of IT governance on business performance be explained?*

An analysis of the nature of the relationship of IT governance and business performance provides numerous insights for different stakeholders. First, a contribution to theory in IS is intended to be made by addressing the research gap regarding the impact of IT governance on business performance and developing a mid-range theory that, first, sheds light on the determinants and implications of mechanisms triggered by IT governance and, second, explains how and why those mechanisms increase business performance. Moreover, this study draws partly on theories that originate in reference disciplines, like the resource-based view of the firm (RBV), the knowledge-based view of the firm (KBV) or the theory of complementarities, and applies them to the IT governance domain. As a consequence, the findings also have implications for theory development in these related disciplines. Third, as IT governance is a highly significant topic in practice and, thus, on the agenda of every CIO, the outcomes of this study are likely to be relevant for practitioners by answering what IT governance can achieve and what has to be considered before, during and after the implementation of ITG. The research framework is depicted in Figure 1.

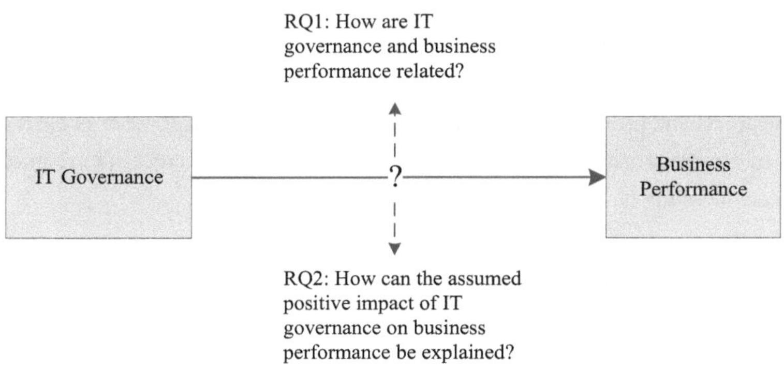

Figure 1: Research framework

1.3 Research Design

For opening the black box between ITG and business performance, the case study method is applied. In an effort to close the previously identified gap in the existing research, this study integrates two empirical phases of which the first is exploratory in nature and aims at theory building, while the second phase is focused on empirical substantiation and refinement of the developed mid-range theory. The object of analysis is determined as the organisation that implements ITG. Due to the fact that previous literature does not provide theoretical models on ITG, a qualitative research design is chosen. Qualitative case study research is according to previous literature well suited in order to answer the question of *how* ITG and business performance are related (Yin 2009).

The research endeavour starts with a thorough review of IS as well as non-IS literature. Thereafter, within the first empirical stage, exploratory case studies of major multibusiness corporations are conducted for theory building. The data is gathered from various industries, making sure the observations are comparable, but not industry specific. The perspective taken is that of the top management. In order to guide the expert interviews, preliminary conceptualisations of the basic constructs *IT governance* and *business performance* are derived from existing literature (Eisenhardt 1989b).

In line with Eisenhardt (1989b), the insights gained from the exploratory case studies are then again compared with the relevant literature in order to develop a theoretical model that analyses and explains the relation between ITG and business performance. This approach helps to build a model that is based on empirical data as much as on a rigorous theoretical background.

In order to substantiate the findings and refine the theoretical model, a second empirical endeavour is undertaken. To avoid a selection bias, a new case sample is chosen. The constructs and propositions employed in the developed model serve as basis for the design of a more structured second interview guideline so as to meet the requirements of the corroborating nature of the second data collection.

1.4 Study Organisation

The structure of this study is developed according to the design of the research endeavour.

Chapter 2 provides the basis for this thesis with the deduction of the fundamental constructs that are framing the research questions and a thorough discussion of the theoretical lens and foundations of the conducted research project. Therefore, a detailed overview of the terminology and the emergence of information technology are given before past and contemporary concepts of the management of IT are introduced. This leads on to the discussion of the value that is provided by IT and a review of essential literature – both in the area of IS as well as in related disciplines – on business performance, which is the dependent construct in the research framework presented in Figure 1. Next, previous work on IT governance is reviewed in detail, leading to a conceptualisation of the independent construct of the research framework. Summing up, based on a literature review, Chapter 2 provides a conceptual framework that guides the exploratory empirical phase of the research endeavour.

Chapter 3 offers the motivation and theoretical justification for the qualitative research design that was chosen in order to answer the proposed research questions. The ontological and epistemological stance of this thesis is discussed and the design of the research project as a whole is elucidated in more detail.

Building upon the literature analysed and the first empirical phase, an explanatory model that answers this study's research questions is developed in Chapter 4. In doing so, the findings of 11 exploratory case studies are presented and analysed based on existing theories.

Following the design of the research endeavour, Chapter 5 presents the substantiation and refinement of the developed model. In doing so, a second data-set comprising 10 case studies was gathered and is, first, introduced in depth case by case. Thereafter, a cross-case analysis is undertaken in order to either substantiate or neglect the theoretical links that were proposed by the developed model, leading to a refined mid-range theory of the relationship of IT governance and business performance. Causal relationships revealed by a mid-range theory are generalisable to certain extent, but do not offer an abstract overarching explanation that is valid in every feasible context (Gregor 2006; Merton 1968).

The results and the contribution of this research endeavour are discussed in detail in Chapter 6. After the implications for theory and practice are presented, existing limitations are assessed and opportunities for future research, which emerged in the course of this study, are suggested.

Chapter 7 provides a summary and conclusion of the study.

2. Theoretical Foundations

This chapter aims at providing the theoretical foundations of the study. Thus, it is serving as the basis for the first phase of the empirical research. Even though this first phase is exploratory in nature, Eisenhardt (1989b) recommends deriving preliminary conceptualisations of the basic constructs to guide the data collection.

In order to assure a basic understanding, this chapter offers an introduction of fundamental terms along with a brief historical overview of the emergence of information technology and the IT function in business. Thereafter, a thorough review of previous work – both in IS literature and adjacent disciplines – on the value that IT can provide to business is introduced. Subsequently, the term IT governance and previous work on the topic is discussed in detail. The chapter closes with a summary introducing the preliminary research framework.

2.1 Information Technology

Information technology and the term "IT" became ubiquitous and pervasive in our every-day lives to a stage where science and media are referring to those born after 1980 as *"digital natives"* (Jones et al. 2010; Palfrey and Gasser 2010; Prensky 2006), implying that they grew up with information technology as a natural part of their (i.e. our) environment.

Nevertheless, in order to be able to discuss the meaning, importance and impact of corporate IT, it is instructive to study the emergence and development of information technology and the IT function within corporations in the last decades.

2.1.1 Terminology

The term *information* is derived from the Latin word *informare* (Oxford Dictionaries 2012c), which stands for *shape, fashion, describe* (Oxford Dictionaries 2012b). It is regarded in this context following Heinrich et al. (2011) as purposeful, action determining knowledge of past, present and future states of reality and events within reality. Information, which is dynamic, has not only to be distinguished from knowledge, which is more persistent, but as well from signs and data, as it stands in a hierarchical relation to those (Heinrich et al. 2011). Pure signs from a certain alphabet need to be enriched with syntax (principles and rules of arrangement) in order to gain data. The latter, additionally, needs to be enriched with semantics (meaning) to generate information. Information is converted into knowledge by humans in a social process of shared understanding and sense making (Borghoff and Pareschi 1998). Throughout this process, it is linked to other information fragments and already extant knowledge in the reference system of the processing actors (Heinrich et al. 2011).

The term *technology* is derived from the Greek word *technologia (τεχνολογία)* which stands for the term *systematic treatment* (Oxford Dictionaries 2012d) and is applied in two distinct domains. First, technology stands for the collection of applicable and actually applied utile artefacts, their use and as well the applied knowledge, methods, processes and tools to craft them (Heinrich et al. 2011; Krcmar 2005). The second application of the term technology is to be found, following Chmielewicz (1994), in the area of purposeful design. Here, a technological statement represents a goal-means relationship which asserts appropriate means for intended goals (Heinrich et al. 2011). In the context of this work, the term technology is understood and applied as described in the first notion.

In information systems research, *Information technology (IT)* is often regarded as an umbrella term for the collection of all tangible and intangible resources being concerned with information, its storage, processing, acquisition and distribution, as well as the way these resources are organised (Checkland and Holwell 2005; Krcmar 2005). While tangible resources encompass physical assets like computers, networks or mobile phones, intangible assets comprise e.g. applied knowledge, techniques or practices employed in this context. This view is very close to the definition of the International Organization for Standardization (ISO) with IT referring to *"[r]esources required to acquire, process, store and disseminate information"* (ISO 2008, p. 4). Further, resources are defined as *"[p]eople, procedures, software, information, equipment, consumables, infrastructure, capital and operating funds, and time"* (ISO 2008, p. 4).

While the terms *information technology (IT)* and *information system (IS)* are often used interchangeably (Ward and Peppard 2002), many scholars advocate a clear distinction between IT and IS (Avison and Fitzgerald 2003; Peppard and Ward 2004). Doing so, IT is seen as referring only to a narrow notion of technology, merely encompassing hardware, software and communication networks. A (computer-based) IS, however, stands for a more general concept, referring to *"the means by which people and organizations, utilizing technology, gather process, store, use and disseminate information"*

(Ward and Peppard 2002, p. 3). Heinrich et al (2011) describe IS as encompassing humans, tasks and technology. Even though the distinction between the terms IS and IT is reasonable, it did not become prevalent in general management language and literature. General management scholars treat IS and IT as synonyms and refer with established terms such as IT strategy, IT management or eventually IT governance to IT as the broader concept of information systems (Krcmar 2005).

In order to ensure consistency with previous literature on IT governance, this work is based on the notion of the term IT as defined by the ISO (2008), namely as equivalent to the broad notion of IS.

2.1.2 The Emergence and Management of Corporate IT

After defining the term information technology, the following chapter discusses the emergence of corporate IT and provides a brief overview of the changing role and impact of information technology as well as the challenges involved with managing the IT function.

The utilisation of IT in business was initiated in the early 1950s with the selective introduction of isolated systems, devoted to particular tasks or purposes (Heinrich et al. 2011). It took another 10 to 15 years until IT really started playing a significant role in the way corporations were working. Ward and Peppard (2002) justify this development with a major increase of processing power provided by the rise of multi-purpose mainframe computers, accompanied by a contemporaneous improvement in storage capacity along with decreasing prices for hardware in general during the 1960s. This era is referred to as the data processing (DP) era, where the primary goal of the IT support for business was the enhancement of operational efficiency (see also Heinzl 1996).

While mainframes were widely used for central data processing, controlled and operated by dedicated and specifically trained IT staff, minicomputers with further increasing power and the opportunity of a decentral deployment, emerged in the 1970s. The latter era is referred to as the management information systems (MIS) era, where the purpose of the enhanced IT available in businesses was an increase in management effectiveness. These upcoming systems facilitated not only the IT support of tasks and processes which were not feasible or economically manageable in a mainframe environment, but furthermore empowered non-IT staff to directly employ IT for business tasks through an increasing decentral deployment (Ward and Peppard 2002). Consequently, not only the way work was done and managed within business functions changed, but the way IT and the IT function were managed eventually had to be adapted as well. Effected by these transitions, theoretical and managerial concepts and models moved further into the focus of scholars, aiming to explain and enhance the application of IT as a means to support business (Heinrich et al. 2011; Krcmar 2005; Ward and Peppard 2002).

The personal computer (PC), as introduced in the 1980s, brought along end-user friendly multi-purpose software, such as word processors or spreadsheets. While the PC thus intensified the trend towards decentral end-user computing (EUC), so-called strategic information systems (SIS) were introduced centrally during the 1980s and took off to *"improve competitiveness by changing the nature or conduct of business"* (Ward and Peppard 2002, p. 23). While IT had started to extensively change and improve the way business was conducted (i.e. business processes were redesigned), the management of IT became increasingly complex. Not singular systems had to be managed anymore, but an organisational collective of central and decentral, mutually interdependent systems, altogether with the required mechanisms for appropriate planning and controlling (Heinrich et al. 2011). This increase in complexity was reflected by an intensified discussion about information management, grinding out new explanatory models of IT support for business and revised management concepts (e.g. Benbasat et al. 1984; Drury 1983; Horton 1981; King and Kraemer 1984; Österle 1987; Scheer 1988; Szyperski and Eschenröder 1983; Wollnik 1988; Zachman 1987).

The latter era is still ongoing and referred to as SIS era (Ward and Peppard 2002). The development and introduction of more powerful hard- and software continued during the 1990s and 2000s, with business processes today being entwined with IT in such a way that business without IT is hard to imagine. Even though standard software packages developed by vendors (e.g. by SAP or Oracle) partly replaced singular legacy systems in many corporations and industries, other uprising trends, such as e.g. outsourcing, offshoring or globalisation in general, represent entirely new challenges for IT management (Heinrich et al. 2011; Ward and Peppard 2002).

The past decade brought a stronger focus on strategic objectives like business/ IT alignment, in addition with a heated discussion about the value that IT provides to business. These facts, altogether with the vast accounting scandal of Enron in 2001, drove especially large corporations to implement an organisational divide of the IT function into *IT management* and *IT governance*. Before discussing the emergence of IT governance, a thorough reflection of the debate on the value of IT is essential.

2.2 IT and Business Performance

The previous review of the historical development of IT showed that the role of IT, and thus the value delivered by IT to business, substantially changed over time. The discussion provided in the following is solely focused on the value delivery of IT within the third and latest era, the so-called strategic information systems era. Starting with the clarification of basic terms, this chapter goes on to introduce the chosen theoretical perspective that serves as a frame for analysing the value that IT provides to business. Thereafter, the value delivered by IT and the sustainability of competitive advantages that can be achieved with information technology are discussed. The chapter closes with a discussion of the measurement of IT impacts on business performance and the introduction of an appropriate operationalisation of a dependent variable regarded as suitable for this study.

2.2.1 The Notion of Value

The definitions of the term *value,* as found in the Oxford Dictionaries (2012e), point out its potential for subjective interpretation, e.g.: *"the regard that something is held to deserve"*, or *"the importance, worth, or usefulness of something"*. In other words, an absolute value of something, detached from its context and the actors involved is hard to determine. This subjective perception of the word is also stressed in IT-specific literature, as shown by Wiggers et al. (2004, p. 11) who define value as the *"worth attached by someone to something at a particular moment"*. Heinrich et al. (2011) describe value as the capability of an object (e.g. a technology, an information system, an IT appliance) to enhance business success, in other words, the contribution of the object to the achievement of strategic business objectives.

Due to the vague concept of value, it is not surprising that the value provided by IT to business is defined and referred to in various ways (Cronk and Fitzgerald 1999). To name some examples, IT business value (ITBV) can stand for the value added as equal to revenue minus purchases (Strassmann 1990), the economic contribution that IS can make to the management's goal of profit maximisation (Banker and Kauffman 1991), the performance of the IS department and the impact of IS (Katz 1993), the ability of IS to gain competitive advantage (Hitt and Brynjolfsson 1994) or the impact of IS on business performance (Mukhopadhyay et al. 1995).

Cronk and Fitzgerald (1999, p. 44) summarise IT business value as *"the sustainable value added to the business by IS, either collectively or by individual systems, consid-*

ered from an organisational perspective, relative to the resource expenditure required". Mooney et al. (1996, p. 69) provide a more specific thesis and state that *"Firms derive business value from IT through its impacts on intermediate business processes. Such intermediate processes include the range of operational processes that comprise a firm's value chain and the management processes of information processing, control, coordination and communication."* They add furthermore that the potential IT business value rises with increased permeation of business by IT.

The last named definition is already very close to the one provided by Melville et al. (2004, p. 287), where ITBV is defined as *"the organizational performance impacts of information technology at both the intermediate process level and the organization-wide level, and comprising both efficiency impacts and competitive impacts."*. Being among the most recognised and cited contemporary works on ITBV, the latter definition on ITBV serves as a basis for this study.

2.2.2 The Resource-Based View as a Theoretical Lens

IT business value was one of the most discussed topics in IS literature in the last two decades. It was studied by academics mainly from two rivalry theoretical perspectives (Duhan et al. 2001); one being market-based and the other resource-based (Rivard et al. 2006). While the basic assumption that firms are eventually striving for competitive advantages in order to enhance business performance (Teece et al. 1997) is fundamental in both perspectives, the proposed explanations of how these competitive advantages are being achieved, differ significantly.

The concept of competitive advantage is regarded within this work in line with Barney (1991, p. 102) as given for a firm *"when it is implementing a value creating strategy not simultaneously being implemented by any current or potential competitor"*. It is important to add that the notion of competitive advantage is generally in contradiction to neo-classical economic models, where perfect competition on all markets is assumed (Cournot 1838).

In the following, the two prevailing theoretical lenses for the analysis of competitive advantage are introduced and the choice of the resource-based view as a basic frame for this study is justified. The link between competitive advantage and business performance is introduced thereafter.

2.2.2.1 The market-based perspective

The market-based perspective is rooted in classic organisation literature (Henderson and Mitchell 1997) where a firm is widely regarded as incapable of influencing the industrial conditions (Bain 1956; Mason 1939). Thus, this perspective in which the environment is carrying the deterministic role (Henderson and Mitchell 1997) can be characterised as *external* (Hannan and Freeman 1977; Spanos and Lioukas 2001). While traditional organisation literature primarily focuses on the industry (Spanos and Lioukas 2001) rather than on the firm, Porter (1980; 1985; 1991) moved the focus of the market-based perspective towards strategic decisions within corporations. In his seminal works, Porter (1980; 1985; 1991) relaxes the former basic assumption of a fully exogenous and constant industry (Bain 1968; Caves 1964) and proposes that actions of firms can affect their environment.

Contradicting neo-classical models, representatives of the market-based perspective regard markets as imperfect (Barney 1986a), allowing actors to achieve super-normal returns through a strategic positioning of their firm. Porter (1980; 1985; 1991) proposes five forces which shape a market and which have to be taken into consideration for a strategic positioning of a firm, aiming at the generation of competitive advantages. Porter (1991) further asserts that a firm needs to be able to defend its attractive relative position in order to be successful in the long term. Such a market position is regarded either as the result of lower costs or a differentiation of the end-product which makes the customers willing to pay a premium price. Therefore, the way a firm selects its position should be hard to imitate and result in an arrangement, where the market forces can be influenced in the firm's owns favour (Porter 1985; Rivard et al. 2006).

This strong focus on the market and the industrial, political and competitive environment as the primary determinative component in relation to the firm's competitive position goes hand in hand with a rather low emphasis of the idiosyncratic attributes of the organisation in regard (Conner 1991; Porter 1990). Following Porter (1980), after analysing the competitive environment and selecting a strategy and positioning of the firm, the management acquires the crucial resources for the implementation of the selected strategy. This argumentation is based upon the implicit assumption that competing firms are either equal regarding the resources they dispose of, or have a comparable access to such resources (Barney 1991; Porter 1991; Rumelt 1984; Scherer 1980). This assumption closely relates to the second heavy assumption of the market-based perspective, namely that potential resource heterogeneity within an industry segment has only a relatively short life-cycle due to high resource-mobility (Barney 1986a; Barney 1991; Hirshleifer et al. 2005). In consequence, unequal distribution of resources and imperfect mobility of resources, as postulated by other scholars (Penrose 1959; Rumelt 1984; Wernerfelt 1984), would not be taken into account as possible sources of competitive advantage.

Within the discussed paradigm, Porter and Miller (1985) describe IT as a means to alter the competitive forces that collectively determine industry profitability by either lowering cost or enhancing differentiation (Rivard et al. 2006).

Summing up, while the external, market-based perspective is considered to be an efficient basis for the analysis of the impact of the environment on the performance of a firm and its generation of competitive advantage, it can be regarded as inapt for an analysis of the link between an organisation's internal characteristics/ peculiarities and its performance (Barney 1991). This is due to the aforementioned basic assumptions of high resource mobility and thus resource homogeneity in the long-term (Rumelt 1984; Wernerfelt 1984).

These shortcomings have lead to the development and evolvement of a second perspective, which is being introduced in the following chapter.

2.2.2.2 The resource-based perspective

In a contrast to the market-based perspective, the resource-based perspective, referred to as the *resource-based view* (RBV), emphasises the strengths and weaknesses of the firm (Mata et al. 1995; Wade and Hulland 2004). Regarded from the point of the resource-based view, firms are considered as collections or bundles of distinct resources which can be heterogeneously distributed among competitors (Barney 1991; Penrose 1959; Peteraf 1993). The resource-based view relaxes the assumption of perfect mobility of input factors, which implicitly means that resource heterogeneity among firms within a certain industry may exist and may even be enduring due to imperfect markets (Barney 1991; Mata et al. 1995; Wade and Hulland 2004). Penrose (1959), who developed the basic ideas of the RBV, posits that the growth of corporations is highly dependent on the best usage of available resources (Rivard et al. 2006). Consequently, whereas the market-based perspective goes hand in hand with an external analysis of the environment, the resource-based perspective is associated with an internal analysis of the firm and the relevant resources that it needs to possess in order to develop competitive advantages (Barney 1991). The impact of the firm's environment is not neglected by the

RBV, but incorporated in such a way that it is argued that the structure of the industry and the competitive arena are the determining factors for the relevance of certain resources (Amit and Schoemaker 1993; Astley and Fombrun 1983).

Before looking in detail at the relationship between resources and competitive advantages, it is important to clearly define what organisational resources are. To do so, the terms *assets* and *capabilities* need to be introduced. Following Teece et al. (1997), assets constitute input, and respectively output factors of the processes of a firm and can be tangible or intangible (Itami and Roehl 1991). This is in line with a definition of assets provided by Sanchez (2004, p. 519) as *"Anything tangible or intangible the firm can use in its processes for creating, producing and offering its products (goods or services) to a market."* Assets are in close interplay with capabilities, as those refer to *"repeatable patterns of actions in the use of assets to create, produce, and/ or offer products to a market"* (Wade and Hulland 2004, p. 109). Hence capabilities transform inputs into outputs of greater value and encompass e.g. processes, skills or managerial capabilities (Daft 2009).

Building upon these two concepts, this study adopts the view of Barney (1991, p. 101), where resources encompass tangible and intangible factors and are defined as including *"all assets, capabilities, organizational processes, firm attributes, information, knowledge, etc. controlled by a firm that enable the firm to conceive and implement strategies that improve its efficiency and effectiveness"*.

As discussed in the following, Barney (1991) further proposes that resources, in order to be able to provide a competitive advantage, need to be:

- Valuable
- Rare
- Not perfectly mobile/ imitable
- Not substitutable

Resources are *valuable* if they provide the firm with the possibility to implement strategies which improve the organisation's effectiveness or efficiency (Barney 1991; Mata et al. 1995). In other words, resources are valuable if they enable the firm to deploy strategies that either neutralise its weaknesses or increase its strengths.

Due to the fact that a competitive advantage is achieved with value creating strategies that are not simultaneously being implemented by competitors, the resources that enable the firms to implement these strategies have to be *rare*, i.e. not easily available to all competitors (Barney 1991). Hirshleifer et al. (2005) discuss the classification of rareness and emphasise the fact that most resources that are rare, are not in the hands of one corporation. Accordingly, they propose that a resource can be classified as rare, and hence able to serve as a basis for the generation of competitive advantages, as long as the amount of firms possessing it is smaller than the amount of corporations that would be necessary for perfect competition dynamics within a certain industry.

In order to assure sustainability of the competitive advantage that is built upon rare and valuable resources, the resources, in addition, need to be *imperfectly mobile/ imitable* and *not substitutable*.

Following previous research, *imperfect imitability* of resources, as referred to by Lippman and Rumelt (1982), is determined mainly for the following three reasons.

First, in contrast to the market-based perspective (Porter 1980; Scherer 1980), the resource-based view incorporates historical conditions in relation to the possession of a resource (Barney 1991; Liebowitz and Margolis 1995). Dierickx and Cool (1989), who provide a thorough assessment on the immobility of resources, posit that resources that are developed over a longer period of time, cannot be rapidly accumulated by a competing firm through larger investments. This is reasoned with time compression diseconomies. The authors further elaborate on synergies between existing firm-specific resources, the interconnectedness of assets and eventually mass efficiencies as additional reasons for low mobility of resources.

Casual ambiguity of the origin or basis of a competitive advantage is regarded as the second major determinant of imperfect imitability or mobility (Barney 1991; Dierickx and Cool 1989). Hence, if it remains unclear or unobservable which combinations of resources empower firms to implement certain strategies, it is very challenging for competitors to imitate this specific bundle of resources (Blackburn and Rosen 1993; Itami and Roehl 1991; Reed and DeFillippi 1990).

Social complexity of resources is presented by previous literature as the third major determinant of their immobility (Barney 1991). That is, if the resource in question is e.g. tacit, knowledge-based, socially constructed or dependent on interpersonal relationships, it is hard to be observed and copied (Hambrick 1987; Hooley et al. 2005; Wernerfelt 1984), as it is found beyond the scope of the common capabilities of a firm (Barney 1986b). The same applies to the reputation of a person, department or the company as a whole (Klein and Leffler 1981; Porter 1980). Since technological complexity like machine or robots (Howell and Fleishman 1982) is generally highly mobile due to the fact that competitors can acquire the necessary tools and skills for the establishment and maintenance of a technologically complex system, it is not a source of competitive advantage (Barney 1991). Nevertheless, the successful embedding and full exploitation of a complex technological system within the value generating processes of a corporation is often highly dependent on socially complex resources (Mata et al. 1995).

The remaining necessary condition for a resource to be a foundation of sustainable competitive advantage is that it cannot be substituted with another resource (Barney 1991; Dierickx and Cool 1989). If the same strategy that was implemented with a valuable, rare and not imitable resource can be implemented with another resource which is perfectly mobile or not rare, no basis for sustainable competitive advantage is given. The two resources, or bundles of resources respectively, are in such a case regarded as strategically equivalent.

2.2.2.3 Summary and choice of the RBV as a theoretical frame

The way IT enhances business performance was studied by researchers mainly from two perspectives (Rivard et al. 2006), the market-based and the resource-based view. Both of these perspectives are based on the assumption that firms pursue competitive advantages which are further capitalised in the form of super-normal returns; that is, an above-market performance.

The first paradigm, the market-based perspective, is rooted in classic industrial organisation literature and proved to be an efficient foundation for the analysis of the impact of the environment on the performance of the firm, and thus the management's market-related strategic choices. Within this paradigm, IT is described as a means of altering the competitive forces that collectively determine industry profitability by either lowering cost or enhancing differentiation (Rivard et al. 2006). Due to the heavy assumption of perfect markets for primary goods, which means a comparable access to strategic resources for all competing actors in an industry, it is from a market-based perspective inappropriate to study the relationship between the internal characteristics of an organisation and its performance.

The second perspective, the resource-based view, regards the firm as a bundle of resources including assets, humans, knowledge and processes (Rivard et al. 2006). The RBV is based on the fundamental assertion that resources can be heterogeneously distributed among competitors and that some of these resources are imperfectly mobile. Therefore, such resources can provide the basis for sustainable competitive advantage.

Consequently, and in contrast to the market-based perspective, the RBV postulates that the specific internal characteristics of the firm are the origin and the foundation of competitive advantages and, thus, of superior business performance.

In order to decide which of the two perspectives is suitable as a theoretical frame for this study, it is crucial to consider the research questions and objectives of this project.

The aim of this study is analysing the impact of the governance of IT, a major resource, on the business performance of the firm. The nature of the analysis is, therefore, internal. More specifically, the objective of this research endeavour is an explanation of the influence of complex social relationships within the boundaries of a firm on the varying success of the exploitation of its technological systems.

The resource-based view clearly addresses this kind of internal linkages as possible origins of varying performance, while the market-based perspective is not focused on, or even neglects those as a possible source of competitive advantage and hence improved business performance.

In consequence, it appears reasonable to choose the RBV as the theoretical basis for this research, given that it provides a suitable framework and set of tools for this investigation.

2.2.3 Extensions of the Resource-Based View

Before discussing the value of IT from a resource-based view, it is necessary to introduce some extensions of the RBV that provide a more sophisticated view on phenomena which are essential for this study.

2.2.3.1 Dynamic capabilities

In an answer to the critique that the RBV is not fully able to grasp and consider the dynamics that are inherent to some resources (Black and Boal 1994), the notion of *dynamic capabilities* was introduced. Capabilities were previously introduced as *"repeatable patterns of actions in the use of assets to create, produce, and/ or offer products to a market"* (Wade and Hulland 2004, p. 109). Building on that notion, dynamic capabilities are understood as processes and organisational knowledge that provide a firm with the ability to adapt its resources (i.e. assets and capabilities) to changing environmental conditions (Teece et al. 1997). Dynamic capabilities are crucial in relation to information technology due to particularly short life-cycles of this resource (Ethiraj et al. 2005).

2.2.3.2 Knowledge-based view, knowledge specificity and absorptive capacity

The knowledge-based view (KBV) is rooted in the strategic management literature (Cole 1998; Nonaka 1994; Nonaka and Takeuchi 1995; Spender 1996a; Spender 1996b) and extends the resource-based view of the firm.

Within the KBV, services rendered by tangible resources are seen as dependent on the way of their combination and application, which in turn is a function of the firm's know-how (Alavi and Leidner 2001). This know-how, or to call it differently, this knowledge, is embedded and carried within tangible and intangible entities of an organisation. Those can, for example, be individuals, documents, policies, working routines, systems or the organisational culture (Grant 1996a; Grant 1996b; Nelson and Winter 1982; Spender 1996a; Spender 1996b). Due to the complex nature of knowledge, especially if embedded within a social and organisational setting, knowledge based resources are regarded as difficult to imitate. Hence the KBV postulates, based on the insights and conditions of the RBV, that knowledge-assets are unequally distributed among competitors and may produce long-term sustainable competitive advantage (Grant 1996a; Grant 1996b).

Like labour is being vertically and horizontally divided among professionals in firms, knowledge and hence knowledge-assets are as well (Botzenhardt et al. 2011). A chemist in the research and development (R&D) department has specialised knowledge that a mathematician in the finance department does neither have nor need and vice versa. Jensen and Meckling (1995, p. 21) define such specific or idiosyncratic knowledge as *"knowledge of the particular circumstances of time and place"*. This specificity of knowledge can be divided into two domains: context-specific knowledge and technology-specific knowledge (Choudhury and Sampler 1997; Hayek 1945; Jensen and Meckling 1995; Sabherwal and Becerra-Fernandez 2005). Regarding the background of this study, the term technology-specific knowledge is further on associated with IT-related knowledge, while knowledge interrelated with specific processes and production technologies in the regarded industries, firms and departments is classified as context-specific knowledge.

It can generally be argued that in regard to IT, Business Units (BUs) hold primarily context-specific knowledge, while IT departments possess primarily technology-specific knowledge. In order to successfully accomplish IT projects, however, it is necessary to combine these two knowledge assets. Even though the BUs need to understand the potentials and limitations of technology, it is in particular the IT department that has to combine the context- and technology-specific knowledge of a firm during IT projects. Consequently, the IT department consistently has to acquire context-specific knowledge from the business units.

Following the KBV, not only knowledge assets themselves are unequally distributed among corporations, but the capabilities to absorb and use knowledge as well. The latter is referred to as *absorptive capacity* and defined as *"the ability to utilize outside knowledge"* (Cohen and Levinthal 1990, p. 128). The fact that the absorptive capacity of an IT department is even less tangible and deeper rooted in the social and organisational setting than the knowledge assets themselves, makes it even less mobile and hence, following the KBV, more valuable and apt to generate long-term sustainable competitive advantage.

2.2.3.3 Complementarities, synergies and relatedness

Complementary goods show, in contrast to substitute goods, a negative cross elasticity of demand. That is, if the price of one good is decreased, the demand of another complementary good is increased (Mankiw 2011). One can say, in other words, that complementary goods, if consumed or applied together, simultaneously increase each other's value or return.

Milgrom and Roberts (1995, p. 181) define complements as *"doing (more of) any of them increases the returns to doing (more of) the others"*. Transferred to resources, Harrison et al. (2001, p. 680) state that *"Complementary resources are not identical, yet they simultaneously "complement" each other"*. Melville et al. (2004, p. 294) apply the concept of complementarity to the relation between information technology and non-IT resources of the firm and state: *"When synergies between IT and other firm resources exist, we call the latter complementary organizational resources."*

In strategy and economics literature, the concept of *synergy* is divided in terms of *super-additive value* synergies and *sub-additive cost* synergies. The former is defined if the joint value of two units of production is greater than the sum of their individual values (Davis and Thomas 1993; Tanriverdi 2006; Tanriverdi and Venkatraman 2005), whilst the latter arises if the use of common production factors reduces joint production costs of the singular business units (Teece 1982). It is a key proposition in strategic management literature that synergies among businesses increase the overall performance of the firm (Goold and Luchs 1993). However, the examination of the link between synergy and performance becomes problematic, as the latter itself is often defined in terms of super-additive value or sub-additive costs. Consequently, a tautology arises: if synergies are feasible, they must be observable in terms of super-additive value or sub-additive cost, which in turn is the definition of synergy (Tanriverdi and Venkatraman 2005). Focusing on sources of synergy, instead of synergy per se, provides a solution (Davis and Thomas 1993).

The central source of synergy in multibusiness firms is regarded to be *resource relatedness*, which refers to the presence of shared resources and similar activities across business units of the firm (Davis and Thomas 1993). Building on the RBV, it is argued that the sharing of strategic resources across business units creates cross-business synergies that improve the overall business performance (Robins and Wiersema 1995; Tanriverdi and Venkatraman 2005).

While the sharing of mutually independent resources supports firms in achieving sub-additive costs, it is not sufficient to achieve super-additive values. According to the *theory of complementarities* (TOC) (Milgrom and Roberts 1995), the generation of super-additive value requires the combination of resources which are complementary, meaning that the increase of one resource increases the return of the other and vice versa (Harrison et al. 2001).

Taken together, the relatedness of complementary resources helps multibusiness firms to achieve sub-additive costs and super-additive values. Sub-additive costs coming from relatedness are more likely to be imitable and lead, therefore, primarily to temporary competitive advantage. Super-additive values from a complementary set of resources with high relatedness, however, are imperfectly mobile and hard to imitate; therefore, they are a potential source of sustainable competitive advantage.

2.2.4 IT Business Value

After discussing the notion of value and introducing the two prevailing perspectives from which IT business value was studied, the choice of the RBV as a theoretical lens for this analysis was motivated, with extensions and related concepts being presented thereafter.

Building upon this effort and arguing from a resource-based view, the following chapter discusses the *"organizational performance impacts of information technology at both the intermediate process level and the organization-wide level, and comprising both efficiency impacts and competitive impacts"* (Melville et al. 2004, p. 287). This quotation was briefly introduced in Chapter 2.2.1 as the definition of IT business value

(ITBV), with efficiency and effectiveness being the two defining terms of the notion of performance (Melville et al. 2004, p. 287). Efficiency is understood from an internal perspective as emphasising certain productivity or cost metrics ('doing things right') (Drucker 2005); effectiveness is regarded as the achievement of organisational objectives (Barney 1991).

This chapter starts with the presentation of a unified view on IT business value research before going on towards a discussion of the question if IT is a valuable resource of the firm, meaning that it allows the organisation to improve effectiveness or efficiency (Barney 1991). Thereafter, the underlying mechanisms for an IT-enabled performance increase are discussed. The chapter closes with an elaboration of competitive advantages based on information technology and their sustainability.

2.2.4.1 A unified view on IT business value research

> *"You can see the computer age everywhere but in the productivity statistics."*

With these words Nobel Prize winner Robert Solow (1987, p. 32) started a long lasting and heated debate about the value that IT adds to the firm (e.g. Carr 2004; Dedrick et al. 2003; Melville et al. 2004; Mooney et al. 1996; Remenyi et al. 2007; Silvius 2006; Soh and Markus 1995; Turban and Volonino 2008). Introducing the term *productivity paradox*, Brynjolfsson (1993) emphasised the discrepancy between high investments in information technology with rapidly rising performance and a comparatively slow growth of economic productivity at the individual and global level.

Melville et al. (2004) provide the to date most prominent and detailed literature review on the research of ITBV. The authors conclude that IT does add significant value to the corporation but that the value added is not generated directly and is, thus, hard to observe. More specifically, the magnitude and nature of the value added are highly dependent on several factors such as complementary organisational resources or the environment of the firm.

Theoretically building upon the RBV and the works of Barney (1991) and Mata et al. (1995), the authors integrate prevailing research encompassing *"any conceptual, theoretical, analytic or empirical study that examines the organizational performance impacts of IT"* (Melville et al. 2004 p. 288) into a singular IT business value model to provide a unified view on ITBV research. The model comprises three domains: the focal firm, the competitive environment and the macro environment. The model is depicted in

Figure 2. Due to the fact that this research effort is not aiming at industry or country specific insights, the focus is laid solely on the inner domain, the focal firm, which is used as a rough frame for the discussion in the following. The outer two domains of the model, competitive environment and country characteristics are not introduced closer.

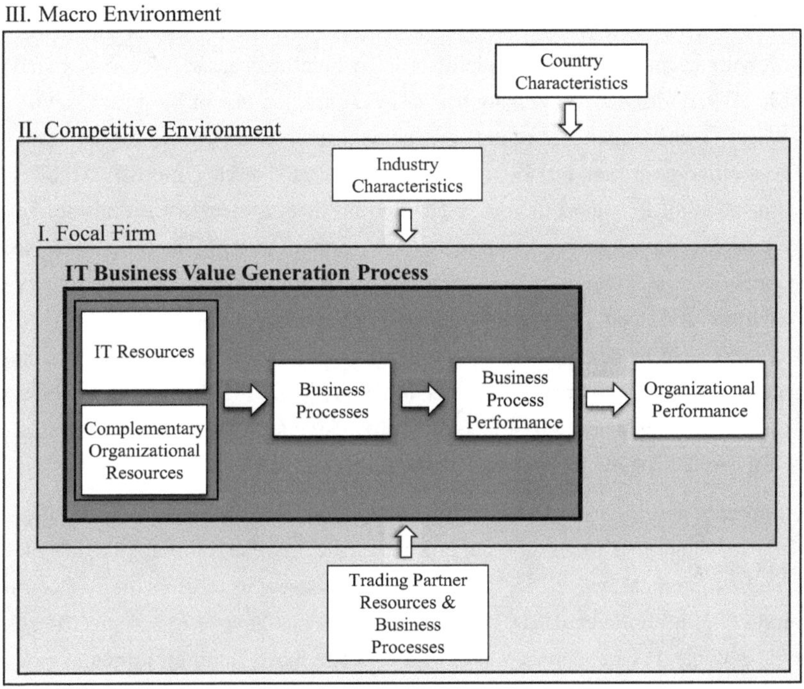

Figure 2: IT business value model (Melville et al. 2004)

2.2.4.2 IT as a valuable resource

When analysing IT as a resource, the major question that has to be answered is, if this certain resource is valuable. That is, in RBV-terms, if IT provides the firm with the possibility to implement strategies that improve the organisation's effectiveness or efficiency (Barney 1991; Mata et al. 1995). In regard of the definitions introduced, this question is equivalent to asking, if IT enables a firm to improve performance.

Empirical studies relying on large data-samples provide support for a positive association between IT (regarded as one singular measure) and organisational performance. Bharadwaj et al. (1999), Lehr and Lichtenberg (1999), Lichtenberg (1995), Siegel (1997) or Brynjolfsson and Hitt (1996) serve as examples. The basic outcomes of these studies remain unaffected under altering econometric specifications, time frames, data sets or assumptions (Brynjolfsson and Hitt 1995; Brynjolfsson and Hitt 2003; Dewan and Min 1997; Melville et al. 2004; Morrison 1997).

Melville et al. (2004) also present studies where business value is associated with specific IT systems. Banker and Johnston (1995) analyse one of the best known examples where IT changed an entire industry, namely reservation systems in the airline sector. A similar case can be found for ATMs in the banking industry (Banker and Kauffman 1988). In regard to cost reduction, the literature review reveals studies that show positive impact of production data management systems in the textile industry (Tatsiopoulos et al. 2002), supply chain management systems in the food industry (Hill and Scudder 2002) or the jewellery business (Newman and Kozar 1994). Hitt et al. (2002) were able to demonstrate that enterprise resource planning (ERP) systems are correlated with a higher financial market valuation, Weill (1992) provided evidence for IT business value generated by transaction processing systems, while Dos Santos et al. (1993) showed the same for the application of innovative IT.

Summing up, there is broad empirical evidence that information technology, regarded as an aggregated measure that is composed of diverse technological IT resources provides economical value, i.e. a higher performance to organisations (Kohli and Devaraj 2003; Melville et al. 2004). Various studies that have analysed specific systems in various contexts can support and extend the introduced findings, allowing a detailed assessment (Melville et al. 2004).

Accordingly, information technology is a valuable resource for a firm, allowing the implementation of strategies that improve the organisation's effectiveness or efficiency, and thus can lead to higher business performance.

2.2.4.3 Business processes and complementary organisational resources as a key to IT-driven performance increases

After presenting studies that showed evidence for the fact that IT as a resource can enhance business performance, the following chapter discusses the related value generation process in detail.

With some exceptions (McAfee 2002), previous research shows that in order to achieve performance gains through IT, extensive organisational changes are to be implemented (Brynjolfsson and Hitt 2000; Brynjolfsson et al. 2002; Cooper et al. 2000). This is due to the fact that IT and other organisational resources are highly intertwined and can only improve performance if aligned to each other. When synergies between IT and other resources of the firm exist, the latter are referred to as complementary organisational resources (Melville et al. 2004). Quantitative and qualitative research shows that complementary organisational resources like e.g. workplace practices, change initiatives or culture interact with IT in the process of value generation.

As illustrated in the integrated ITBV model (Figure 2), it can be generally stated that IT rarely creates value directly. Value is rather created in an interplay of a successful deployment and application of information technology on one hand, and complementary organisational resources on the other hand. That way, business processes are facilitated or improved, which in turn has an impact on organisational performance (Brynjolfsson and Hitt 2000). Business processes are regarded in line with Ray et al. (2004, p. 24) as *"actions that firms engage in to accomplish some business purpose or objective"*.

While quantitative studies were able to provide empirical support for the proposition that ITBV is closely tied to complementary organisational resources and business processes (Black and Lynch 2001; Francalanci and Galal 1998; Oh and Kim 2001; Powell and Dent-Micallef 1997), they did not offer insights for fully grasping and understanding the mechanisms behind that proposition. Therefore, many scholars undertook case study-based qualitative research endeavours looking at specific IT applications in order to open the black box of ITBV (Melville et al. 2004).

One of the first in-depth cases of that nature is provided by Clemons and Row (1988) on an order entry and distribution system. It was possible to demonstrate that the deployment of IT and the adaption of work practices as complementary resources enabled the realisation of large efficiency gains for the business processes concerned; not only for the corporation in question, but as well for its customers. A case study on First American Bank shows how an existing IT database is employed with a new IT infrastructure system in the course of a strategy shift; only after a radical organisational change was undertaken in addition, this lead to thoroughly enhanced business processes (Cooper et al. 2000). Kraemer et al. (2000) present how organisation-wide application of IT over several interrelated business processes enhances online-buying and built-to-order. Other studies where IT enables severe operational efficiencies can be found for example in the travel industry (Clemons and Row 1991), package delivery (Williams and Frolick 2001) or the cotton industry (Lindsey et al. 1990).

However, Brynjolfsson et al. (1997) point out that even a thoughtful and well-designed introduction of IT and organisational changes will not necessary lead to immediate performance increases. Factors like e.g. adjustment costs or learning may need to be taken into account in the transition phase (Chew et al. 1991). The behaviour of employees, their work practices and tacit knowledge might be even strongly contra-productive during the deployment of new IT systems and an associated adaption of complementary organisational assets (Melville et al. 2004).

Altogether, IT resources (human and technical) are highly intertwined with complementary non-IT resources of a firm. The success of an effort to enhance performance by introducing or transforming IT is therefore highly dependent on a consideration of these complementary resources and a deliberate organisational transformation. In the case of success, such an effort leads to improved business processes performance, which eventually leads to improved organisational performance (Melville et al. 2004), or *business performance*, as referred to by Sabherwal and Chan (2001).

To stress the interdependence of information technology and business processes, scholars apply the metaphor of *Siamese twins* (Heinrich et al. 2011) that cannot survive, if torn apart.

2.2.4.4 IT as a possible source of sustained competitive advantage

After showing that IT is a valuable resource and opening the black box of IT business value creation in the past chapter, it is important to enquire the competitive nature of IT business value. This chapter therefore raises the question if *"IT doesn't matter"* (Carr 2004, p. 1) due to the fact that it creates value which is available to every corporation, hence leading to competitive parity, or if IT can be the origin of sustainable competitive advantage.

As shown previously, IT creates value in conjunction with other resources through the enhancement of business processes (Ravichandran and Lertwongsatien 2005; Ray et al. 2004). Seen from the RBV, business processes are capabilities (i.e. resources) that employ, transform or exploit other resources. Due to the basic assumption of the RBV, for a business process to be valuable, the resources that are employed or exploited by it need to be valuable. In order to generate sustainable competitive advantage, the conditions of rareness, non-imitability and non-substitutability apply in addition (Barney

1991). In consequence, those business processes that employ or exploit intangible resources are the most promising for achieving sustained competitive advantage. That is due to the often path dependent, socially complex and causally ambiguous nature of intangible resources (Barney 1991; Dierickx and Cool 1989; Lippman and Rumelt 1982).

While the fact that IT is a valuable resource is commonly accepted, the sustainability of the competitive advantage that can be achieved with IT is still under discussion (Melville et al. 2004), as presented in the following.

For the purposes of a more detailed analysis, information technology can be divided into a technological and a human domain, referred to as technological IT resource (TIR) and human IT resource (HIR) (Barney 1991; Bharadwaj 2000; Dehning and Richardson 2002; Melville et al. 2004).

The technological IT resource (TIR)

While both components of IT, TIRs and HIRs, are valuable, there seems to be broad consensus on the view that the competitive advantages created by TIRs can only be of temporary nature. TIRs are progressively commoditised as shown by Carr (2004), allowing a very effective acquisition thorough markets (Hayes and Wheelwright 1984). This applies to hardware as much as to software. Following office applications, central databases and ERP solutions, even niche-functionalities are transformed into standards that can be plugged onto commonly used platforms (Kude et al. 2012). It is therefore very unlikely that value creation which is based solely on hard- or software can be protected from imitation. A very well known example is the deployment of the computerised airline reservation system SABRE. Even though this resource was valuable and rare to an extent that the created competitive advantage was large enough to drive some competitors out of business, it eventually was imitated and lead to a competitive parity in the long run (Hopper 1990).

To sum up, value generated from TIRs is widely regarded as leading only to a temporary competitive advantage which eventually turns into a competitive parity. This view is very much in line with the prospects of the RBV that classifies even very complex technological systems as mobile or imitable (Barney 1991; Carr 2004; Mata et al. 1995; Melville et al. 2004).

The human IT resource (HIR)

Yet, there is empirical support for the assumption that firms which invest in strategic information systems do achieve sustained competitive advantage and an enhanced market valuation (Brown et al. 1995; Kettinger et al. 1994). There is broad consensus in previous literature that this is due to the characteristics of the second crucial component of IT – the human IT resource (Melville et al. 2004). The HIR forms a socially complex system which can be imperfectly mobile, and therefore a source of sustained competitive advantage (Barney 1991).

Looking back at Chapter 2.2.4.3, where the mechanisms of ITBV are discussed, the availability of TIRs is presented as a necessary but not sufficient precondition for the enhancement of business processes (Clemons and Row 1991; Copeland and McKenney 1988). The availability of appropriate human IT resources is inevitable in order to realise possible synergies between IT and complementary organisational resources (Jarvenpaa and Leidner 1998).

Mata et al. (1995), who have adopted Barney's (1991) seminal work on the RBV to information technology, provide five attributes that are related to the IT resource and might lead to sustained competitive advantage. These are:

- Customer switching costs
- Access to capital
- Proprietary technology
- Technical IT skills
- Managerial IT skills

Thoroughly analysing each of them, the authors conclude that, even though all of these attributes are highly valuable, only managerial IT skills can be a basis of sustained competitive advantage. ITBV which is based upon any of the other attributes, or a combination of those, is very likely to result in a competitive parity due to the mobility or substitutability of these resources/ attributes (Mata et al. 1995).

Managerial IT skills on the other hand are yet imperfectly mobile (Melville et al. 2004) and generally not substitutable. Mata et al. (1995, p. 498) define managerial IT skills as comprising the *"management's ability to conceive of, develop, and exploit IT applications to support and enhance other business functions"*, which encompasses:

- Understanding and appreciating business needs of other functions, suppliers and customers.
- Collaborating with these actors in order to develop appropriate IT applications.
- Coordinating IT activities in a supportive manner for all affected actors.
- Anticipating future needs of other functions, the companies suppliers or customers in regard to the usage of information technology.

Comparing these qualities to the three determining factors of non-imitability within the resource-based view, one can see that all of them are matched. In contrast to technical IT skills which can be relatively easy sourced externally, managerial skills are often developed over time by trial and error (Katz 1974) and accordingly in a 'learning by doing' manner (Williamson 1975). Such a process always involves historical and social peculiarities of a firm and inevitably leads to causal ambiguity, also because *skills* in general are highly tacit (Castanias and Helfat 1991). The extremely collaborative nature of managerial IT skills makes them socially complex and deeply intertwined with an organisation's culture. All these facts explain why managerial IT skills are hard to imitate.

Taken together, in order to create value with IT through the enhancement of business processes, a corporation needs to possess technological IT resources as well as managerial and technical human skills for realising synergies between IT and complementary organisational resources. Technological IT resources, including hard- and software can efficiently be acquired over the market. The same applies for technical human skills. These resources, therefore, cannot be a source of sustained competitive advantage. The necessary managerial IT skills on the other hand are rare, not perfectly mobile and not substitutable. Consequently, managerial IT skills can be a source of sustained competitive advantage.

This proposition is fully in line with the basic assumptions of the RBV, namely that technological complexity is generally highly mobile due to the fact that competitors can acquire the necessary tools and skills for the establishment and maintenance of a technologically complex system. Nevertheless, successfully embedding and fully exploiting a complex technological system within the value generating processes of a corporation is often highly dependent on socially complex resources (Barney 1991; Mata et al. 1995).

Empirical studies support the view that HIRs are crucial for creating ITBV and the key to competitive advantage (Melville et al. 2004). Brynjolfsson and Hitt (1996) as well as Lichtenberg (1995) show that the output generated by IT labour is higher than the output generated by non-IT labour. Bharadwaj (2000) can show that HIRs are related to business performance and applies the mediator *IT capabilities*. Santhanam and Hartano (2003) confirm these findings. Once more it is qualitative studies which allow a closer analysis. Cooper et al. (2000) show that after a new data warehouse was technically implemented at First American Corporation, it took numerous years for the HIRs to implement changes in thinking and culture, involving a steady learning process in order to reap the synergies and benefits that were enabled by the new technological IT resources. This applies not only to service processes which are information-centric. Brynjolfsson et al. (1997) report that manufacturing practices, even though technologically determinated to a much wider extent, show similar characteristics. The build-to-order business process at Dell Inc. is a prominent example here. After implementing the technological basis for the build-to-order method, it took several years of developing and refining the business process itself. Once the technological basis was erected, the success or failure of the project was fully dependent on the managerial capabilities resident in the corporation (Kraemer et al. 2000).

While in the early 1990s IT specialists insisted that new hard- and software are central to process redesign, scholars later claimed that *"the challenge is increasingly one of the implementation of organizational change and the visioning involved in that change, rather than the technology itself"* (O'Neill and Sohal 1999, p. 574; Wastell et al. 1994). Due to fact that such processes change the way a corporation operates as a whole, historical conditions and the cultural background of the corporation play a central role and need to be fully understood by the managerial HIRs. With other words, the managerial HIRs need to be rooted and intertwined with the organisation in order to obtain full support from the respective staff. Melville et al. (2004), therefore, conclude that complex business processes that heavily rely on managerial HIRs, if imitable at all, would require years for imitation.

Therefore, in contrast to the TIRs and technical HIRs, the managerial HIRs cannot be imitated or effectively sourced from the market, thus they are imperfectly mobile and a source for sustainable competitive advantage (Mata et al. 1995; Melville et al. 2004).

2.2.4.5 Summary

The previous chapters in detail introduced the notion of IT business value regarded from a resource-based perspective. After showing that information technology does generate value for a corporation, the mechanisms behind ITBV generation were analysed. It was shown that IT, in synergetic interplay with complementary organisational resources, generates value through the enhancement of business processes. Thereafter, the competitive nature of ITBV was discussed. It was shown that IT can generate both temporary competitive advantages, leading to a competitive parity, as well as sustained competitive advantages. The latter is most likely to be achieved with superior managerial HIRs.

2.2.5 Business Performance

Having discussed how IT creates value and enhances performance for a corporation, altogether with the related competitive implications, it remains unclear how the impact of IT on business performance can be measured. As discussed in Chapter 2.2.4, (business) performance is defined by two terms: efficiency and effectiveness (Melville et al. 2004, p. 287). In the following, the choice of an outcome construct, or, in other words, an appropriate dependent variable in resource-based ITBV research is discussed.

Wade and Hulland (2004) point out that a consistent approach with regard to the measurement of IT value or impact on business performance is neither generally available (DeLone and McLean 1992; Seddon 1997), nor consistent across resource-based analyses, even though the latter are focused on sustained competitive advantages. More recently, RBV scholars analysing the impact of IT have reoriented from trying to measure ITBV or IT-generated competitive advantage, towards directly measuring the eventually related dependent construct business performance (Wiggins and Ruefli 2002). This is due to the fact that competitive advantage or ITBV itself are, if at all, very hard to operationalise (Wade and Hulland 2004). IT creates value conjointly with complementary resources throughout a myriad of other resources and processes. These add up towards a better performance and in some cases to a competitive advantage of the firm (Melville et al. 2004; Wade and Hulland 2004).

Accordingly, analysing the business performance of firms when investigating the impact of IT proves to be a good solution and a logical first step: the concept of a valuable resource in the RBV (see Chapter 2.2.4.2) and the concept of business performance (see Chapters 2.2.4 and 2.2.4.3) are highly related, as both constructs are indicators of an increase of effectiveness or efficiency. More explicitly, a valuable resource is a formative indicator, while business performance is a reflective one. Subsequently, in a second step, the variation in business performance has to be carefully scrutinised in order to identify and understand the underlying effectiveness or efficiency gains, which then have to be examined in relation to IT. Eventually, the sustainability of the achieved competitive advantages has to be assessed according to the conditions of the RBV.

Strategic management literature often relies on business performance metrics like return on investment (ROI), return on assets (ROA), sales or market shares (Bharadwaj 2000; Robins and Wiersema 1995). However, IS-scholars state that confining resource-based analyses to such singular firm-level variables would be too restrictive for investigating the impact on IT, due to the fact that the IT affects the firm at various levels (Wade and Hulland 2004). Especially singular firm-level dependent variables are not able to capture the broad context of the impact of IT onto business performance (Ray et al. 2004). Therefore, scholars regard the use of intermediate-level dependent variables/ constructs, e.g. at the project-, department- or business process-level, as particularly beneficial (Ray et al. 2004; Wade and Hulland 2004).

In view of that and with regard to the exploratory character of this study, which aims at opening the black box between IT governance and business performance, Sabherwal and Chan (2001) provide a suitable and wide-reaching construct. The authors operationalise business performance encompassing eight items (Sabherwal and Chan 2001, p. 19):

- Reputation among major customer segments
- Frequency of new product or service introduction
- Return on investment
- Net profits
- Technological developments and/ or other innovations in business operations
- Product quality
- Market share gains
- Revenue growth

Building up on prior research which is showing that managerial assessment of company performance is highly correlated with both objective performance indicators obtained from secondary data sources (Venkatraman and Ramanujam 1986) as well as internally obtained key performance indicators (KPIs) (Dess and Robinson Jr 1984), Sabherwal and Chan (2001) advocate perceptual measures (Chan et al. 1997; Venkatraman 1989) obtained from senior management.

2.2.6 Summary

The preceding chapter introduced the notion of value and discussed the two prevailing theoretical lenses used in IT business value research; the market-based perspective and the resource-based view. The RBV proves to be a suitable framework for studying the impact of IT governance on the performance of a firm, since it provides an adequate set of tools for investigating the internal linkages within corporations. Such links are inherent to the research question pursued and neglected within the marked-based perspective as a possible source of competitive advantage. Valuable extensions of the RBV such as dynamic capabilities and the knowledge-based view were introduced as well as the related theory of complementarities. The latter alleviates the assessment of the interplay of organisational resources. Crucial for such an analysis are furthermore the concepts of synergies and the relatedness of resources, which were briefly introduced.

Building on the resource-based view, the chapter is based on research showing that IT is a valuable resource for the firm and that the value is mostly achieved through the enhancement of business processes, which eventually can lead to competitive advantages. The sustainability of such competitive advantages is dependent on several factors which were discussed in detail. Previous research indicates that advantages generated by managerial IT capabilities are most promising to be sustainable, while advantages based on pure technology are very prone to imitation.

The chapter closes with the insight that a consistent approach towards the measurement of the impact of IT on business performance is not available. Due to the fact that the operationalisation of ITBV or sustained competitive advantages proved to be too complex, measuring a dependent performance construct in a first step, and relating it to IT-enabled efficiency or effectiveness gains in a second step got established as an alternative in previous research. Regarding the broad context of IT-enabled efficiency and effectiveness gains, Sabherwal and Chan (2001) provide a suitable operationalisation of the construct business performance, which is applied as the dependent construct in this study.

The previous sections illustrate how far and in which way information technology is capable to influence the business performance of a firm. Further, a suitable framework for the study's research question is provided, altogether with an operationalisation of the dependent construct, business performance.

In the following, extant work on IT governance, the independent construct, is presented.

2.3 Previous Work on IT Governance

Even though the term IT governance is used in research and practice for more than a decade now (Brown and Grant 2005; Webb et al. 2006), it is still debated what IT governance actually stands for. An ancient Indian fable which is recurrently being cited in relation to the definition of the term ITG clearly illustrates its ambiguity (Lewis and Millar 2009; Peterson 2004b; Turnbull 1997):

Six blind men, curious about the appearance of an animal called elephant, decide one day to find out about its appearance by touching it. While the first one, touching its trunk, proclaims an elephant is very much like a snake, the second blind man, touching its side, states an elephant is nothing but a wall. Sensing the sharpness of its tusk, one of the blind men is reminded of a spear, while another one, embracing its leg, imagines an elephant just a tree (e.g. Bosson et al. 2000).

In order to elucidate the comparable ambiguity behind the term IT governance, which is regarded in this work in line with Weill (2004, p. 3) as *"the framework for decision rights and accountabilities to encourage desirable behaviour in the use of IT"*, the following chapter starts with a discussion of the root concept of corporate governance. Thereafter, the effort of finding a general definition of ITG is discussed before the four major streams of ITG research are reviewed and introduced. Leading to the research gap and question, the independent construct of the study is derived. For reasons of completeness, commonly used field driven ITG frameworks are introduced briefly in order to provide a complete and sound picture of the subject. The chapter closes with a summary of the literature review.

2.3.1 Corporate Governance

Publications on ITG clearly point out a hierarchical relationship between IT governance and corporate governance (CG) – to name a few: *"good IT governance draws on corporate governance principles to manage and use IT to achieve corporate performance goals."* (Weill 2004, p. 3), *"The governance of IT is a part of, and inseparable from, corporate governance."* (Lewis and Millar 2009, p. 7 f.), or *"IT Governance can be regarded as the application of the concept of corporate governance to the IT domain."* (Lee et al. 2009, p. 3). Consequently, a basic understanding of CG and its principles is inevitable for studying ITG.

The broad definition of the term governance as *"the action or manner of governing a state, organization, etc."* (Oxford Dictionaries 2012a) points out the interdisciplinary manner of the idea of corporate governance that led to a vast number of approaches and definitions employing varying terms such as 'regulate', 'control', 'manage' and so forth (Daily et al. 2003; Turnbull 1997). A similar myriad of perspectives can be found concerning the subject of matter in relation to CG, namely the firm. Some scholars link the concept of CG to very generic definitions of firms, encompassing private, non-profit or state-owned corporations (Daily et al. 2003; Turnbull 1997), while others claim that CG is primarily aiming at publicly traded firms (Blair 1995). For a detailed elaboration on the general topic of an organisation, please refer to Kieser and Walgenbach (2010).

Due to the vast amount of literature and approaches on the subject of CG (Daily et al. 2003), only an overview and some predominant approaches can be introduced in the scope of this thesis. Neither underlying theories nor frameworks applied in practice or performance impacts of CG are discussed.

2.3.1.1 Origins of corporate governance

The origin of the necessity of what is understood as corporate governance today is seen in the increasing separation of financial supply and managerial decision power within corporations in the age of industrialisation. Caused by an extensive need for capital, large firms were increasingly owned by a varying group of shareholders, especially if capital markets were involved in the process of funding. In consequence, a collective management of such corporations by (all) their owners became impracticable, often leading to complete separation of ownership and decision power (Daily et al. 2003; Jensen and Meckling 1976b; Shleifer and Vishny 1997).

After Adam Smith (1776, p. 800) had already described the core of the uprising problem: *"The directors of such companies, however, being the managers rather of other people's money than their own, it cannot well be expected, that they should watch over it with the same anxious vigilance with which the partners in a private copartnery frequently watch over their own."*, Berle and Means (1932), together with Coase (1937), were among the first to academically describe and investigate the basic problem arising in consequence, namely potential conflicts of interest and opportunistic behaviour of executive management at the shareholder's expenses (Gill 2008). While the largest fraction of the latter usually seek long-term yield returns, managers might target goals like short-term success motivated by bonus payments or personal goals like e.g. so-called "empire building", despite being aware of potentially harmful consequences for the corporation in the long-run. Theft of infringement represents the most extreme form of opportunistic behaviour.

Tirole (2000, p. 1) provides some examples for undesirable behaviour which is repeatedly observed: *"They [managers] exert insufficient effort when overcommitting themselves to external activities, when finding it convenient to accept overstaffing, or when overlooking internal audit. They may collect private benefits by building empires, enjoying perks, or even stealing from the firm by raiding its pension fund, by paying inflated transfer prices to affiliated entities, or by engaging insider trading. Last, they may entrench themselves by investing in mature or declining industries that they are good at running, by taking risk that is either excessive (as when their position is endangered) or insufficient (as when it is secure), or by bending over backwards to resist takeover."*

Due to the fact that management is closer to the business, it has an information advantage regarding e.g. the business situation or the financial figures of the corporation, which means that so-called information asymmetries between the owners and the managers of a corporation are in place. In consequence, the former often cannot be fully aware if the actions of the latter are in their interest (Jensen and Meckling 1976a; Küpper 2008).

Problems arising from the separation of ownership and control are labelled *agency problems* (Jensen and Meckling 1976a; Shleifer and Vishny 1997) and are in the focus of the principal-agent theory (PAT), which is closely related to the contractual view of the firm, as introduced by Coase (1937) (for details on the PAT, please refer to Jensen and Meckling 1976a). Often based on the PAT, corporate governance practice and research in the 20th century was focused on the relationship between executive management (so-called agents) and the corporation's shareholders (so-called principals). Hence CG was meant to mitigate agency conflicts and secure a value based management, meaning that preservation and increase of shareholder value was regarded as the primary goal.

2.3.1.2 The shareholder value concept in North America and the UK

This original focus of corporate governance is reflected for example in Shleifer and Vishny's (1997, p. 737) definition in the Journal of Finance:

"Corporate governance deals with the ways in which suppliers of finance to corporations assure themselves of getting a return on their investment. How do the suppliers of finance get managers to return some of the profits to them? How do they make sure

that managers do not steal the capital they supply or invest it in bad projects? How do suppliers of finance control managers?"

The shareholder value-centric concept is often referred to as *"Anglo-Saxon corporate governance system"* (Shleifer and Vishny 1997, p. 737) and mostly shows a narrow perspective, primarily concerned with the two parties representing ownership and control.

Other well-cited definitions include Hambrick et al. (2008, p. 381): *"We see corporate governance as referring to the formal structures, informal structures, and processes that exist in oversight roles and responsibilities in the corporate context."*, or Turnbull (1997, p. 181): *"Corporate governance describes all the influences affecting the institutional processes, including those for appointing the controllers and/ or regulators, involved in organizing the production and sale of goods and services."*

2.3.1.3 The stakeholder concept at the example of Germany

While the shareholder value concept is originated in North America, constituting the predominant approach as well in the United Kingdom (UK) (Daily et al. 2003; Shleifer and Vishny 1997), a different understanding of CG, the so-called stakeholder concept, is more common in Continental Europe and Japan (Schmidt 2003; Shleifer and Vishny 1997; Wentges 2002) due to several historical and legal factors.

Starting with the historical background, compared to the USA and UK, a rather late and moderate adoption of the stock-markets as sources of capital took place in Continental Europe and Japan (Jürgens et al. 2000; Wentges 2002). While the stock-market capitalisation in relation to the GDP in 2007 represented 148% in the USA and 160% in the UK respectively, the figures for Germany (57%), the euro zone (79%) or Japan (106%) (Deutsche Bank Research 2008) indicate a less significant role of stock markets for corporate financing.

This difference is further illustrated using Germany as an example for the stakeholder concept. A significant historical difference can be found regarding the ownership/ shareholder structures of large corporations in the second half of the 20th century, resulting in diverging governance requirements. Windolf and Beyer (1995, p. 1) summarise the differences between the UK and Germany: *"In Germany ownership is highly concentrated i.e. shareholdings [...] tend to be sufficiently large to allow the owners to dominate the firm. In Britain ownership is much less concentrated, with almost half of all shareholdings [...] amounting to less than 5% of company stock."* Baums and Fraune

(1995) conclude that despite significant cross-ownerships between German corporations (the so-called Deutschland AG (Streeck and Hoepner 2003)) large amounts of voting rights were eventually concentrated in the hands of German banks. This was due to own stocks and investment funds on the one hand, and proxy voting rights on the other hand. The banks were consequently able to protect shareholders' interests directly with seats on the supervisory boards. If this was done, or even possible in an effective manner remains a subject of heated discussions (OECD 1995; Schmidt 2003; Wenger and Kaserer 1998; Wentges 2002; Windolf and Beyer 1995).

However, the major difference between the shareholder- and stakeholder-concept can be found, as the denotation already implicates, in a stronger consideration of interests of all participating parties, the employees in particular (Shleifer and Vishny 1997; Wentges 2002).

The so-called *co-determination* of the workforce (Jensen and Meckling 1979) is legally guaranteed in Germany and gives elected representatives of employees information-, advice- and veto-rights concerning certain corporate decisions. In fact, co-determination in Germany is much stronger than in other industrialised countries, according to Oechsler (2006). Among others, the co-determination act (MitbestG 1976) enforces an equal representation of employees and shareholders on the supervisory boards of corporations with more than 2,000 employees. The shareholders are given the right to name the chairman who has a double vote in a standoff situation. The co-determination act for the mining and steel-producing industries (MontanMitbestG 1951) gives employees' interests even more weight: it applies to all firms with more than 1,000 employees and guarantees real parity on the supervisory boards, including a neutral chairman. In corporations between 500 and 2,000 employees, one out of three seats of the supervisory board has to be assigned to an employee representative (BetrVG 1952; DrittelbG 2004).

The introduced facts elucidate why the understanding of corporate governance in Germany and other countries, where the stakeholder concept is prevailing, is dissimilar to Anglo-Saxon countries, where the shareholder value concept, and as a consequence the singular aim of preservation and increase of shareholder value is prevailing.

Whether the stakeholder concept with co-determination is positive or negative for a corporation (or a society as a whole) cannot be answered unambiguously. While the social debate (Streeck and Hoepner 2003) is beyond the scope of this thesis, it is interesting to see that a clear answer concerning the performance impact of co-determination is not available, either. 30 years ago, Jensen and Meckling (1979, p. 474) declared co-determination as harmful to shareholders (*"The fact that stockholders must be forced by law to accept co-determination is the best evidence we have that they are adversely affected by it."*). However, empirical data is failing to confirm or neglect this proposition undoubtedly, as shown by Frick and Bermig (2011).

Schmidt (2003, p. 3) provides a definition based on the boarder view of CG as represented in the stakeholder concept: *"Corporate governance takes in legal regulations and arrangements regarding the way in which the highest-level decision-making rights are distributed in a company; it also encompasses other aspects of company law, the product markets, the markets for capital and labour, and finally, both the formal organisational structure of a company and any informal organisational arrangements which may exist and function alongside the formal structures."*

2.3.1.4 Approximation of the two concepts in light of corporate risks

Neither the shareholder value nor the stakeholder concept is fully existent in its pure form anymore (Daily et al. 2003; Hambrick et al. 2008; Schmidt 2003). Mallin (2011) describes how the desire for more transparency and accountability was reinforced by financial scandals, corporate collapses, an ongoing globalisation and, eventually, recurring global crises in the last 15 years. In consequence, a large number of countries have enacted legal regulations and corporate governance codes, which changed the playing field and partly contributed towards an approximation of the two concepts.

It was the Sarbanes-Oxley Act of 2002 (SOX 2002) which had major impact, not only on the regulations of the United States of America (US) where it originates, but also on all corporations which were listed for trading on a stock market in the US (Romano 2005). Today, SOX is primarily associated with the collapse of Enron and WorldCom. However, there was a larger number of massive scandals at the turn of the millennium which convinced regulators to enact SOX (Gill 2008). A large portion of attention and discussion about SOX focuses on the sections 302 and 404 which regulate that the chief executive officer (CEO) and chief financial officer (CFO) are personally liable to certify financial statements and the existence and effective operation of disclosure controls and procedures. In consequence, this means that each filing to the SEC has to comprise certifications of these two executives stating that they have performed an evaluation of the design and effectiveness of such controls, i.e. their governance mechanisms (SOX 2002). SOX further requires the external auditors to independently attest this declaration of the executive officers (Damianides 2005; Romano 2005). An enactment of related legal regulations can be found in Germany prior to SOX (KonTraG 1998) as well as in reaction to it (BARefG 2007) based on an European directive (EC 43 2006), often referred to as *EuroSOX*. These in parts comparable regulations and the fact that large corporations often have to comply to several directives due to listings and affiliations in different regions, force multi-national corporations to live in both worlds of corporate governance.

On one hand, increased orientation towards the capital markets and a significant reduction of cross-ownerships among German corporations (Streeck and Hoepner 2003), in addition to the aforementioned eruptions on the financial markets, promoted the formulation of the German Corporate Governance Code (GCGC 2010) in 2002. The code addresses major international criticism, primarily the inadequate focus on stockholders' interests (Schmidt 2003; Teubner and Feller 2008), moving the shareholder value idea further into the focus of the stakeholder concept. However, the GCGC is signed on a voluntary basis and does not represent a legal regulation.

On the other hand, a trend towards multiple stakeholder interests can be observed in Anglo-Saxon countries. Daily et al. (2003, p. 371) define CG in their Academy of Management Review article entitled *"Corporate Governance: Decades of Dialogue and Data"* as *"the determination of the broad uses to which organizational resources will be deployed and the resolution of conflicts among the myriad participants in organizations"*. In their contribution, the authors add: *"This definition stands in some contrast to the many decades of governance research, in which researchers have focused primarily on the control of executive selfinterest and the protection of shareholder interests in settings where organizational ownership and control are separated."* Gill (2008) summarises that in the years after the two major company collapses of Enron and WorldCom corporate governance moved its traditional focus from agency conflicts towards issues of ethics, accountability, transparency, disclosure and eventually corporate social responsibility (CSR), hence benefiting stakeholders like employees, consumers and communities.

Instead of evaluating if the stakeholder- or shareholder approach is superior, it is instructive to read Shleifer and Vishny (1997, p. 737 f.) stating that *"United States, Germany, Japan, and the United Kingdom have some of the best corporate governance systems in the world, and the differences between them are probably small relative to their differences from other countries."* Comparing the CG systems of the named countries on one hand with systems of e.g. Italy or Russia on the other, the authors explicate how weak CG inevitably retards or even completely obstructs the flow of external capital to firms, causing harm to national industries or societies as a whole. Being beyond the scope of this work, please refer to Ammann et al. (2011) for a recent enquiry on CG and firm performance.

The previous chapters offer an overview and basic understanding of corporate governance, providing crucial comprehension for a review of IT governance literature. Due to the fact that one single concept of corporate governance is not available, it is not possible to pinpoint one single definition, principle or concept that serves as a unique basis for IT governance research. However, given the fact that IT governance research is originated in the US and based on US literature, where the shareholder value approach is prevailing, it is the latter which shaped the foundation of ITG research and development.

2.3.2 Defining IT Governance

After discussing the concept of corporate governance, the following chapter provides a detailed discussion of the term ITG, serving as a basis for a review of ITG-related literature.

As a starting point for outlining the concept of ITG, Van Grembergen et al. (2004) emphasise the hierarchical relationship of CG and ITG by breaking down Shleifer and Vishny's (1997) characterisation of corporate governance towards IT-centric questions, as shown in Table 1.

Corporate governance questions	IT governance questions
How do suppliers of finance get managers to return some of the profits to them?	How does top management get their CIO and IT organisation to return some business value to them?
How do suppliers of finance make sure that managers do not steal the capital they supply or invest it in bad projects?	How does top management make sure that their CIO and IT organisations do not steal the capital they supply or invest in bad projects?
How do suppliers of finance control managers?	How does top management control their CIO and IT organisation?

Table 1: Relationship between ITG and CG (adapted from Van Grembergen et al. 2004)

Despite being an important first step, it is not enough to transform CG principles towards information technology to define ITG. Even though a red line between governance and management on the corporate level cannot be explicitly drawn in every case, the distinction between owners and executive managers in combination with their respective interests is relatively clear. This distinction helps to separate the central objectives and stakeholders of the two concepts and define what CG is. Within the domain of information technology, this differentiation of interests and stakeholders is not as obvious, especially regarding the various organisational approaches which can be found today. In consequence, various definitions of ITG evolved out of varying basic assumptions.

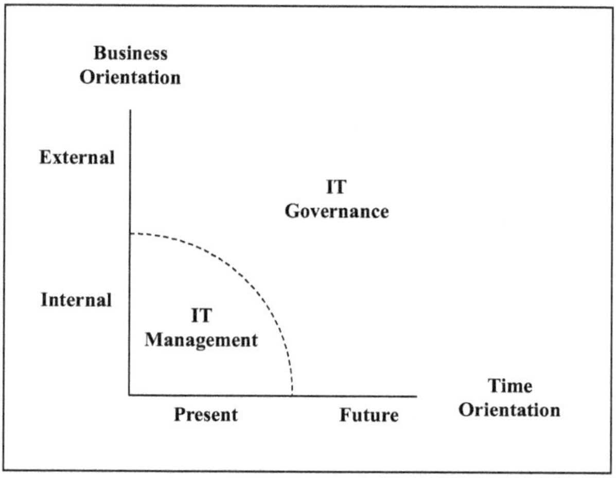

Figure 3: IT governance and management as illustrated by Peterson (2004b)

Peterson (2004b) proposes the two dimensions business orientation and time orientation to distinguish management from governance within the IT domain. Figure 3 provides an illustration. In his view, IT management is concerned with the administration and management of present IT operations as well as the effective internal supply of IT services and products. IT governance on the contrary has a much broader focus in his view and is concerned with performing and transforming the company's IT to meet present and future demands of internal and external stakeholders (Peterson 2004b; Van Grembergen et al. 2004). Weill (2004), on the contrary, separates governance from management by stating that management is about specific decisions which are eventually made, while governance is about the decision rights serving as a basis.

The denotation *IT governance* appeared in academic literature for the first time in the early 1990s (Henderson and Venkatraman 1993; Loh and Venkatraman 1992) and was applied to a set of instruments for ensuring the availability of crucial IT capabilities (Brown and Grant 2005; De Haes and Van Grembergen 2005). The term was reused by Luftman (1996) and shortly followed by Brown (1997, as IS governance), but did not become prominent in academic literature until two years later Sambamurthy and Zmud (1999) published a seminal paper on IT governance frameworks (Brown and Grant 2005; Webb et al. 2006). Even though research on what we understand as IT governance today goes back as far as to the 1960s (Brown and Grant 2005), Sambamurthy and Zmud's (1999) paper can be regarded as the kickoff for the academic application of the term IT governance and various attempts to define the expression (Simonsson and Johnson 2006; Webb et al. 2006).

Going back to the introduction of Chapter 2.3 and the ancient Indian fable, one could say that the construct of IT governance to scholars is even more ambiguous than the elephant to the blind men. This is due to the fact that IT governance is not only very complex on its own, including various different facets which are connected to each other, but that the term is in addition applied to different entities in different industries (Webb et al. 2006). Table 2 provides an overview of prominent definitions of ITG.

Definition	Source
IT governance [is the] selection and use of relationships such as strategic alliances or joint ventures to obtain key IT competencies. This is analogous to business governance, which involves make-vs.-buy choices in business strategy. Such choices cover a complex array of interfirm relationships, such as strategic alliances, joint ventures, marketing exchange, and technology licensing.	(Luftman 1996, p. 27)
[...] three spheres of activities [IT infrastructure management, IT use management, and IT project management] are directed, controlled, and coordinated through IT governance arrangements. Governance arrangements, hence, represent an organization's IT-related authority patterns.	(Sambamurthy and Zmud 1999, p. 262)
[ITG is] the organizational capacity to control the formulation and implementation of IT strategy and guide to proper direction for the purpose of achieving competitive advantage for the corporation.	(Van Grembergen 2001, p. 201, citing the Japanese Ministry of International Trade and Industry)
IS/ IT governance concentrates on the structure of relationships and processes to develop, direct and control IS/ IT resources in order to achieve the enterprise's goals through value adding contributions, which account for balancing risk versus return over IS/ IT resources and its processes.	(Korac-Kakabadse and Kakabadse 2001, p. 9)
IT governance is the organizational capacity exercised by the Board, executive management, and IT management to control the formulation and implementation of IT strategy and in this way ensure the fusion of business and IT.	(De Haes and Van Grembergen 2004, p. 1; Van Grembergen 2002, p. 240)
IT governance is the responsibility of the board of directors and executive management. It is an integral part of enterprise governance and consists of the leadership and organisational structures and processes that ensure that the organisation's IT sustains and extends the organisation's strategies and objectives.	(ITGI 2003, p. 10)

Definition	Source
[...] we have defined governance as the "IT related structures or architectures (and associated authority pattern) implemented to successfully accomplish (IT imperative) activities in response to an enterprise's environmental and strategic imperatives."	(Schwarz and Hirschheim 2003, p. 131)
IT governance is the system of structures and processes for directing and controlling information systems.	(Sherer 2004, p. 2)
[ITG is defined] as specifying the framework for decision rights and accountabilities to encourage desirable behaviour in the use of IT.	(Weill 2004, p. 3)
IT governance is basically about IT decision-making: The preparation for, making of and implementation of decisions regarding goals, processes, people and technology on a tactical and strategic level.	(Simonsson and Johnson 2006, p. 14)
IT Governance is the strategic alignment of IT with the business such that maximum business value is achieved through the development and maintenance of effective IT control and accountability, performance management and risk management.	(Webb et al. 2006, p. 7)
The system by which the current and future use of IT is directed and controlled. Corporate governance of IT involves evaluating and directing the use of IT to support the organization and monitoring this use to achieve plans. It includes the strategy and policies for using IT within an organization.	(ISO 2008, p. 3)

Table 2: Prominent IT governance definitions

The numerous available definitions have heavily varying foci and scopes, reaching from very generic ones, where ITG is regarded as a set of decision rights, to very specific definitions where ITG is equated with strategic alignment.

Looking at citation counts, the ITG definition by Weill (2004) evolved to become the most prevalent one. The definition goes in its core back to Boynton et al. (1992) and appeared in similar forms in earlier, non peer reviewed sources like working papers or talks (all of them related to Peter Weill's research group at the Center for Information Systems Research (CISR) at the Massachusetts Institute of Technology (MIT), e.g.:

Broadbent 2002; Weill and Woodham 2002). Without using the term ITG, Boynton, Jacobs and Zmud (1992) already highlighted the distinction between the *"location and distribution of the IT resources themselves [... and] the location, distribution, and pattern of managerial responsibilities and control that ultimately affect how IT resources are applied [...]"*. These roots can be clearly pointed out in the extended definition as provided by Weill (2004, p. 3):

"We define IT governance as specifying the framework for decision rights and accountabilities to encourage desirable behavior in the use of IT. A desirable behavior is one that is consistent with the organization's mission, strategy, values, norms, and culture, such as behavior promoting entrepreneurship, sharing and reuse, or relentless cost reduction. IT Governance [sic] is not about what specific decisions are made. That is management. Rather, governance is about systematically determining who makes each type of decision (a decision right), who has input to a decision (an input right), and how these people (or groups) are held accountable for their role. Good IT governance draws on corporate governance principles to manage and use IT to achieve corporate performance goals."

This ITG definition offers accuracy and clarity without being too exclusive or disregarding the wide scope of the ITG domain. In addition, it offers a clear delineation between management and governance, whilst pointing out and assessing the hierarchical relation between ITG and CG. Regarding the scope of this research effort, which aims at general and non industry specific effects of IT Governance seen from a top-level view, it seems reasonable to choose the above definition as a basis. In consequence, the basic concept of IT governance is regarded in this work in line with Weill (2004).

After introducing the general notion of (corporate) governance and breaking the concept down to the IT domain, the previous chapter has provided a general understanding and top-level definition of what is understood as IT governance in this research effort. Even though the term ITG does not date back further than to the early 1990s, research on what is understood as ITG today is done for more than five decades and can be assigned to four different research streams as discussed in the following.

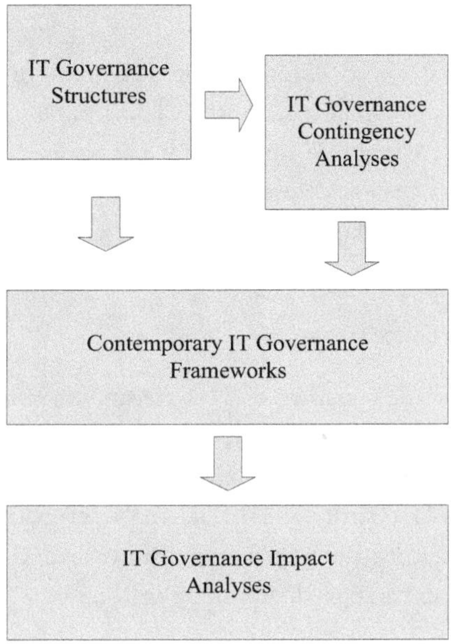

Figure 4: Streams of IT governance research

The classification, as illustrated in Figure 4, was introduced by Brown and Grant (2005) and extended by Lazic et al. (2011b). Brown and Grant (2005), build on previous work (e.g. Brown 1997; Sambamurthy and Zmud 1999; Schwarz and Hirschheim 2003) and divide the first two streams of ITG literature into related but still distinctly separated parallel paths of research, namely IT governance structures and IT governance contingency analyses. These streams converged in contemporary ITG frameworks as found in the first half of the 2000s. After consensus was partly reached in the aforementioned streams (Brown and Grant 2005; Brown and Magill 1994; Sambamurthy and Zmud 2000) and well developed ITG became a necessity in practice (De Haes and Van Grembergen 2009), scholars started inquiring the mechanisms behind the postulated positive effects of ITG on the business performance of a firm. This most current stream of ITG research is classified in this study (building on Lazic et al. 2011b) as ITG impact analyses.

The following chapters are organised according to the aforementioned classification. Each stream is discussed in detail.

2.3.3 IT Governance Structures

As shown in chapter 2.1.2, the possibilities of the early forms of information technology were confined and often determinated the way IT had to be managed. However, after large-scale computers were available, allowing for a centralised data analysis on the one hand, and minicomputers, deployed decentrally and empowering non-IT departments to independently employ IT for business tasks on the other hand (Ward and Peppard 2002), the debate about the locus of IT decision making emerged.

2.3.3.1 Basic IT governance structures

The first efforts that can be classified as ITG research, hence, date back to the late 1950s/ early 1960s (e.g. Burlingame 1961; Thompson and Bates 1957) and were attempting to determine the right IT decision-makers, who would be able to maximise the return on investment in IT (Garrity 1963). The debate eventually focused on bi-polar extremes of centralisation vs. decentralisation (Brown and Grant 2005; Cross et al. 1997). The latter two can be applied, according to King (1983), with respect to three dimensions:

- Control (locus of the decision making authority)
- Physical location (locus of facilities and physical IT resources)
- Function (locus of activity/ responsibility within the organisational structure of a firm)

It was primarily the dimension of control which was in the centre of a heated debate. From the 1960s on, top-level managers in many cases wished to delegate as much control as possible to a central IT department for achieving economies of scale and ensuring company-wide standards (Boynton and Zmud 1987; Olson and Chervany 1980). Most scholars agreed on such benefits of centralisation, but pointed out in addition that a decentral allocation of control, as promoted by line managers who claimed to understand their local business needs best (Gerrity and Rockart 1986), increases customisation of solutions radically. Consequently, decentralisation leads to better responsiveness concerning end-user requirements and, hence, a better competitive positioning of business units on the market (Brown and Grant 2005; Burlingame 1961; Garrity 1963; Golub 1975; Jelinek 1977; Keen 1981; Von Simson 1995; Wetherbe 1988).

2.3.3.2 Expanded IT governance structures

A classification of IT decision making authority into the two extremes central/ decentral proved inapt, as firms were aiming to combine the best of both philosophies. While pursuing centralisation in some aspects of information technology, decentralisation efforts were observable in the same firms regarding other facets of IT. This lead to an expansion of research efforts on ITG structures into two domains:

- Refinement of the former bi-polar classification
- Mapping of certain types of decisions to certain governance structures

Within the first domain, academics attempted to map reality better with a refinement of the bi-polar categorisation, including a more detailed analysis of the respective decision making authorities. While one group of scholars replaced the unsuitable bi-polar classification with a continuous one (Ein-Dor and Segev 1978; King 1983; Olson and Chervany 1980; Tavakolian 1987), a second tried to solve the issue with additional discrete classifications. The most prominent example of the latter is labelled as 'federal mode' of governance (Boynton and Zmud 1987; Brown and Grant 2005; Zmud et al. 1986). The denotation was chosen referring to the principles of federally organised states. Transferred to IT, this meant combining guidelines and policies from a central IT department with a certain degree of local autonomy within business units. Comparable concepts are named distributed governance (Rockart et al. 1979), hybrid governance (Brown 1997; Dixon and John 1989; Rockart 1988), equilibrium governance (La Belle and Nyce 1987) or centrally decentralised governance (Brown and Magill 1994; Von Simson 1995; Von Simson 1990). After being able to describe the distribution of control between central and decentral units quite accurately, research focused on the respective decision-making authorities in the decentral units (Brown and Grant 2005); those were not addressed in detail before (Boynton and Zmud 1987; Rockart 1988; Rockart et al. 1996). Following Brown and Grant (2005), this research stream singled out a group of line managers in business units, which understood their business lines and respective technological requirements better than a central IT department (Gerrity and Rockart 1986; Rockart 1988). As a consequence, it deemed appropriate to confer the responsibility for decisions about the use of technology upon this group of managers, while having authority over core services, e.g. infrastructure, situated in a central IT department (Boynton et al. 1992; Dixon and John 1989; Rockart 1988).

These ideas are in close relation to the second domain in which research on ITG structures was expanded (Brown and Grant 2005). Instead of studying the locus of the entire decision making authority, or the IS department as a whole, more recent studies were going further into detail by investigating specific (types of) decisions instead (Sambamurthy and Zmud 1999). Olson and Chervany (1980) analysed which structure of governance related best to each of the three IT service functions as defined by Norton (1973): operation, development and management. In the same manner, Boynton and Zmud (1987) and Byrd et al. (1995) investigated the relation between IT planning and ITG structures. In summary, this stream of research argued that authority over specific types of decisions could be distributed to central/ decentral units independently of the overall organisational governance structure (Brown and Grant 2005). Most prominent is the aforementioned example of the decision about the use of technology (Allen and Boynton 1991; Brown and Magill 1994; Dixon and John 1989; Zmud et al. 1986).

2.3.3.3 Summary

The previous chapter provided a discussion of early works on ITG and introduced numerous sub-classifications of the literature stream for easier comprehension. Due to the nature of the topic, these classifications are in parts overlapping. Even though not labelled as IT governance, research on IT decision rights and accountabilities started in the late 1950s. The first works on the topic can be subsumed under the term basic IT governance structures and were focused on the fundamental question, if decision making authority concerning IT should be situated in a central department or rather be distributed in business units. While providing valuable insights into pros and cons of central- and decentralisation, the discussed bi-polar classification was not able to reflect reality. In an attempt to solve this issue, research on ITG proliferated into different directions. One group of scholars worked on refined classifications of governance structures, a second focused on the respective decision making authorities in decentralised settings, while a third group of academics analysed the fit between certain types of decisions and certain governance structures. These streams of literature can be subsumed under the term expanded IT governance structures.

2.3.4 IT Governance Contingency Analyses

The second stream of ITG research evolved in parallel to the expansion of research on ITG structures at the end of the 1970s/ beginning of the 1980s. After findings of basic studies on ITG structure clearly showed that both central and decentral governance have pros and cons (see Chapter 2.3.3.1), one group of scholars introduced a new research stream. These academics moved the focus away from refining the structural options (like done in the expanded ITG structure stream) towards investigating external and internal (contingency) factors that may explain success or failure of a certain types of governance.

Despite being related to insights from ITG structures research, the works on ITG contingency analyses should be classified as a distinct research path due to a fairly independent development of the stream, but particularly due to a strong theoretical grounding in organisational research (Weill and Olson 1989). The largest part of the introduced works on ITG structures, on the contrary, can be regarded as descriptive (Orlikowski and Baroudi 1991).

After providing a short introduction into the general ideas of contingency theory, this chapter successively discusses works on contingency analyses for basic and expanded ITG structures.

2.3.4.1 Contingency theory

Contingency theory (CT) should be regarded as an umbrella term for various approaches and theories being developed from the 1950s on as a response to previous organisational theories (Kast and Rosenzweig 1972; Weill and Olson 1989).

In contrast to these organisational theories, where mostly one best way to manage an organisation is proclaimed, the contingency approach *"attempts to understand the interrelationships within and among organizational subsystems as well as between the organizational system as an entity and its environments. It emphasises the multivariate nature of organizations and attempts to interpret and understand how they operate under varying conditions"* (Szilagyi et al. 1980, p. 370). In other words, CT claims that a unique best way of organisational design and management does not exist. On the contrary, the ideal way to manage a firm depends on the fit between the organisation's environment, its subsystems and other additional factors, e.g. the specific task or the culture of the firm (Fiedler 1964; Weill and Olson 1989). Despite being seen as rather outdated due to weak explanatory power in its originating field from the 1980s on, CT and related approaches were still applied in the area of IS after the turn of the century. For a closer assessment and critique on the contingency approach and its various applications in IS, please refer to Weill and Olson (1989).

2.3.4.2 Contingency analyses for uniform ITG structures

The first studies in this stream aimed at identifying which individual factors affect company-wide ITG design (Brown and Grant 2005). While often analysing up to a dozen different contingencies per study, the authors did not consider possible interactions in these first models. The contingencies most often analysed were:

- Organisational and/ or decision-making structures
- Competitive and business strategy
- Firm size
- Industry

Organisational structures and decision-making structures were regarded as the most promising predictors of an IT governance design and were part of most early contingency analyses (Allen and Boynton 1991; Boynton et al. 1992; Dixon and John 1989; Ein-Dor and Segev 1978; Henderson and Venkatraman 1993; King 1983; Olson and Chervany 1980; Tavakolian 1987; Wheelock 1982). Despite recurring attempts to find evidence for the generally accepted assumption that a centralised/ decentralised organisational structure leads to centralised/ decentralised ITG (Brown and Magill 1994; Tavakolian 1989), it was not possible to show that the choice of a certain ITG design is related to an organisational or decision-making structure, or that a specific value-adding fit exists (Brown and Magill 1994). Olson and Chervany (Olson and Chervany 1980) actually presented very early evidence of the contrary.

Competitive and business strategy was as well expected to be a major predictor for the ITG design (Boynton et al. 1992; Henderson and Venkatraman 1993; King 1983; Tavakolian 1989; Venkatraman 1997). In fact, some evidence was found that companies with a conservative/ defender strategy tend to adopt a centralised ITG structure more often than comparable corporations following a more aggressive competitive strategy (Henderson and Venkatraman 1993; Tavakolian 1989).

Another popular object of analysis was the firm size. Ein-Dor and Segev (1982) were able to show that in their specific dataset revenue (but not headcount) was associated with a specific ITG design. However, the general opinion that firm size is not an antecedent of a specific ITG structure was established after the failure of several attempts to show the contrary (Ahituv et al. 1989; Clark Jr 1992; Olson and Chervany 1980).

The proposition that industry affiliation could be an important factor determining a particular ITG design was neglected clearly (Ahituv et al. 1989; Clark Jr 1992).

Despite testing further variables as contingencies (for details please refer to Brown and Grant 2005), scholars were convinced that this kind of studies will not lead to a breakthrough. The hypotheses based on the assumption that one single organisational variable could influence the company-wide design of ITG proved to be too simplistic and limited in scope (Allen and Boynton 1991; Brown and Magill 1994; Brown and Magill 1998; Clark Jr 1992; Sambamurthy and Zmud 1999).

However, the previously introduced works provided an essential foundation for up-coming, more complex analyses. Based on a number of empirical studies, substantial conclusions were available on how and why specific contextual factors influenced the design and adoption of ITG (Brown and Grant 2005).

Scholars consequently moved the focus away from studying the influence of singular contingencies towards a set of multiple interacting and in parts conflicting contingencies (Brown and Magill 1994; Sambamurthy and Zmud 1999). Previous studies were used as blueprints but got in parts enriched with up-to-date findings of the stream on ITG structures. Thus, additional discrete classifications, such as hybrid governance were included (Allen and Boynton 1991; Brown and Magill 1994; Brown and Magill 1998; Clark Jr 1992; Sambamurthy and Zmud 1999).

For example Brown and Magill (1994) used an empirical study of six companies to find a relation between four discrete, company-wide classifications of ITG-structures, namely highly centralised, re-centralised, hybrid and highly decentralised as well as interacting patterns containing the following contextual factors:

- Corporate strategy
- Corporate vision
- Culture
- Locus of control for system approval
- Overall firm structure
- Satisfaction with management of technology
- Satisfaction with use of technology
- Senior management of IT
- Strategic grid of applications
- Strategic IT role

As an outcome, the authors published a contingency pattern for each of the four aforementioned ITG designs, hoping to deliver a predictor model for the design of IT decision making structures (Brown and Grant 2005). While moving away from the bipolar classification by including a refined categorisation of ITG-designs, the scholars of this stream already followed insights from the expanded ITG structures research. However, they adhered to the idea of a consistent company-wide ITG-design which proved to be outdated and not reflecting reality.

2.3.4.3 Contingency analyses for non-uniform ITG structures

In an attempt to move contingency analysis closer to reality and respond to critique, some scholars expanded the scope of their studies and broke the governance specifications further down towards business lines or specific IT services. Doing so, they developed very complex contingency frameworks for non-uniform ITG structures and tried to include all relevant insights from the parallel streams of research.

The most cited of these works was published by Sambamurthy and Zmud (1999). Based on eight detailed case studies, the authors developed a complex system of multiple contingencies which were classified into the three clusters reinforcing, conflicting and dominating. On the other side, nine patterns of centralised, decentralised and federal governance models were introduced. Abandoning the idea of a uniform company-wide ITG design, Sambamurthy and Zmud (1999) did not tailor the contingency patterns for corporations as a whole, but for three distinct IT services – IT infrastructure, IT use and IT project management. The framework was established on the theoretical grounding concerning fit and misfit of multiple contingencies as provided by Gresov (1989).

Sambamurthy and Zmud's (1999) work can be regarded as the productive peak of contingency analyses, containing a high portion of explanatory power in relation to antecedents and determinants of ITG design (Brown and Grant 2005). A comparably complex framework was published by Brown and Magill (1998) and is based on Brown's (1997) work, in which the fit between a pattern of interacting contingencies and an ITG design for individual business units was analysed. In the refined study, the authors (Brown and Magill 1998) analysed one specific IT service and compared multiple business units. Doing so, they tried to include all previous findings as far as possible, including multiple and interacting contingencies, a business line of analysis, individual IT services as well as refined categorisations of ITG designs. As a result, Brown and Magill (1998) presented a complex model very much comparable to the well-known framework by Sambamurthy and Zmud (1999), which was published one year later. The major difference is that the latter has a wider scope, while the former is tailored to the IT systems development function.

2.3.4.4 Summary

Works on contingency analyses formed a research stream parallel to works on ITG structures. Despite including insights form the latter research stream, scholars working on contingency analyses established a distinct research path, rooted in organisational theory. Based on the conviction that one right way of organisational design and steering does not exist, scholars were trying to identify relations between ITG designs and patterns of contextual variables in the external and internal environment of corporations. The aim was to establish an explanatory and predictive model of ITG designs relating to a number of interacting contextual factors. Starting with singular contingencies and aiming at uniform firm-wide ITG designs, scholars refined their models, added interacting multiple contingencies and tailored their analyses down to singular business units and specific IT services. Eventually, this stream of research was saturated with very complex, though explanatory powerful models. The insights of ITG contingency analyses represent an important basis of today's research on IT governance.

2.3.5 Contemporary IT Governance Frameworks

Sambamurthy and Zmud's (1999) paper represents a demarcation line between two eras of ITG research. After the academic community agreed on the fact that a saturation and consensus was reached in many points (Brown and Grant 2005; Sambamurthy and

Zmud 2000), a lull in publishing on ITG was observed in the following years. However, that did not mean that research in this area stopped; instead, a reorientation took place.

Meanwhile, the economic and particularly the legal environment changed profoundly. Accounting scandals related to cases of enormous fraud lead to corporate collapses and huge shareholder losses like in the cases of Enron, WorldCom, Tyco International or Peregrine Systems (Gill 2008). The resulting enactment of SOX made the CEO and CFO of US-listed corporations personally liable to certify the existence and effective operation of disclosure controls and procedures (for details see Chapter 2.3.1.4). In other words, a clearly defined framework for decision rights, including information technology, became obligatory. These circumstances coupled with frequently missing expertise on ITG in practice (Weill 2004) lead to a strong knowledge demand from industry, which was served primarily by two relatively distinct but complementary schools of thought. Those were lead by Peter Weill and Jeanne Ross (Weill 2004; Weill and Ross 2004) on the one hand and Wim Van Grembergen and Ryan Peterson (e.g. Peterson 2004a; Van Grembergen 2004) on the other.

In the following years, these researchers and scholars related to them dominated both academic and practice-oriented literature on ITG. Studies linked to Weill and Ross (2004) can be seen as continuation of previous works on structures and contingencies, resulting in a new system of ITG archetypes. Research related to Van Grembergen (2004) and Peterson (2004a) is much closer to practice and focuses on mechanisms that are central to ITG (Brown and Grant 2005; Weill 2004).

2.3.5.1 IT governance archetypes

The insights of the most-cited study on ITG (Weill 2004; Weill and Ross 2004) are based on a series of research projects between 1999 and 2003 (e.g. Broadbent 2002; Ross and Beath 2001; Weill et al. 2002; Weill and Woodham 2002). This collection of research comprises empirical studies in more than 300 corporations worldwide and received input from various scholars (for details see Weill and Ross 2004). The aggregated results of the various research projects and articles were published as a peer reviewed journal article by Weill (2004) and in a more detailed form as a textbook by Weill and Ross (2004). Referring to the study as a whole, including its sub-projects, this work quotes the journal article.

Weill's (2004) work can be seen in close relation to earlier research on decision rights and accountabilities. He draws on both previous streams of ITG (see Chapters

2.3.3 and 2.3.4) and manages to aggregate those into a new framework (Brown and Grant 2005). Revising traditional ITG classifications, which converged towards a triangular structure of centralised, decentralised and federal designs, Weill (2004) proposes six archetypes which he denotes according to political systems:

- Business monarchy – IT decisions are in the hands of CxOs
- IT monarchy – IT executives have the authority to decide
- Federal – Hybrid form of decision making
- Feudal – Autonomy of business units concerning IT
- Anarchy – Users are free to act as they like
- IT duopoly – IT and one business group make decisions

The two monarchy archetypes represent a finer granulated categorisation of a centralised decision structure, as introduced in Chapter 2.3.3, with diverging decision owners. The federal archetype is adopted with minor modifications from previous research while the feudal archetype can be clearly assigned to the former classification of a decentralised ITG structure.

Consequently, only anarchy and IT duopoly really represent novel classifications. As the matter of partial IT anarchy in corporations is a widely known fact, it is rather surprising that it was not clearly addressed in earlier research. However, it seems to be a logical reaction to the described turmoil in industry, causing an enactment of SOX, to include anarchy as a classification and delineate it from decentralisation or feudal governance. IT duopoly is in parts similar to a federal mode of ITG, but represents some cases in reality with much more accuracy. This is due to the fact that IT solutions are often developed in a federal arrangement between a central IT department and one specific BU before being rolled out company-wide.

Weill (2004) uses a matrix to combine these archetypes with five major IT decisions (broken down to decision rights and input rights):

- IT principles – Strategic role of IT use
- IT architecture – Basic technological choices
- IT infrastructure strategies – Budgeted IT capabilities .
- Business application needs – IT applications for business needs
- IT investments – How and where to invest in IT

Due to the comparably large and detailed data set, Weill (2004) offers an excellent and unprecedented insight into IT decision making patterns of corporations, as illustrated in Figure 5.

		Decision Domain									
		IT Principles		IT Architecture		IT Infrastructure Strategies		Business Application Needs		IT Investment	
Governance Archetype		Input	Decision	Input	Decision	Input	Decision	Input	Decision	Input	Decision
	Business Monarchy	0	27	0	6	0	7	1	12	1	30
	IT Monarchy	1	18	20	73	10	59	0	8	0	9
	Feudal	0	3	0	0	1	2	1	18	0	3
	Federal	83	14	46	4	59	6	81	30	93	27
	Duopoly	15	36	34	15	30	23	17	27	6	30
	Anarchy	0	0	0	1	0	1	0	3	0	1
	No Data or Don't Know	1	2	0	1	0	2	0	2	0	0

[shaded] Most common pattern for all firms

The numbers in each cell are percentages of the 256 enterprises studied in 23 countries. The colums add to 100%

Figure 5: IT decision making patterns of firms (adapted from Weill 2004, p. 8)

Weill (2004) then goes one step further and combines the archetype-decision matrix with patterns of five contingencies:

- Strategic and performance goals
- Organisational structure
- Governance experience
- Size and diversity
- Industry and regional differences

The author states that the presented variations in decision making patterns can be explained with variations in the respective contingency patterns. The richness in data and detail represent a significant progress in ITG research, despite the fact that most of the applied factors are known from prior studies.

Effective IT governance

Summing up, Weill (2004) draws on the two previous streams of ITG and aggregates those into a new framework which promotes both ITG structures and contingency analyses (Brown and Grant 2005).

More significantly, however, Weill (2004) modifies one of the basic assumptions of the construct of IT governance. ITG was regarded over decades as the (tripartite) allocation of decision rights, which may fit or misfit contextual factors. The existence of ITG was never questioned before; neither was quality of ITG. Only the fit of the applied ITG mode with certain contingencies was challenged. This is a logical consequence of the way the term was defined and applied by previous scholars (see Chapter 2.3.2), namely as a label for certain types of decision structures or authorities that every firm has by definition; despite the fact that those may not be documented, formally specified or even expressed at all (e.g. in the case of ITG anarchy). Weill (2004, p. 3) asserts to stick to this view by stating that *"[a]ll enterprises have IT governance"*, but he softens this proposition when defining ITG on the same page as *"specifying [...] decision rights [...]"*. This definition is in contrast to the concept of ITG being a label for an immaterial and ever-existing object, i.e. a distribution of specific rights, as it defines ITG as the conscious act of designing or shaping an artefact that represents an explicit specification of decision rights and accountabilities. By modifying this very basic assumption of what ITG is, an assessment of the quality or even existence of ITG becomes feasible.

Consequently, the author speaks of firms *"with above-average IT governance performance"* (Weill 2004, p. 3) and claims that these can achieve more than 20% higher profitability than their competitors. In other words, Weill (2004, p. 3) concludes that there is a difference between effective and ineffective IT governance which can be observed in the form of availability of actively designed ITG mechanisms: *"enterprises with effective governance have actively designed a set of IT governance mechanisms (e.g., committees, budgeting processes, approvals, IT organizational structure, chargeback, etc.)"*.

These ITG mechanisms can be classified into structures, processes and relational mechanisms and were thoroughly studied by another group of scholars, as introduced in the following chapter.

2.3.5.2 IT governance structures, processes and relational mechanisms

In parallel to the introduced series of research projects in relation to Weill (2004), a second stream of IT governance literature has become available with a more practical focus (Brown and Grant 2005). Lead by Peterson (2004a) and Van Grembergen (2004), this stream aims at analysing the implementation of ITG and its mechanisms in enterprises. As these mechanisms are regarded as a key to effective ITG by Weill (2004), the two streams of literature complement each other.

Structural Capability	Process Capability	Relational Capability
Key mechanisms:	**Key mechanisms:**	**Key mechanisms:**
Formal positions and roles Committees and councils	Strategic IT decision making Strategic IT monitoring	Business-IT partnerships Shared learning
Examples:	**Examples:**	**Examples:**
CIO and DIO IT program managers IT relationship managers IT account managers IT project office IT executive councils IT steering committee IT project committees E-commerce advisory board E-CRM task force Centers of competence and excellence	Balanced scorecard analyses Critical success factors Scenario analysis Cost/ benefit/ risk analysis SWOT analysis Service-level agreements IT chargeback system IT delivery management IT benefits management IT performance tracking Shared IT performance database	Active participation of key stakeholders Partnership rewards and incentives Shared understanding of business/ IT objectives Active conflict resolution (nonavoidance) Cross-functional business /IT training and job rotation Business/ IT co-location Business/ IT "virtual connection" and "communities of practice"

Table 3: IT governance capabilities (Peterson 2004b, p. 12)

Peterson (2004b) states that vertical lines of management, hence pure decision rights and accountabilities as specified by IT governance, are only of limited use if regarded in isolation (Galbraith 1994; Peterson et al. 2000). In order to efficiently coordinate formal and informal decision making authority, horizontal integration is crucially needed (Brown 1999). These coordination mechanisms which Weill (2004) labelled ITG mechanisms, are classified by Peterson (2004b) into three so-called ITG capabilities, as introduced in Table 3.

When refining the concept, scholars maintained this proposed trichotomy but dropped the notion of capabilities (De Haes and Van Grembergen 2004; De Haes and Van Grembergen 2008a; De Haes and Van Grembergen 2008b; De Haes and Van Grembergen 2009; Van Grembergen et al. 2004) and referred to ITG structures, ITG processes and ITG relational mechanisms.

IT governance structures

The term IT governance structures subsumes those mechanisms that represent *"structural (formal) devices and mechanisms for connecting and enabling horizontal, or liaison, contracts between business and IT management (decision-making) functions"* (Peterson 2004a, p. 12). These mechanisms depend on the existence of respective functions and committees (Brown 1999; Van Grembergen et al. 2004), their unambiguity and a commonly available understanding and acceptance among staff (Duffy 2002; ITGI 2003). The variety of stakeholders affecting ITG structures highlights that effective IT governance (Weill 2004) is not merely dependent on top-level decision makers. IT governance can only be effective, if it is based on a shared responsibility, horizontally among IT and business functions, as well as vertically among various levels of decision hierarchies (De Haes and Van Grembergen 2006; Peterson 2004b; Van Grembergen et al. 2004). A clear allocation of decision rights ensures that decisions are made by the right people, while well-implemented IT governance structures guarantee a solid decision-making basis and an efficient day-to-day operation and interaction of key stakeholders (Callahan et al. 2004; ITGI 2003; Nolan and McFarlan 2005; Weill and Ross 2004).

IT governance processes

IT governance processes encompass *"formalization and institutionalization of strategic IT decision-making or monitoring procedures"* (Peterson 2004a, p. 13). Such processes shall ensure a rationale or business case as a basis for IT decisions, especially in relation to investment prioritisation, as well as an ongoing monitoring and ex-post analysis of implementation efforts and outcomes (Broadbent and Weill 1998; Lentz et al. 2002; Luftman and Brier 1999; Peterson 2004b). ITG processes denominate to a large extent mechanisms developed in the area of strategic information systems planning (SISP) (Earl 1993; Hammer and Champy 1993; Parker et al. 1988; Rockart et al. 1979; Webb et al. 2006). Summing up, ITG processes constrain IT decision making to follow predefined rules and procedures to a certain degree and provide the basis for tracking ongoing and past implementation performance which serves as a basis for future decision making (De Haes and Van Grembergen 2009; Earl 1993; Peterson 2004b; Van Grembergen 2000; Weill and Ross 2004).

IT governance relational mechanisms

While structure and process mechanisms can be implemented (at least in theory) by resolution, this applies only in exceptional cases to relational mechanisms, which Peterson (2004a, p. 14) describes as *"the active participation of, and collaborative relationships among, corporate executives, IT management, and business management"*. Relational mechanisms are most often tacit and voluntary actions that shall support dialog and shared learning. They cannot be *"programmed"* (Peterson 2004a, p. 14). Instead, a productive environment has to be provided in which these mechanisms, once initiated, can evolve. With a focus on resolving conflicting and diverging stakeholder perspectives, these intangible mechanisms are essential for an effective strategic positioning and promotion of information technology within a corporation (De Haes and Van Grembergen 2009; Peterson 2004b). Concrete mechanisms and techniques were developed in order to e.g. comprise strategic dialog and coalition building, cross functional business/ IT training, shared learning or mutual understanding of business and IT objectives (Brown 1999; Luftman 2000; Monnoyer and Willmott 2005; Peterson et al. 2000; Reich and Benbasat 1996; Smith 2006).

2.3.5.3 An operationalisation of IT governance maturity

Based on Peterson's (2004a) tripartite classification of ITG mechanisms and various refinements (De Haes and Van Grembergen 2004; De Haes and Van Grembergen 2006; De Haes and Van Grembergen 2008a; De Haes and Van Grembergen 2008b; Van Grembergen and De Haes 2005; Van Grembergen et al. 2004; Van Grembergen et al. 2007), De Haes and Van Grembergen (2009) provided an operationalisation of IT governance maturity.

The construct is composed of a set of ITG processes, ITG structures, and ITG relational mechanisms. A thorough literature review served as a basis for the selection of the respective mechanisms, before an empirical study that covered multiple stages and case studies was conducted to validate and refine the set of indicators (De Haes and Van Grembergen 2009).

It is important to note that the availability of ITG mechanisms does not necessarily mean that the ITG of a corporation is in a mature and effective condition. In some cases, organisational overhead can even diminish efficiency and effectiveness of management. The complex system of ITG can only have a positive impact if it is designed in accordance with a corporation's mission and goals, in careful consideration of contextual factors (Weill 2004).

The construct of ITG maturity as introduced and applied by De Haes and Van Grembergen (2009) is a suitable indicator of the maturity and effectiveness of a corporation's ITG (Liang et al. 2011). It builds on Weill's (2004) findings that enterprises with effective IT governance have actively designed a set of IT governance mechanisms. By applying a qualitative methodology that allows a close assessment of each mechanism in the respective corporations, the authors ensure having an accurate perception of the maturity of ITG as a whole, and not only a raw number of enacted processes, which may only exist on paper.

This work follows De Haes and Van Grembergen's (2009) approach to a large extent. Due to the fact that their eventual collection of ITG mechanisms addressed is tailored to the financial industry in Belgium (De Haes and Van Grembergen 2009), a more general observation of ITG mechanisms is targeted in the course of this study.

2.3.5.4 Field driven frameworks

In addition to academic literature, a number of ITG models and frameworks was developed and published by various institutes and found its way onto the market in the course of SOX (Damianides 2005). Being besides the scope of the research at hand, these works are only introduced briefly for the sake of completeness.

The so-called ITG reference models were developed in order to provide guidance to corporations when setting up and assessing ITG mechanisms. To a certain extent, the introduction of such a model can be statutory, e.g. for US listed corporations. The model most frequently applied is labelled Control Objectives for Information and Related Technology (COBIT) and specifies in the current version, 4.1, 34 IT processes, which are separated into four domains (ITGI 2007; Simonsson and Johnson 2006). COBIT integrates various other frameworks and standards, such as IT Infrastructure

Library (ITIL) for service management, British Standard (BS) 7799 for security issues, ISO 9000 for quality management or Capability Maturity Model Integration (CMMI) for project management (Johannsen and Goeken 2006). While COBIT provides a collection of "what" shall be done when revising ITG, ITIL (Behr et al. 2004) offers a collection of practices of "how" and "why" IT services shall be set up (Heinrich and Lehner 2005; Johannsen and Goeken 2006; Meyer et al. 2003). Other frameworks often associated with ITG are Committee of Sponsoring Organizations of the Treadway Commission II (COSO 2004) or The Val IT Framework 2.0 (Val IT) (ITGI 2008). Despite the fact that the aforementioned frameworks are often associated with ITG, providing a helpful guideline for practitioners, they are not to be confounded with academic literature as they constitute to the largest extent not more than a collection of agreed on (best) practices.

2.3.6 IT Governance Impact Analyses

The literature on ITG, as introduced in the preceding chapters, provides insight into IT decision-making structures and mechanisms which are essential for an efficient and effective governance of a corporation's information technology. However, despite the practical value of the literature presented in the first three streams of ITG, the outcomes and models developed within these research endeavours are to a large extent descriptive and prescriptive. Apart from a few exceptions (e.g. Sambamurthy and Zmud 1999) they lack a solid theoretical foundation (see also Lazic et al. 2011b).

In addition to the fact that ITG is legally enforced to a certain extent for almost a decade now (see Chapter 2.3.5), various scholars (De Haes and Van Grembergen 2009; Luftman et al. 2008; Peterson 2004a; Weill 2004) and institutions (ISACA 2010; ITGI 2003) classify it as a critical success factor. But while empirical studies claim that ITG can account for a 20% increase in profits (Weill 2004), it is highly surprising that theory-based explanatory models are missing in this context. In fact, theoretical models explicitly dealing with ITG are in general scarcely available (De Haes and Van Grembergen 2009; Lazic et al. 2011a). Recent exceptions can be regarded as a new stream of ITG research and are labelled as *ITG impact analyses* (Lazic et al. 2011b).

When trying to find an explanatory linkage between IT governance and its impact, most of this contemporary research considers ITG mainly in relation to business/ IT alignment (BITA). The latter in turn is understood in relation to business performance (Sabherwal and Chan 2001). Examples for such efforts were offered by De Haes and Van Grembergen (2009), Silva and Chaix (2008), Csaszar and Clemons (2006), Luftman et al. (2008) or Liang et al. (2011). While De Haes and Van Grembergen (2009) provide a good basis for theory-based research with a validated IT governance construct (see Chapter 2.3.5.3), it is important to note that their model is lacking a theoretical foundation itself. Liang et al. (2011) refine De Haes and Van Grembergen's (2009) concept, grounding it on the Principal Agent Theory (Eisenhardt 1989a).

While representing an important first step towards opening the black box between ITG and its impact on firms, these confined studies are unsatisfying for various reasons. Most significant is the fact that the notion of BITA is still vague and being applied by scholars to various different concepts. Despite being discussed for more than two decades in over 150 publications (Chan and Reich 2007), no agreement is reached on what BITA eventually is (Chan and Reich 2007). In consequence, widely accepted BITA constructs are not available for theory building and need to be developed and validated when BITA is applied to theory-guided IT governance research, as shown by Liang et al. (2011). This fact is not surprising, since BITA is a primarily field-driven concept that was rarely related to theory. The most cited BITA concept and model (Luftman and Kempaiah 2007) is not of theoretical nature, but rather constitutes a guiding frame for practice.

In addition, it is important to note that the formative indicators of BITA (Luftman et al. 2008) are in parts overlapping with several aspects regarded as indicators of mature IT governance (De Haes and Van Grembergen 2009), hence the relationship between ITG and BITA could be classified as tautological (Lazic et al. 2011a; Lazic et al. 2011b).

These facts limit managerial implications, and particularly the theoretical contribution of BITA-related ITG models. The proposition that mature ITG enhances BITA, therefore, does not provide an explanation of the positive impact of ITG, but merely reframes the research question and moves it to the research area of BITA, where a clear answer is not in sight (Chan and Reich 2007). Some scholars (e.g. Chan and Huff 1993; Chan and Reich 2007) even point out that primarily pursuing alignment goals can be even contra productive from an IT governance point of view, as it hinders IT from challenging the business positively, especially if the business strategy is not clear, or in a process of change. If business processes are internally not consistent or left unmaintained over years, achieving alignment can lead to pathologies and IT stagnation as shown by Sauer and Burn (1997).

Summing up, previous research has established a large body of literature on ITG, but theoretically grounded explanatory models of the effects of ITG were not addressed until very recently. Contemporary studies that aim at explaining positive impacts of ITG, as postulated by prior empirical research, can be subsumed under the term IT governance impact analyses. While an operationalisation of ITG maturity is available, an established theoretically grounded explanation of the relation between ITG and business performance is still missing.

2.3.7 Summary

The previous sections have addressed and discussed the concepts of corporate governance and IT governance before extant studies on ITG were introduced in detail. The research on IT governance evolved for half a century and commenced with two parallel streams, one on ITG structures and one on ITG contingency analyses. These distinct fields of research were amalgamated in contemporary frameworks on ITG after the turn of the millennium. Various scandals and related legal action moved ITG further into the focus of practitioners and fostered the development and publication of so-called ITG reference frameworks. These constitute collections of good practices and are not to be confounded with academic literature.

After findings of empirical studies have suggested that ITG can account for a substantial increase in profits, the question of a theory based explanation of the impact of ITG was posed. Studies which aim at answering this question represent a novel stream of research which is yet to evolve. While an operationalisation of the independent construct, ITG maturity, is available, the discussed studies which are trying to explain the relation between ITG and organisational performance are yet unsatisfying.

2.4 Preliminary Research Framework

Following a brief summary of the theoretical foundations introduced in this section of the study, the preliminary research framework is presented in the following.

This chapter provided a thorough discussion and review of the basic terms that are underlying this study's research questions. After the expression information technology was introduced, an overview of the emergence and management of corporate IT was provided.

As IT represents one of the major cost factors in today's firms, the notion of value provided by IT is of central importance in this context. Therefore, works on the two prevailing approaches for analysing IT business value, namely the market-based and the resource-based perspective, were reviewed in the second part of this chapter. Since the RBV provides a more adequate set of tools for the addressed research questions, it was chosen as a basis for this study and introduced in detail with extensions and related theories. An operationalisation of the construct business performance as presented by Sabherwal and Chan (2001) was chosen to guide the case studies in this research.

The third part of the chapter at hand gave an overview of previous works on IT governance. After a review of the evolvement of the concept of ITG, contemporary frameworks were presented. An operationalisation of the construct ITG maturity by De Haes and Van Grembergen (2009) was introduced and chosen to guide the empirical part of this study. Despite the fact that a far reaching consensus regarding the concept of ITG is found, the discussion revealed a significant research gap in relation to the postulated positive impact of ITG. To date, only empirical studies that propose such an impact can be found, but an established explanatory model is still missing. First attempts to derive such a model are based on the assumption that the relationship between ITG and business performance is primarily mediated with the concept of BITA. Various shortcomings of this approach were presented, emphasising the need for a novel approach as pursued in the course of this thesis.

In order to successfully promote such a novel approach, however, Eisenhardt (1989b) and Yin (2009) describe a thorough review of literature as a crucial basis. Furthermore, they advocate that preliminary conceptualisations of the basic constructs that form the research questions should be deduced from literature; not only to shed light on the research gap in place, but also to be able to guide the exploratory case studies. Hence, the constructs of IT governance maturity (see Chapter 2.3.5.3) and business performance (see Chapter 2.2.5) were derived from extant literature and serve as a basis for the preliminary research framework.

Figure 6 provides an illustration of the preliminary research framework; the definitions of the basic constructs are provided in Table 4. Following the discussed literature, a resource-based perspective is taken and a positive relationship between IT governance maturity and business performance is assumed. That is, the higher the IT governance maturity, the higher is the firm's business performance (De Haes and Van Grembergen 2009; Weill and Ross 2004; Weill and Woodham 2002).

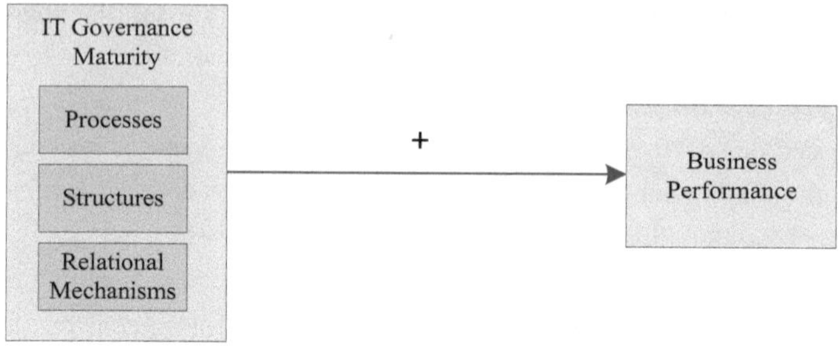

Figure 6: Preliminary research framework

Construct	Conceptualisation
IT Governance Maturity	Maturity of the framework for decision rights and accountabilities to encourage desirable behaviour in the use of IT. Regarded as a combination of ITG processes, ITG structures and ITG relational mechanisms (based on De Haes and Van Grembergen 2009; Peterson 2004a; Weill 2004).
Business Performance	Combination of (1) reputation among major customer segments, (2) frequency of new product or service introduction, (3) return on investment, (4) net profits, (5) technological developments and/ or other innovations in business operations, (6) product quality, (7) market share gains and (8) revenue growth. (based on Chan et al. 1997; Dess and Robinson Jr 1984; Sabherwal and Chan 2001; Venkatraman 1989; Venkatraman and Ramanujam 1986).

Table 4: Conceptualisation of basic constructs

3. Research Design

In an effort to close the previously identified gap in existing research, this study aims at developing a mid-range theory that is amenable to theory testing and able to explain how IT governance influences business performance (Gregor 2006). The selection and application of an appropriate research design represents an essential fundament for such a task. First, the following chapter presents the ontological and epistemological stance together with the research endeavour's object of analysis. Thereafter, the selection of a multiple case study strategy is discussed and the related research process is presented in detail, followed by the data collection and analysis.

3.1 Ontological and Epistemological Stance

Any scientific endeavour comprises an inherent ontological and epistemological stance. Examples for such positions are positivism, constructivism, interpretivism or postmodernism (Chalmers 1999; Crotty 1998). Most commonly, IS researchers classify their work as positivist or interpretative (Myers and Avison 1997; Weber 2004).

Positivism is based on the ontological assumption that the observer and reality are separate and that an observable reality exists beyond human consciousness and cognition (Orlikowski and Baroudi 1991; Weber 2004). The epistemological stance of positivist scholars implies that knowledge can be created and formed through experiences and observations of the world (Chalmers 1999). These observations of facts are understood as reflecting an objective and independent reality which forms the foundations of human knowledge (Weber 2004).

Interpretative scholars on the other hand do not believe that the observer and reality can be separated (Weber 2004), but that reality is a product of social construction (Orlikowski and Baroudi 1991). This ontological point of view implies the epistemological stance that knowledge is intentionally constituted, reflecting particular experiences, cultural backgrounds, history, etc. Thus, knowledge is built through social construction (Weber 2004).

Positivist scholars presume fixed relationships between entities in reality and posit that those shall be formulated and tested in the form of propositions and hypotheses (Dubé and Paré 2003; Straub et al. 2004; Weber 2004). That is in contrast to interpretative research, where the primary goal is found in the understanding of phenomena, rather than in building and testing of causal relationship models (Miles and Huberman 1994; Orlikowski and Baroudi 1991; Weber 2004).

While a strong line was drawn between positivist and interpretative information systems research in the past, mixed approaches are receiving attention from both schools of thought lately, as they offer a bridge between the two concepts (Mingers et al. 2011). Examples are soft positivism, scientific realism (Kirsch 2004; Madill et al. 2000; Ravishankar et al. 2011) or critical realism (Mingers et al. 2011). E.g., critical realism, despite being based on a strongly realist ontology, defends the necessity for both observation of facts, on one hand, and interpretation on the other, so as to allow an access to the understanding of why things occur and to what effects they may lead (Mingers et al. 2011). Adopting the approach of scientific realism, Ravishankar et al. (2011) point out that combining an ontologically positivist stance with interpretative epistemological approaches allows to conduct data analysis with expectations based on prior theory without losing valuable and unexpected findings emerging from the data.

The aim of this study is to open the black box between IT governance and business performance. To be able to do so, this study builds on prior theory, but relies on knowledgeable individuals as a primary source of information (see Chapter 3.5), being open to unexpected findings. Consequently, the researcher has to interpret the statements of the interviewees and assign meaning to their assertions in the context of their organisation. Doing so, the goal is eventually to explain organisational mechanisms in the form of relationships between constructs in the organisation's context (Straub et al. 2004). The study at hand aims, therefore, at building a theoretical model which comprises such constructs and relationships and is able to answer the underlying research question. The developed model shall be generalisable to comparable settings and amenable to statistical testing. Therefore, the constructs forming the model have to be clearly defined and measurable independently of the observer.

In consequence, this study follows the aforementioned mixed approaches between the positivist and interpretative extremes. This work is based on a strongly realist ontology implying an *"existing, causally efficacious, world independent of our knowledge"* (Mingers et al. 2011, p. 1), altogether with a theoretical model that is deemed promising to answer the posed research questions. However, the study acknowledges the need for interpreting the individual actors' statements in order to gain an understanding of determinants and implications of organisational behaviour. This includes the incorporation of unexpected findings potentially emerging from the data.

After clarifying the basic ontological and epistemological stance of a research project, it is essential to elucidate the unit of analysis before selecting a research strategy. The work at hand explores corporations that apply and redefine IT governance in order to enhance business performance. Therefore, the unit of analysis is predetermined by the research question and located at the organisational level.

3.2 Research Strategy

Social science encompasses a multitude of research strategies that can be applied in order to answer a particular research question. Examples are among others laboratory experiments, surveys, simulations, field experiments, field studies or case studies (Creswell 2007; Kerlinger and Lee 1999; Yin 2009). A one-best research method is not available and each strategy has different implications. Therefore, a research strategy has to be chosen carefully according to several dimensions of a research question and setting.

Yin (2009) proposes three dimensions as a guiding frame for the selection of a research strategy, as presented in Table 5. This study poses the research question of *how* IT governance influences business performance and is focused on contemporary events regarding the fact that the perception of ITG has changed radically in the last decade. The control of behavioural events is not practicable in this research endeavour. In consequence, according to Yin (2009), case study research represents the most suitable research strategy.

Strategy	Form of research question	Requires control of behavioral events?	Focuses on contemporary events?
Experiment	how, why?	yes	yes
Survey	who, what, where, how many, how much?	no	yes
Archival analysis	who, what, where, how many, how much?	no	yes/ no
History	how, why?	no	no
Case study	how, why?	no	yes

Table 5: Relevant dimensions for the selection of a research strategy (Yin 2009, p. 8)

Further dimensions that can be applied as a basis for the choice of an appropriate research strategy are provided by Stone (1978). Similarly to Yin (2009), Stone (1978) highlights the control of the investigator over the participants as a major determinant for the choice of a research strategy. In this study, as described above, such a control is not feasible. The second dimension is represented by the realism or naturalness of a research setting. Regarding the fact that this study analyses the decision rights and accountabilities of large corporations, a replication in an unnatural setting, such as a laboratory experiment, seems not promising. Another dimension is shaped by the question, if the research findings are generalisable (Kerlinger and Lee 1999). The primary goal of this study is to open up the black box of the relationship between ITG and business performance and thus provide results transferable to related settings.

Similar to Yin (2009), the set of dimensions by Stone (1978) advocates for the application of the case study research strategy in this context. The research question needs to be studied in a natural setting where no control over the participants can be executed by the observer. It is important to note that case studies may be exposed to certain biases and entail a reduced statistical generalisability. However, insights of case studies can be transferred to other settings by analytical generalisation (Yin 2009).

Stone (1978) argues that case studies are in particular suitable for theory building when on-site analysis of complex natural scenarios is crucial, as case studies allow for a flexible and detailed investigation of reality. In the research endeavour at hand, this is eminently important regarding the complexity of the introduced constructs of the preliminary research framework. The respective discussion about the independent construct (see Chapter 2.3.5.3) accentuates the need for a close assessment of available ITG mechanisms and suggests a qualitative approach. The same applies to the dependent construct. Chapters 2.2.4.3 and 2.2.4.4 discuss prior research in this context and show that qualitative case studies proved most promising in the effort of understanding ITBV generation, which is the core goal of this study.

Following the introduced taxonomies (Stone 1978; Yin 2009), as much as implications discussed by prior research in the context of ITG maturity (De Haes and Van Grembergen 2009), ITBV (Melville et al. 2004) and business performance (Melville et al. 2004; Ray et al. 2004), qualitative case study research (Benbasat et al. 1987; Eisenhardt 1989b; Lee 1989; Yin 2009) was chosen as research method.

3.3 Case Study Design

After the ontological and epistemological stance, the object of analysis and eventually the specific research strategy were introduced, the following section is concerned with details of the empirical part of the research effort. Accordingly, the case study organisation is discussed in detail due to various available case study implementations. A case study approach can be either of exploratory or confirmatory manner, it can be focused on a singular case or encompass multiple case studies and eventually, a case study can rely on qualitative or/ and quantitative data.

Exploratory case studies can form a basis of theory building (Eisenhardt 1989b; Eisenhardt and Graebner 2007; Yin 2009). In other words, exploratory case studies can be applied to discover constructs and corresponding relations among them (Kerlinger and Lee 1999). Meanwhile, confirmatory case studies are applied to either substantiate a conceptual framework deduced from literature or to corroborate findings of an exploratory theory building effort (Cavaye 1996). Guillemette and Paré (2012) even apply a set of interviews to test and confirm a theory building effort.

This study draws in parts on both of these concepts. Regarding the fact that case study research is generally an iterative and cyclic endeavour, Yin (2009) proposes continuous redesign, involving selection of alternative cases and changes in the data collection protocol. Following this suggestion, this study is organised in two phases encompassing an exploratory stage as well as a corroborative one. Within the first phase, an exploratory approach is applied, based on the preliminary research framework as presented in Chapter 2.4. Grounded on the resource-based perspective, the preliminary framework provides the cornerstones to guide the exploratory approach as advocated by Eisenhardt (1989b) and Yin (2009). Meanwhile, the preliminary framework leaves enough space for the exploration of new constructs and relationships as requested by Kerlinger and Lee (1999). While the first, exploratory phase is conducted with the goal of theory building, the second empirical phase is undertaken with the aim of theory substantiation and refinement. Moreover, the second phase shall provide the groundwork for further generalisation and validation of the developed explanatory model.

In pursue of a high generalisability of results, both phases of empirical research were based on multiple case studies. When choosing such an approach, theoretical and literal replication of cases have to be distinguished. Aiming at varying observations, theoretical replication demands for a heterogeneous choice of cases, while literal replication is conducted with a sample that predicts similar results (Yin 2009). Despite the fact that the exploratory phase was undertaken in a very open manner, the case sampling was done in a fashion which was promising for the collection of varying insights, given the goal to develop a model of far-reaching explanatory power. Hence, a theoretical replication was pursued. The same applies for the second empirical phase, where the aim was a substantiation of the developed mid-range theory. Based on the proposed constructs and relationships, a systematic sampling of cases for a theoretical replication was feasible.

Eventually, it is important to clarify if the case study approach of this research is focused on qualitative or quantitative data. Case study research is most commonly seen as a qualitative approach, relying on e.g. interviews, observations or documents as primary sources of information (Eisenhardt 1989b; Yin 2009). However, quantifiable information and quantitative analysis of obtained qualitative data can amend the investigation and enrich case study findings thoroughly, as shown e.g. by Dibbern et al. (2008) or Kude et al. (2012). Generally, a multitude of data sources is appreciated in the context of a case study so as to allow for triangulation of data and increase validity of findings (Eisenhardt 1989b; Yin 2009).

This research effort relies primarily on qualitative data in both case study phases. However, during the exploratory phase, text coding is used in order to quantify available information to a certain extent and enable a more reliable identification of key themes in the dataset. The details pertaining to the case sampling procedure and the collection and analysis of data in both phases are discussed in detail in the following sections.

3.4 Case Sampling Procedure

Regarding the goal of this study, namely the development of a mid-range theory that explains the impact of IT governance on the business performance of a firm, the deliberate choice of case sites, i.e. the case sampling (Yin 2009), is crucial to ensure a high comparability and generalisability of insights. In other words, the explanatory power of the developed mid-range theory is highly dependent on a purposive case sampling procedure.

As introduced in the theoretical foundation, the concept of IT governance was endemic to large organisations before being increasingly adopted by small and medium sized companies these days. That is not only due to a confined legal enforcement of SOX, which only applies to US-listed corporations, but reflects the general fact that the need for governance mechanisms rises with the number of actors and parties involved in the management of a corporation (see Chapter 2.3.1). Therefore, it seemed reasonable to focus on large multibusiness firms in this study and confine the data collection to such corporations so as to ensure comparability of results. Despite being multibusiness firms, many large corporations are residing in specific sectors or even industries. This requires a heterogeneous case sample which reflects various industries in order to circumvent biased conclusions and ensure generalisability of the explanatory model.

Generalisability and comparability of insights, however, are always to be regarded in a trade-off to rising complexity. Previous literature shows that culture is an important determinant of hierarchical relationships and hence ITG design (see Chapter 2.3.4). In regard of the inherent complexity of the topic at hand, it seemed reasonable to focus the initial theory building effort on one cultural domain. In consequence, only German corporations were chosen as case sites so as to ensure comparability, while keeping complexity manageable.

Another significant factor for ensuring comparability of insights across case sites is the comparability of the respective source of information. This is particularly important for the research question at hand due to a varying perception of the concept of IT governance (see Chapter 2.3.2). Regarding the fact that this study is focused on the top-level perspective on IT governance as well as firm-wide business performance impacts, knowledgeable high-level executives should be interrogated in the course of the data collection. The ideal dialogue partner in this case is the CIO, who should be able to provide sufficient insights about both ITG and IT related impacts on business performance. This assumption is justifiable due to the fact that the specification of IT decision rights and accountabilities is mostly in his/ her responsibility. Meanwhile, the CIO is responsible for the tracking of IT business value and has access to performance data of the company due to his/ her positioning near to the board of directors, or, in some cases, as a member of it.

Aiming at a theoretical replication in both empirical phases, an additional determinant of the case sampling logic is represented by an adequate heterogeneity (i.e. variance) of the independent construct. In other words, the ITG maturity of the case-companies should be diverging within both case samples. The applied ITG maturity measure was based on De Haes and Van Grembergen (2009). Previous literature does not provide a rigid number of cases that should be pursued. Eisenhardt (1989b) suggests a rough corridor between 4 and 10 cases for theory building purposes, so as to ensure generalisability of findings while avoiding vast complexity. Others do not give a specific number at all, but advocate that *"the analytic benefits from [multiple] cases may be substantial"* (Yin 2009, p. 60).

In order to guarantee that the case samples meet the described requirements, all firms traded on the German blue chip stock market (Deutscher Aktienindex, DAX) as well as in size comparable private firms were approached for the data collection (for details see Chapter 4.1). An ongoing analysis of the ITG maturity and industry sector of the participating firms ensured that both samples offered the required heterogeneity before the data collection was closed. This lead to 11 cases in the first and, respectively, 10 cases in the second data collection.

The case sites and interview partners are presented in detail in the Chapters 4 and 5. In order to meet the requirements of the corroborating nature of the second data collection, the two case-samples needed to be completely disjoint.

Summing up, in both empirical phases a purposive case sampling was conducted in order to ensure a collection of research sites that is represented by large multibusiness firms from varying industries with a varying level of IT governance maturity. To ensure comparability of results, exclusively top-level ITG decision-makers were interrogated (for details see Chapter 3.5). The case companies of the two samples were completely differing so as to enable an unbiased substantiation and refinement of the explanatory model.

3.5 Data Collection and Analysis

After previous sections have specified the theoretical framing of the empirical analysis, the case sampling procedure was clarified. Building on that spadework, the data collection and analysis process are introduced in the following.

The exploratory as well as the corroborating case study phases were based on expert interviews and document analyses as primary sources of information (Yin 2009). In addition, the exploratory phase encompassed a round table with researchers and members of various case companies where potential weaknesses and omissions of the developed explanatory model were discussed.

The expert interviews of both phases were conducted in a semi-structured manner, that is, a predetermined set of questions was used as a guiding frame for the conversations, while the interviewees were given the opportunity to speak freely (Yin 2009). Semi-structured interviews allow both parties to move away from the questionnaire and focus on upcoming issues which may be of interest (Stone 1978). Particularly in the exploratory phase this is of major significance in order to expand the preliminary research framework and discover constructs and corresponding relations among them (Kerlinger and Lee 1999).

The interview guideline of the first phase (see Appendix 2.1) was based on the preliminary conceptualisations and the RBV as introduced in Chapter 2.4. Due to the exploratory character, the guideline represented a broad framing, especially for the outset of the conversations. Once the dialogue was going into the right direction, the interviewees were given the opportunity to set course towards topics which were regarded as of major importance in their corporations while the guideline was used to keep the interview in the right corridor. This procedure allowed discovering new constructs and relations while acquiring in-depth insights of the ITG mechanisms of the case companies.

The constructs and propositions employed in the explanatory model that was developed on the basis of the exploratory phase served as basis for the design of a more structured second interview guideline (see Appendix 2.2). Despite following a semi-structured approach as well, the interviews of the second empirical round were held closer to the interview guideline and a thorough collection of crucial answers was ensured. This approach allowed meeting the requirements of the corroborating nature of the second data collection, while enough flexibility was available to gather novel insights.

Most of the interview partners in both case rounds were willing to provide access to internal documentation like e.g. ITG manuals and guidelines, governance presentations, organisational charts, quality manuals, snapshots of project management tools etc. These documents were of essential significance for the triangulation of data and hence for increasing the internal validity of the results.

All interviews were fully transcribed and provided to the interview partners for inspection and approval before the analysis was initiated. Following Patton (2002), an analysis of the core content of qualitative material is facilitated by identifying and labelling patterns in the data by means of categorisation and classification. To do so, the first step is coding of the transcribed interviews. Codes are described by Miles and Huberman (1994) as tags or labels which assign units of meanings to descriptive or inferential information that is gathered in the course of a data collection. Various intersecting codes can be attached to singular words, sentences or whole paragraphs.

The coding procedure in the exploratory phase was facilitated in the course of this study with the software tool NVivo in an iterative way. After starting out with two codes representing the initial constructs ITG maturity and business performance, the data was recurrently analysed in the search for central themes, emerging patterns and relationships between constructs. Doing so, new codes were defined, others redefined and yet others dropped. This procedure was reiterated until a theoretical concept emerged that was promising for the explanation of all cases (Miles and Huberman 1994; Patton 2002). To ensure intercoder reliability, the entire dataset was re-coded independently by a second person. In line with Eisenhardt (1989) as well as Dubé and Paré (2003), insights gained from the data analysis were continuously compared with relevant literature in order to guide the defining of the codes and eventually develop a theoretical model that explains the relation between ITG and business performance. This approach helps to build a model based on empirical data as much as on a rigorous theoretical background.

Due to a deviating goal in the second, corroborating phase of the empirical enquiry, the data analysis was modified in a way that allowed for substantiation and refinement of the model that was developed in the exploratory round. Based on the compiled qualitative data, each previously defined construct and relationship was evaluated for each case separately (the complete coding scheme is provided in Appendix 3) before a cross-case analysis was conducted (Miles and Huberman 1994). Again, an independent evaluation of the constructs by two individuals ensured intercoder reliability.

3.6 Summary

This chapter has introduced the design that forms the basis and framing of the research effort at hand. Starting with the ontological and epistemological stance, this study is based on a strongly realist ontology and aims at explaining observations in reality by means of relationships between constructs in the respective context. This context is represented by large organisations which were determined as the object of analysis in this research effort. Eventually, the goal is to answer the research questions with a theory-guided explanatory model which is composed of objectively measurable constructs and respective linkages, expressed by propositions.

To do so, various available research strategies were compared and a justified selection of the case study method was presented. The chosen case study design is represented by a two-staged approach which comprises an exploratory phase for theory building and a corroborative phase for theory substantiation and refinement. Both phases are composed of qualitative multiple-case studies aiming at a theoretical replication of insights.

The case sampling was conducted in a way that ensures high comparability of case sites for internal validity, but at the same time a certain degree of heterogeneity, so as to ensure a high generalisability of insights and the opportunity of a theoretical replication. The latter requirement necessitates an adequate variation of the independent construct across case sites.

Both phases of case studies rely primarily on semi-structured interviews and the analysis of internal documentation for triangulation purposes. In addition, the exploratory phase encompassed a round table, with researchers and members of the case companies, where the developed explanatory model was discussed. The analysis of data was based on an iterative coding-approach in comparison with relevant literature.

Following Dubé and Paré (2003), Appendix 1 provides a detailed overview of the research design, the context description, the elucidation of the data collection process, the data collection methods and an elucidation of the data analysis process.

The findings of the exploratory case studies are introduced in the following section, Chapter 4 – *Empirical Exploration and Theory Building*. Based on the presented insights and existing literature, an explanatory model answering the research questions of this study is developed. Chapter 5 - *Empirical Substantiation and Theory Corroboration* - comprises the results of the corroborating phase.

4. Empirical Exploration and Theory Building

After the previous chapters have elaborated the theoretical foundations and the methodological approach of the study at hand, the following section introduces the empirical part of the research, which is divided into two phases, one being exploratory in nature and a second with the goal of substantiation and refinement. The following chapter presents the results of the first empirical phase which aimed at developing a theory-guided explanatory model that is able to explain the impact of IT governance on business performance. The multiple-case study approach was guided by the theoretical foundations and preliminary framework presented in Chapter 2 and included constant review of relevant literature in the case of novel emerging insights.

After a detailed introduction of the case sites and data collection procedure, the developed explanatory model is presented first, before it is discussed in depth in the subsequent chapters.

4.1 Data Selection and Analysis

As elucidated in Section 3.4, this study is focused on large German corporations and a top-level perspective on ITG. Therefore, the highest ranking IT executives (usually the CIO) of all DAX corporations as well as in size comparable private firms were approached in the course of the first empirical phase of the study. The first written enquiry led to the participation of six corporations and a minor number of negative answers. After the data was collected at these six sites, those corporations which did not react to the first written enquiry were re-approached via telephone. When doing so, the case sampling strategy as described in Chapter 3.4 served as a basis for the sequence of the performed telephone calls, which were stopped after the desired amount and variation of cases was at hand. This approach allowed a purposive sampling that fully met the previously introduced requirements of a theoretical replication without wasting contact data. Doing so, those firms which did not respond to the first enquiry and which were not approached via telephone were set aside and re-approached in the course of the second empirical data collection. Table 6 provides an overview of the case sample.

Case company	Core business	Turnover 2011	Bal. Sheet 2011
ALPHA	High-tech industry	> € 20 bn	
BETA	Chemical industry	> € 20 bn	
GAMMA	Chemical industry	> € 20 bn	
DELTA	Heavy industry	> € 20 bn	
EPSILON	Chemical industry	> € 10 bn	
ZETA	Media industry	> € 10 bn	
ETA	Telecommunication industry	> € 20 bn	
THETA	Transportation industry	> € 20 bn	
IOTA	Financial industry		> € 350 bn
KAPPA	Financial industry		> € 350 bn
LAMBDA	Financial industry		> € 350 bn

Table 6: Case sample of the exploratory phase

As described above, in each corporation the CIO was approached and at six sites a personal interview was determined. At four sites the available timeframe did not allow for a personal interview with the CIO due to scheduling issues. In these cases, the interviews were arranged with the respective heads of the CIO offices. In the latter cases, the CIOs received the interview guidelines a priori and assured that the substituting interview partners are fully knowledgeable about the topics in question. In one case, the CIO passed the interview request on towards a division CIO, one organisational level underneath. The reason at this particular case site was that the respective division was responsible for an ongoing redesign of the corporate IT governance. As a consequence, the concerning division CIO was considered to be the right respondent for the study.

Case company	Interview partner(s)
ALPHA	Chief Information Officer
BETA	Chief Information Officer Head of controlling CEO of IT service provider
GAMMA	Head of CIO office
DELTA	Chief Information Officer
EPSILON	Head of CIO office Head of IT quality management
ZETA	Chief Information Officer
ETA	Department Chief Information Officer Head of Department-CIO office
THETA	Head of CIO office Head of IT strategy and alignment
IOTA	Chief Information Officer
KAPPA	Chief Information Officer
LAMBDA	Head of CIO office

Table 7: Interview partners in the exploratory phase

After the guidelines for the semi-structured interviews (see Appendix 2.1) were dispatched, four case companies announced that more than one interview partner will take part in the conversation. All interviews were carried out in person and took place on-site. The conversations were held in German and had an average length of 90 minutes. Nine interviews were tape recorded and fully transcribed. In two cases, ETA and IOTA, recording was not permitted onsite. Therefore, comprehensive notes were taken during the interviews and a protocol was tape-recorded by two interrogators right after the dialogues. Building on these records, a transcript was written for ETA and IOTA as well. All transcripts were sent to the case companies for inspection and returned with minor modifications. The conducted interviews resulted in more than 82,000 words (approx. 160 pages) of approved qualitative data.

As stated previously, most of the case companies were willing to provide access to internal documentation like e.g. ITG manuals and guidelines, governance presentations, organisational charts or quality manuals. These documents were complementing the insights from the conversations and allowed for triangulation of data and an increase of the internal validity of the study. The documentation was particularly valuable for analysis of the independent construct, ITG maturity.

As introduced in Section 3.5, the data was analysed in an iterative manner. A cyclic assignation of codes to chunks of text was followed by feedback from literature and an assessment of gathered documentation from the case-sites. When following this approach, new codes and constructs were introduced for emerging concepts while others were redefined or dropped in the process of sense-making. Meanwhile, the preliminary research framework was expanded with these emerging constructs and associations, while being persistently compared to relevant theories and concepts from previous literature. This led to the steady evolvement of an explanatory model which was then used to provide feedback for the ongoing procedure of analysis. This process was re-iterated until saturation was reached, meaning that the developed theoretical model was able to explain the impact of IT governance on the business performance for the analysed case companies, while further analysis of the data did not provide novel insights. The results of the exploratory case studies are presented in the following.

4.2 Proposed Explanatory Model

In the subsequent chapters, the developed explanatory model is presented first and thereafter discussed in detail. While doing so, the discovered constructs and associations are introduced in close relation to the referring themes and examples that were found in the course of the exploratory case study research. As introduced in Chapter 3.5, novel concepts were formulated in comparison to extant literature and theory that guided the defining of new constructs and setting up of propositions.

The theoretical model illustrated in Figure 7 integrates the findings of the exploratory case-studies and offers an answer to the research question of how IT governance impacts business performance of a firm. Table 8 provides the definitions of the employed constructs. These are based on previous work presented in Chapter 2 and further literature that is introduced in the following.

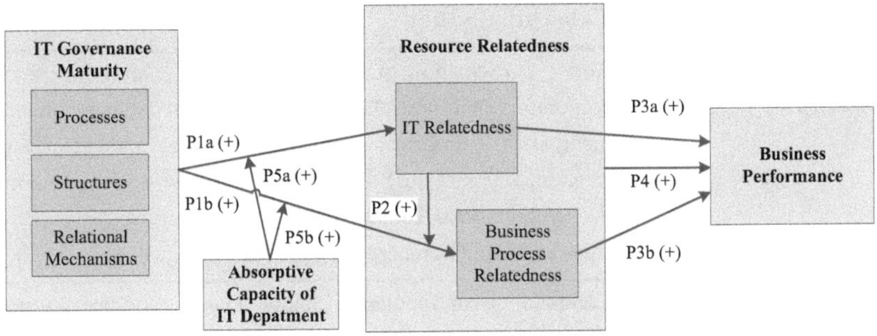

Figure 7: Explanatory model of the impact of IT governance on the business performance of a firm

Construct	Conceptualisation
IT Governance Maturity	Maturity of the framework for decision rights and accountabilities to encourage desirable behaviour in the use of IT. Regarded as a combination of ITG processes, ITG structures and ITG relational mechanisms (based on De Haes and Van Grembergen 2009; Peterson 2004a; Weill 2004).
ITG Processes	Formalisation and institutionalisation of strategic IT decision making or IT monitoring procedures, such as charge back arrangements, SLAs, portfolio management processes, performance measurement processes, specific frameworks (e.g. COBIT, ITIL), project governance processes, IT budget control processes or IT reporting processes (based on De Haes and Van Grembergen 2009; Peterson 2004a).
ITG Structures	Structural (formal) devices and mechanisms for connecting and enabling horizontal, or liaison, contacts between business and IT management (decision-making) functions, such as IT strategy committees, IT steering committees, IT architecture committees or IT project steering committees (based on De Haes and Van Grembergen 2009; Peterson 2004a).

Construct	Conceptualisation
ITG Relational Mechanisms	Active participation of, and collaborative relationship among, corporate executives, IT management, and business management, such as informal meetings, knowledge management (job rotation, KM-systems), IT leadership, business-IT account management, internal communication addressing IT (based on De Haes and Van Grembergen 2009; Peterson 2004a).
Business Performance	Combination of reputation among major customer segments, frequency of new product or service introduction, return on investment, net profits, technological developments and/ or other innovations in business operations, product quality, market share gains and revenue growth. (based on Chan et al. 1997; Dess and Robinson Jr 1984; Sabherwal and Chan 2001; Venkatraman 1989; Venkatraman and Ramanujam 1986).
Resource Relatedness	The use of common resources (i.e. common factors of production) across business units (Davis and Thomas 1993).
IT Relatedness	The use of common IT resources and common IT management process across business units (Tanriverdi 2006).
Business Process Relatedness	Usage of common business processes and managerial practices across business units (based on Campbell and Goold 1998; Milgrom and Roberts 1995; Tanriverdi 2005; Tanriverdi 2006; Tanriverdi and Venkatraman 2005).
Absorptive Capacity of the IT Department	The ability of the IT department to consistently gain and utilise context-specific knowledge situated within business units (based on Cohen and Levinthal 1990).

Table 8: Definition of employed constructs

4.3 The Impact of IT Governance

When conducting and analysing the exploratory case studies, two major themes of IT governance impact were observed. The first is represented by technology-related changes, encompassing infrastructure, applications as well as IT services. The other is related to the amendment of business processes and the corresponding process logic in the observed corporations. The following section is organised accordingly.

4.3.1 Infrastructure and Applications

As a common theme throughout all analysed companies, the consolidation of IT infrastructure has been found to be one of the primary goals and actions after initiating activities of an active revision of ITG. Excerpts from the cases of GAMMA, LAMBDA, DELTA and ZETA are provided in order to illustrate this correlation.

The exploratory analysis further suggests that ITG has an effect on the application landscape of the regarded firms. The cases of THETA and KAPPA, together with further insights from LAMBDA, are introduced to demonstrate these finding.

Based on the insights of the case-descriptions, Proposition P1a is suggested. Thereafter, a discussion of the applied constructs and a theoretical positioning of the suggested proposition are offered.

4.3.1.1 Consolidation of IT infrastructure – empirical observations

GAMMA

GAMMA is an industrial corporation specialised on the production of health care and nutrition products, as well as high-tech materials. The three respective divisions have high degrees of managerial freedom, which accounts for IT as well. However, three to four years prior to the interview, the board decided that it should be evaluated, where mutual approaches in the area of IT are sensible. Following that decision, a CIO office was introduced. Currently, GAMMA is in the process of an ITG redesign and evaluates first results. According to the head of the CIO office, before redesigning ITG, there was no informed or responsible body for company-wide decisions relating to IT. Hence, no coordinated actions across different departments were possible, despite a centralised and shared IT department that was in place. The redesign of ITG did not change decision rights to a large extent, but ensured that responsibilities were assigned to certain actors and that it became possible to discuss certain topics, as reported by the interviewee:

> *"Before we had a CIO office, certain things were recognised as an open issue, but there were basically no decisions made."*

The first results that are attributed to the redesigned ITG at GAMMA are a technical consolidation of data centres and a unified communication system. Furthermore, the head of the CIO office emphasised minor historical issues, which never constituted a technical difficulty, but remained open due to vague or missing responsibilities:

> *"Before having actively pursued IT governance, it was not possible to consolidate e-mail addresses. These were based on a two-digit number of top-level domains before. Another topic was identity and access management, which did not allow using one single key card across the firm's facilities."*

According to the interviewee at GAMMA, such rather simple projects, which were directly affecting staff, had a prominent psychological effect that helped to familiarise the organisation with the newly founded CIO department, opening doors to larger projects.

LAMBDA

The initial situation at LAMBDA, where a CIO was introduced recently as well, was quite similar, yet for other reasons. LAMBDA grew very rapidly during the last years; mainly through acquisitions. The head of the CIO office stated that this phase was formative for the currently dismembered state of the corporate IT. A CIO or a comparable position was not existent in the corporation for years and IT was regarded as a pure service provider. According to the interviewee, this led to severe problems:

> *"The integration of acquired companies was barely makeshift and IT governance was not further emphasised than required by regulators. Strategic IT considerations were practically inexistent."*

The interviewee reported further that IT staff was working to full capacity to keep the daily business running, but that the daily routine was highly inefficient:

> *"Every department was doing the best they could do, but without looking left or right, as no collaborative structures or authorities were in place."*

LAMBDA got into severe problems in the course of the financial crisis in 2008, with IT being part of the problem according to the interviewee:

> *"The eventual mess in the IT heavily contributed to what was happening."*

Basic functions like financial risk management were bounded to the constrained possibilities of the IT, which was not adequately integrated among the acquired firms. After a major spin-off in the aftermath of the crisis pushed the IT staff at LAMBDA to the limits of their capabilities, a significant change of the way IT was organised and working was regarded as inevitable. The first step was the implementation of a CIO position. The new executive introduced a framework for decision rights and accountabilities, which was in such a form not available before, and announced major operational changes:

> *"Looking back at the feudal time before the CIO was onboard, everyone was doing whatever he wanted, e.g. getting freelancers for IT projects or buying end-user solutions for his department. Now it is different, there are rules, like for IT investments that have to go through a separate board or the obligation to calculate a business case."*

One year later, the IT of LAMBDA was undergoing a complete reorganisation. The entire hardware stack was re-designed from scratch and is being currently implemented with an external partner. The interviewee explicated:

> *"Our main strategy at the moment is to get rid of the inhomogeneous system landscape. From there we will move on towards further optimisation."*

The head of the CIO office at LAMBDA admitted that the corporation is still at the very beginning of the way they want to go, but that a lot of progress was done:

> *"The new ITG framework is in place and we see first results. However, the framework has to be lived consequently [and] stands or falls with the acting people."*

DELTA

Related observations were made in the case of DELTA. Compared to GAMMA and LAMBDA, the organisational and historical background is a different one. Despite being active in closely related industries, DELTA is organised as a conglomerate with a very decentral governance. According to the CIO, this meant a lot of freedom in the past:

> *"In some extreme cases it was common for small subsidiaries to go to ALDI and get a few computers there to equip their offices."*

Basically, corporation-wide ITG was nonexistent. Two years prior to the interview, a board decision led to the introduction of a CIO office at corporate level, which was charged with the development of a corporate-wide IT governance and IT strategy. The CIO stated:

> *"[ITG was introduced] to enable a constructive collaboration of different departments. This starts with cost savings through synergy effects, the reduction of interfaces, the decrease of communication processes, or, first things first, with the implementation of communication processes."*

The CIO explained that the first step was a major revision of company-wide authorities in relation to information technology, which was a tough process:

> *"It is hard to explain to the CEO of an eight-man subsidiary why he in future will have to stop buying cheap hardware [..., but] a common IT infrastructure is the basis for all strategic considerations concerning IT."*

DELTA is focusing currently on a revision of its basic infrastructure; the CIO reported:

> *"The first steps are consistent desktop solutions, wide area networks and data centres. Simultaneously an analysis is ongoing to determine which things can be done similarly e.g. in steel production, in plant construction or in ship building."*

Eventually, the ITG initiative is seen at its beginning at DELTA, as described in the course of the interview:

> *"The new IT governance structure at DELTA is in place for ten months now, hence the whole mission is at the very beginning of the journey."*

ZETA

ZETA, one of the key players in the media industry, is governed in a similarly decentralised fashion as DELTA. The case study at ZETA does not report a success story, but rather offers insights into the course of a major project failure. The findings at ZETA provide crucial insights for a better understanding of the relationship between IT governance and the consolidation of IT infrastructure. The CIO at ZETA reported that the corporate IT landscape is not only dismembered to a large extent, but that even an overview of the implemented hard- and software is missing:

> *"If we stick to the finance topics – some departments use SAP, others Oracle and others use Dynamics for these topics. I see only who uses which system when I have to sign off the bills of orders. Actually, that is the only way for us [the CIO office] to see which [technological] progress is going on in the firm."*

A company-wide framework for IT decision rights and accountabilities is not available, giving subsidiaries almost the full authority over their IT. Basically, this would represent a fully decentralised (IT) governance.

However, what makes this specific case study extremely interesting is the fact that ZETA tried to consolidate their IT infrastructure a few years ago, without a holistic revision of corporate ITG. Reasoned with a unique culture at ZETA, authorities and accountabilities remained unchanged, while decisions about corporate-wide IT projects, like a consolidation of data-centres or a harmonisation of desktop solutions, were made centrally by the CIO, backed by the board. These projects all failed spectacularly as reported by the CIO:

> *"The idea at the beginning of the 2000s was a central IT delivery for all operative departments. In 2003 we realised that it is very hard to roll out such a project without heavily changing the structure of this firm. Consequently it was decided to return to the former principle where the business units can coordinate their IT topics - more or less actively - on their own."*

The CIO reported that it was not possible for his office to manage the execution of such projects on the fly, without implementing an overreaching matrix of authorities and decision rights that encompassed all affected entities. However, the interviewee explicated that such an approach was not welcome:

> *"Implementing such an instrument was interpreted as equivalent to a partial cession of management rights within subsidiaries, which is contravening organisational culture at ZETA."*

In consequence, all consolidation projects, planned or ongoing, were cancelled. The CIO of ZETA summarises:

"We are aware that there is a significant delta between calculated optimal IT costs, or even industry benchmarks on one hand, and the numbers that we are measuring here, on the other. However, adjusting this delta [with ITG] would mean altering the basic structure [of the corporation]."

4.3.1.2 Harmonisation of the IT application landscape – empirical observations

Not only a relation between IT governance and the consolidation of hardware was observed in the exploratory case study, but a similar link was also reported for applications and IT services.

LAMBDA

Whilst DELTA and GAMMA were focused on the redesign of infrastructure after introducing new ITG guidelines, LAMBDA simultaneously initiated a major revision of its application landscape. However, the head of the CIO office at LAMBDA reported that these two projects cannot be compared regarding their complexity. While the consolidation of the hardware stack mainly required an adjustment of the IT decision rights, the revision of the software stack involved by far more parties, especially in the business units:

"The original state in the business units was a typical 'candy shop' situation. But a simple withdrawal of decision rights would not have worked out. We need the business units to be involved in the redesign of the software-stack."

Therefore, various mechanisms proposed in ITG literature, especially relational ones, had to be implemented in order to move along, as reported by LAMBDA:

"I need strong promoters in the business units, with a lot of guts. These managers, who handle the demand management, need to understand the daily routines in the business units and they need to know how to negotiate with the local business units. If they are weak, the ITG will not work, and we can't move along."

The head of the CIO office added:

> *"We learned one thing, namely that establishing such a process bottom-up is impossible. These mechanisms need to be implemented top-down, promoted by the right people."*

KAPPA

KAPPA is among Europe's system relevant banks and has, similar to other major financial institutions around the globe, a long record of acquisitions, especially in the last 10 years. The CIO of KAPPA states that IT is seen as a *"migration machine"* for the corporation as a whole. The infrastructure is to a large extent consolidated and the next big goal of KAPPA is going towards a unified platform for banking and back-office support systems. The CIO reported that the latter task is not seen as a serious problem. A competence centre for human resource (HR) functions was established and the first results are regarded as satisfying. However, the consolidation of core-banking and front-office systems is a serious challenge. The adaption of authorities and hence a redesign of IT governance was the first step. The CIO reported:

> *"Business units were since ever approaching the IT from a product-perspective stating 'we need application X, to be able to offer product Z' mostly with the addendum 'immediately'. IT had to deliver; this is how the balance of power was for decades. In order to move on, this had to be changed. And it has changed, firmly and throughout the corporation."*

Nevertheless, KAPPA emphasises, similarly to LAMBDA, that the pure shift of decision rights, which in part works for hardware, does not lead anywhere in the context of the application landscape:

> *"The shift of authorities can impede the uncontrolled growth of application-heterogeneity, but to re-integrate it, several mechanisms are essential to animate business units and the IT staff to work on solutions together."*

This, once more, leads to a purposeful redesign of IT governance as reported by the interviewee:

> *"Eventually, it is ITG that ensures these mechanisms. An example is the requirements engineering that now has to be done in mixed teams, composed of representatives of the business units and IT experts."*

Such approaches are deemed appropriate to ensure the necessary balance of interests among all involved parties, which is seen as a basis for a successful transformation of the application landscape at KAPPA.

THETA

The final case study that is presented in this section is THETA. Due to fact that THETA did not follow the same sequence of actions as observed in the previously introduced cases, the analysis of THETA offered additional insights. While many major transportation firms got into severe financial problems, or even went bankrupt in the course of the liberalisation of the airline industry, THETA expanded and acquired several competitors. ITG has always been receiving a lot of attention at THETA as reported in the interview:

> *"The labels changed over the years [...] but what you call IT governance today is actively pursued since the 1980s at THETA, keeping the IT landscape, including hard- and software, highly streamlined and consolidated. I am talking now about the core-corporation."*

However, the numerous acquisitions changed the status quo and brought along new challenges. The interview partners at THETA reported that the acquired competitors, which are still operating under their original brand names, were run relatively independently in the beginning. This was possible since THETA provides major services for competitors, such as catering, technical support or IT solutions for the aviation market.

> *"Economies of scale can be achieved rather quickly. Full integration of IT was not pursued in the case of the acquired companies. When necessary, e.g. for payroll systems, linkages between the systems were established. [...] An intelligent harmonisation policy, that's how I would call it."*

The head of the CIO office at THETA stated that costs were under control but that THETA was confronted with problems at the level of business processes:

> *"We emphasise the perspective of our customers, and we want to offer the best possible service for our clients. This involves seamless services across all our brand names. We want our customers who booked with THETA-SUB1 to be able to check in at all THETA check in machines, all around the globe."*

Such requirements proved to be serious challenges on the basis of a heterogeneous infrastructure. THETA emphasises the need for a certain degree of local autonomy for subsidiaries, but the head of the CIO office states:

> *"If advantages of the network are not reaped, THETA is not much more than a collection of medium sized companies."*

Consequently, THETA is currently acquiring information all across its subsidiaries in order to develop a consolidation plan that allows coping with the problems at the process level. According to the interviewee, this is where the topic of governance comes into play, as it forms the basis for the design and redesign of corporate IT. Well developed ITG relational mechanisms were emphasised particularly by the head of the CIO office for the current challenges at THETA:

> *"For THETA, IT governance is not only about decision rights, IT governance goes far beyond the common matter of hierarchy, towards communication, information and awareness."*

While a large-scale data collection is ongoing to get an overview of the systems in use, a deliberate set of ITG relational mechanisms got enacted to improve communication and alleviate implementation procedures:

> *"The goal [of ITG] is to establish a better communication. The ability to reach all staff is far more worth than a setup where a CIO has direct access to exactly five people. A CIO with a toolbox that enables him to reach the whole community has great opportunities to achieve his goals."*

While the established ITG instruments are relatively similar to the ones introduced in the previously described cases, THETA does not aim at an incremental bottom-up procedure, where a consolidation of hardware is pursued first, before strategic considerations are developed for the application-stack. According to the head of the CIO office, the approach is primarily guided by the customer perspective. The strategy is to decide top-down which application is required across all brands and, thereafter, to design the hardware stack accordingly.

To sum up, the exploratory case studies suggest that the maturity of an IT governance framework is strongly related to the consolidation of IT infrastructure and the application landscape of corporations. Proposition P1a is suggested on the basis of the presented empirical insights. The applied constructs and theoretical positioning of Proposition P1a are provided subsequently.

Proposition P1a: The higher the maturity of IT governance processes, structures and relational mechanisms, the higher the IT relatedness.

4.3.1.3 IT relatedness and IT governance maturity – deduction and refinement of constructs

In line with the described research design (see Chapter 3.5), the iterative analysis of the exploratory cases was closely linked to an ongoing review of related literature. This provided the basis for the definition and formulation of constructs which are forming the developed explanatory model.

IT relatedness

As introduced in Chapter 2.2.3.3, extant literature offers the construct of resource relatedness, which refers to the presence of shared resources and similar activities across business units of the firm (Davis and Thomas 1993). Tanriverdi and Venkatraman (2005) show that the construct of relatedness was applied and adapted to several organisational functions and resources, such as product relatedness (Rumelt 1974), manufacturing relatedness (John and Harrison 1999), technological relatedness (Robins and Wiersema 1995; Silverman 1999), R&D relatedness (Chatterjee and Wernerfelt 1991), marketing relatedness (Capron and Hulland 1999), advertising relatedness (Chatterjee and Wernerfelt 1991), managerial relatedness (Ilinitch and Zeithaml 1995; Prahalad and Bettis 1986) or human resource relatedness (Farjoun 1994).

Based on these works, Tanriverdi (2006, p. 59) derives the construct of *IT relatedness* which he defines as *"the extent to which a multibusiness firm uses common IT resources and common IT management processes across its business units"*. Tanriverdi (2006) provides an operationalisation of the construct with the four dimensions IT infrastructure, IT Strategy, IT Human Resources and IT Vendor Management, which he relates to corresponding organisational resources as presented by Campbell and Goold (1998). The author states that the number of the dimensions of the construct is only limited to the number of distinct IT resources and management processes within the regarded firms.

The construct of IT relatedness is particularly well suited to map the findings of the exploratory case studies in relation to the observed consolidation of IT infrastructure and the application landscape.

Some scholars (e.g. De Vries 1999; Lee and Kim 1999; Manrodt and Vitasek 2004; Wüllenweber et al. 2008) applied the construct of standardisation to comparable contexts in the IS-literature. However, the construct of standardisation proved to be too confined to fully encompass and describe the observed findings of the exploratory case studies, especially in firms which were in an early stage of IT governance initiatives. While some of the interviewees considered standards as a good means for consolidation efforts, especially regarding the hardware stack, others claimed that the introduction of rigorous standards would be too early in many contexts. These dialogue partners often described their efforts with expressions such as 'harmonisation of approaches', 'convergence of way departments are working' etc. This approximation of involved parties and perspectives was described as a crucial stopover towards a harmonised application landscape in almost every corporation. While the construct of relatedness has the depth to map and describe these tacit observations and findings, the construct of standardisation has not.

In consequence, the construct of IT relatedness (Tanriverdi 2006) was chosen in this study to model the observed IT consolidation conditions and efforts in the conducted case studies.

IT governance maturity

The semi-structured interviews were guided by the preliminary framework as introduced in Chapter 2.4. The applied independent construct that was meant to map the IT governance in the observed corporations was provided by De Haes and Van Grembergen (2009). It follows a maturity-based concept (see Chapter 2.3.5.3) which is theoretically rooted in the seminal works on ITG by Weill (2004) and Peterson (2004a). A maturity perspective is chosen due to the fact that an objective evaluation of *good* or *effective* IT governance is not feasible. However, Weill (2004, p. 3) states that firms *"with effective governance have actively designed a set of IT governance mechanisms (e.g., committees, budgeting processes, approvals, IT organizational structure, chargeback, etc.)"*. The construct of ITG maturity builds on the evaluation of the availability of these mechanisms. Moreover, an in depth analysis of the application and quality of these ITG instruments is crucial to assure that they add up to a mature ITG framework.

A collection of guidelines on paper has no impact as long as it is not 'lived' by the corporation.

The construct of ITG maturity proved to be very well suited for both the guidance of the exploratory studies as well as for the mapping of gained insights. ZETA, which claimed that ITG is no topic of interest, had a marginal number of the mechanisms described by the construct of ITG maturity. Companies like DELTA and GAMMA, which were assessed at the beginning of their ITG venture, have enacted a number of ITG mechanisms. Yet, they are still at the stage of designing an overreaching ITG framework with a focus on the setup of decision rights or even basic accountabilities like in the case of GAMMA. Firms which asserted that ITG was pursued actively for a longer period, or which claimed to have made good progress regarding their ITG-targets, showed not only a higher number and variety of ITG mechanisms, but provided evidence that those were tailored to their companies' needs, often accentuating relational mechanisms. Examples of exceptionally well developed ITG frameworks were offered by ALPHA and BETA. In these cases, emphasis was not only laid on numerous well designed ITG mechanisms, but also on appropriate staffing that ensures effectiveness and efficiency of these frameworks (see Chapter 4.3.2). However, the assumption that the pure number of enacted ITG mechanisms does not describe the effectiveness and maturity of an ITG framework, was as well substantiated in this study. An example was provided by EPSILON, where the interviewee stated:

> *"The development and enactment of a redesigned ITG framework showed no results for months as staff was still living in the old governance structure, asking each other for favours on the telephone and ignoring the new accountabilities."*

4.3.1.4 Theoretical positioning of Proposition P1a

The deliberated redesign of ITG provided many observed companies for the first time a platform for company-wide information aggregation, analysis and discussion, which in turn allowed for mutual and sensible decision making. Regarded from the RBV, IT represents one of the fundamental resources of the firm. In consequence, management will utilise the available information and related control structures in order to fully exploit it and achieve the maximal output that can be generated by that particular resource (Barney 1991; Mata et al. 1995). Since resource relatedness is a major source of synergies in multibusiness firms (see Chapter 2.2.3.3), it will be pursued by management with zeal.

Consequently, the more mature ITG is, the more capabilities are available for information gathering, decision making and eventually enforcing of IT related topics throughout the corporation. This includes the possibility to raise IT relatedness and, thus, to achieve synergies that lead to higher profits.

Proposition P1a is thus fully in line with the basic assumptions of the RBV. The related detailed discussion of the performance effects of IT relatedness is provided in Chapter 4.4.

4.3.2 Business Processes

While evidence for Proposition P1a was found in all conducted cases, the three case companies ALPHA, BETA and EPSILON added a new perspective to the previously introduced findings. An analysis of these three companies suggests not only a relation between ITG maturity and IT relatedness, but as well an impact of ITG on the way business processes are designed.

In line with the preceding chapter, excerpts from the cases are followed by the suggested Proposition P1b. Thereafter, a discussion of the applied constructs and a theoretical positioning of the suggested proposition are offered.

4.3.2.1 Harmonisation of business processes – empirical observations

ALPHA

ALPHA is a market leader in various industries and has a long-lasting tradition in engineering. The CIO of ALPHA reported that the topic of ITG is high on the agenda for more than two decades now. According to the interviewee, ALPHA has started implementing mechanisms, which are today classified as ITG instruments, in the early 1990s, long before they were at the agenda of other corporations or field driven frameworks like COBIT or ITIL. The ITG framework at ALPHA was steadily refined over the years according to the CIO and goes beyond technology today:

> *"A large organisation like ALPHA works only if you have compulsory guidelines. [...] ALPHA started 20 years ago [with guidelines focused on infrastructure] and moved up the stack very quickly. That is why we ended up with [a focus on] processes earlier than others."*

While new ITG mechanisms were implemented due to changing requirements, the CIO reported that other mechanisms were not essential anymore, as the culture and attitude of the staff assimilated the basic ideas and guidelines behind these mechanisms:

> *"In the 1990s we had a serious dispute with our staff when we decided that the implementation of certain applications has to be coordinated with the central IT, and that the IT will not support different software products in various versions for the same task anymore. We had raging users on the telephone stating 'if you take this tool away, I cannot do my work anymore'. I am talking about e-mail clients. [...]*
>
> *Today it is the other way around; we would get angry telephone calls if different clients would be in use, involving e.g. scheduling problems."*

A variety of evidence for the previously suggested Proposition P1a was found at ALPHA. While the ITG maturity can be regarded as high, the IT relatedness at ALPHA is exceptional. The CIO reported:

> *"Infrastructure and data-centre consolidations were started almost 20 years ago. [...] It takes only a few hours to update more than 200,000 PCs world-wide, from China via South Africa to Brazil. [...] If you look at the topic cloud computing – this does not make sense for ALPHA as our data centres are set up in a highly efficient manner."*

ALPHA is running a largely harmonised application platform on its own data centres. Wherever possible on the level of processes, unified solutions are applied. This is exactly where ALPHA provided a novel perspective on ITG. According to the CIO at ALPHA, the current goal of IT governance is finding a way to further promote the slogan 'one solution for one problem' towards the process level in the business units:

> *"The director I report to states that ALPHA should only have one solution for one problem, throughout the whole corporation. That is why the concepts behind the solutions have to be unified. [...] This brings along very high requirements [... and ...] huge discussions."*

The interviewee explained that after 20 years of controlled ITG campaigns, ALPHA came to a point where the further optimisation of the IT support for the company's business was only possible in close interdependence with the reengineering of the supported business processes. Like IT is not an end in itself, IT governance is neither and needs to be designed purposefully. If it is not effective, it needs to be adapted and developed further. The CIO provided following example for such a case:

> *"IT governance assured that ALPHA was running only SAP on unified hardware, but the BUs were defining their processes themselves, and gradually the SAP R/3 was no standard anymore, but merely a basis for various highly customised proprietary solutions [... which ...] basically represent very expensive custom made software."*

With full support of the board, the CIO office at ALPHA was able to redesign the IT governance in a way, which ensured full involvement of IT representatives in process design all across the corporation. The CIO explicated:

> *"It is not only about decision power or even about enforcing of unpopular decisions. Often, it is simply about knowing what is possible with our running solutions; regularly in the past, this knowledge was missing in the BUs, leading to a process design that enforced unnecessary new applications. If a department has a request, we first analyse if we can map this request to our platform. If not, we first try to redesign the process. If this is not possible, we are happy to build a new solution."*

The conducted redesign of decision rights and accountabilities raised the conception of ITG at ALPHA to a new level. However, various new problems arose. While the IT is well aware that a single e-mail client is able to serve all needs of most of the users, the situation with specific process designs in the business context is different. The CIO department realised that the major hurdle would not be designing the new ITG framework, but acquiring the right people which could fill it with life. The resolution that two departments have to move on to one production process can be blocked by the involved parties by asserting that this is technically not possible. In consequence, the CIO office started hiring people with strong process knowledge from the BUs to successfully solve this problem:

> *"Many of our staff came from business units. Often we have more process knowledge today in our organisation [i.e. the CIO department], than the business units themselves. The solutions we are replacing these days were often even developed by our people 20 years ago in the BUs."*

The CIO added that in some cases his department has to take care that the BUs do not lean back in the course of process design, as input from the BUs is crucial. The interviewee emphasised that the process owners are not resident in the IT or the CIO department. However the IT governance is designed in a way, that every process design or re-design is aligned with the IT.

BETA

The observations and findings of the BETA case study compare on various domains very well with the results of the case study at ALPHA. BETA is represented on a multitude of markets related to the chemical industry. Similarly to ALPHA, BETA is pursuing the topic of IT governance for longer than a decade, however, based on a very different organisational approach. While all domains of information technology at ALPHA were subordinated to the CIO, IT at BETA is organised in another way. Comparably to ALPHA, the CIO is located directly under the board, but all operational topics are bundled in a fully owned but distinct external organisation. This IT organisation is separated organisationally as well as physically. In order to get a comprehensive picture, interviews with the CIO of BETA and the CEO of BETA's IT organisation were conducted. The former was accompanied by the head of controlling. What makes the case-study at BETA exceptionally interesting is the distinct separation of roles between the CEO of the IT organisation, which is located outside of BETA, and the CIO.

It was instructing to see that BETA, despite a very different organisational structure and ITG design, had a similar experience curve in the context of IT governance as ALPHA. In line with a constant redesign of ITG, BETA consolidated its hardware stack. The CIO stated:

> *"The ITG department was installed in 2000 [...and ...] is connected to the question how to reach our business goals best. Integration and synergies are a central concept here. Cost- and process efficiencies are the central topics of our ITG. [...] Productivity and efficiency gains linked with less costs – 'more for less', this is what we were aiming for [with ITG], and what we were able to achieve."*

The CIO repeatedly stated 'more for less' to be his guiding principle and goal in the domain of infrastructure. The interviewees claimed that this goal – 'more efficiency with lower costs' – was achieved with a highly standardised hardware stack and a harmonised application platform.

Besides examples like unified desktop-solutions around the globe, the conversation partners exemplified high relatedness of their IT with the fact that a full integration of a major competitor is achievable in less than six months.

The ITG maturity at BETA is regarded as high, not only based on the fact that a multitude of deliberately tailored ITG mechanisms is in place. What is more in the case of BETA is the fact that ITG efficiently serves as a vital connector between the industrial corporation, the CIO office and the external service provider. These observations support the previously suggested Proposition P1a.

However, after the infrastructure and application landscape was transformed to certain degree, BETA reported that a major barrier was hit on the way towards a better IT support of the corporation. Again, varying business processes among different departments were referred to as the central issue in the interviews:

> *"Within the HR, for example, we are trying to [...] explain that if Spain, Italy and Germany keep running their own processes, not only the development of the HR application [i.e. SAP module] is a problem, but we constantly get overlapping and clashing change requests. The system becomes extremely complex and problematic to maintain. [...] But there [in the HR] is absolutely no understanding."*

The CIO of BETA emphasised that after certain steps are done, IT governance has to go beyond the borders of IT towards the core of the problem:

> *"The definition of requirements, in whatever corner of this company, has eventually an effect on the operation [of IT], and if everything is implemented what the BUs wish for, we end up with something that no one can run or maintain anymore. And once implemented, these things deter us from other process amendments."*

In consequence, IT governance was redesigned a few years ago in a way that business units cannot bypass the IT in the design phase of processes. However, the CIO of BETA pointed out that this redesign was not equal to a transfer of decision rights to the IT organisation or the CIO office. On the contrary, he stated that a centralised approach, with IT as a key authority, would result in inefficiencies as well:

"What we are looking for is a coordinating process which assures transparency and involvement of all parties. [It's about answering] Who can do what, independent of where on the planet he is sitting; how can we connect all these actors, how can we coordinate?"

However, he pointed out:

"Some things have to be promoted with certain imperialism, but in balance with the involved stakeholder groups. A collaborative structure will generate more efficiencies and effectiveness than a centralised structure can achieve."

The CEO of the IT organisation reported that process redesign was already conducted successfully in some areas based on this involving approach, e.g. for the supply chain or in the procurement division. The largest part of the commercial areas was under revision in the time of the case study. The goal was to harmonise all employed ERP solutions towards one system. The CEO of the IT organisation stated that this project only has chances of success if all involved parties work together and find a compromise between process amendments and software customisation.

The impression at BETA so far was that wherever physical goods are involved, it is relatively easy to communicate the need for an equal process across divisions. The situation is different in departments like the HR, where the users are missing the understanding why their daily routine should be aligned with the one of their colleagues all across the globe. The CIO explicated:

"The whole mission of harmonisation went along with discussions. Now, it got accepted by most of the actors in the core areas like supply chain or order management. In other areas, like HR, there is absolutely no understanding [... because ...] it is the first time for these people to be involved in such a project. There is absolutely no understanding, let's say in France compared to Italy [why processes should be aligned]."

EPSILON

The historical background at EPSILON, another firm active in the chemical industry, is very different compared to ALPHA and BETA. While ITG in the latter two cases was pursued for more than a decade, EPSILON started its ITG campaign a few years ago, basically from zero. In consequence, the case study at EPSILON added a new perspective and provided extremely valuable additional insights. Though, it is important to note that EPSILON is somewhat smaller than the other case sites.

The ITG redesign at EPSILON was started three years prior to the interview and pursued rather radically. The head of the CIO office described the time before:

> *"Live and let live was the motto in the old days. As long as money was transferred from e.g. Brazil, we did not care how they earned it."*

After a new CEO was named, however, the basic structure of the company was redesigned and a CIO position, which did not exist before, was implemented. The CIO established an entirely new unit, consisting of about 50 people. These were recruited internally from the IT and various operational departments and complemented with experts from the market. When being asked for how long EPSILON has had documented IT governance, or even any active ITG mechanism, both interview partners stated *"since three years now"*. This exemplifies the clear cut and highlights the value of the case study at EPSILON.

After the new department was set up, EPSILON developed an extraordinary detailed ITG framework, which was printed under the label *IT quality manual* and distributed on paper to every EPSILON desk around the world. This manual includes all accountabilities and decision rights in relation to IT, from very basic end-user requirements like desktop support, to top-level concerns like IT architecture. The head of the CIO department explained that technical goals were achievable quite well on the basis of a strict set of rules and guidelines. As a consequence, a targeted redesign and harmonisation of infrastructure, including a large fraction of the software stack, was accomplished in a very short period of time. These insights again provide support to the suggested Proposition P1a.

However, the formulation of an ITG framework and quality manual proved not to be a silver bullet. The head of IT quality management, a position introduced in the new CIO department, stated in the course of the case study:

> *"Three years ago, we thought that the problem is having all those [ITG] mechanisms designed well and the manual written, published and distributed. Now, we think we were wrong. The problem is having those things read by the corresponding people. This is much tougher."*

The head of the CIO department explained that after the new authorities were enacted, nothing happened besides the technological changes, which were actively pursued by the CIO department. According to him, more tacit goals in relation to organisational processes were not accomplished as the staff continued working the way they did before:

> *"We turned around the organisation quite substantially, and nothing happened."*

The head of quality management explicated that e-learning initiatives, video conferencing or comparable approaches failed. In a reaction, the largest part of the EPSILON CIO department, 42 people, was assigned to an active ITG rollout project, meaning that they physically travelled around the world, spending about two weeks at each EPSILON site in e.g. Brazil, South Africa or China. The interview partners stated that this physical ITG-rollout was the key enabler for a subsequently accomplished business process redesign and ERP harmonisation:

> *"You need to go there, you need to coach and you need to talk to them [the employees abroad]. This is why we travelled a lot - we went to Asia, South America or Africa; we coached on the global scale. If we would have tried to do it solely by video conferences and e-learning, it would not have worked out. Human nature needs that."*

Comparably to BETA, EPSILON defined its IT governance in a way that BUs cannot bypass the IT in the design phase of business processes. Meanwhile, the IT was deterred from becoming a new hegemon in the subject of business process design, as reported in the interview:

> *"On one end you have the business owner and on the other you have basically the IT owner. And in here somewhere you maybe have a business process manager [...] and the critical thing is starting to happen [...] in this area, where we have the system architect and the process architect. [...] I strongly believe that you need to have [...] a positive tension between those two because they are coming from fundamentally different angles and I'm extremely happy that this decision has been made here to separate them, because otherwise you are not getting that tension. If you put the system architect in the business, you end up in chaos. If you put the business process architect in the IT, then you end up*

exactly in the situation where IT starts telling business how they should do their job and when you do that you are lost, because they pay the bills."

To ensure this positive tension on the basis of a separation of duties, a newly founded department called 'business process and data ownership' took over the responsibility for the collection and bundling of requirements as well as a first rough design of processes. It is then the 'business process and data ownership' department which collaborates with the IT on the final process design and development of the software solution. Eventually, the IT governance enforces collaboration between IT and business units in the course of process design. The head of the CIO office reported:

> *"You have to keep these things separated, if you don't, you end up in a conflict of interests. It can be very dangerous, to start building your processes solely based on what the existing ERP can deliver. [...] the business process and data ownership [department] is therefore responsible for the processes and the IT [department] for the technology; they have to find a solution mutually, none of them has the right of command."*

Summary

Summing up, all three introduced case companies came to a point where they were persuaded that a further enhancement of the IT support for the firm depends on a close interplay between business and IT, accompanied with a revision of the underlying business processes. This meant, in consequence, that the way these business processes were governed had to be redesigned as well. Nevertheless, the approaches chosen by the three case companies were varying.

Neither EPSILON nor BETA transferred a significant proportion of decision rights in the context of business process design towards a central IT department. However, both firms established a deliberate IT governance system that enforces transparency, communication and collaboration among all actors so as to impede the implementation of multiple solutions for similar tasks. Compared to EPSILON and BETA, ALPHA chose a more centralised approach, with extensive decision rights residing in the IT. However, an analysis of the historical background at ALPHA shows a very similar course of actions as reported by EPSILON and BETA. A gradual redesign of ITG first enforced collaboration between BUs and the IT department, deterring the former from implementing multiple solutions for similar problems. Thereafter, in a second step, ITG ensured an active role of the IT department in the design of the business processes, before the decision rights were eventually transferred to the IT department of ALPHA.

Despite the varying approaches, as an outcome a highly streamlined business process landscape can be observed in all three case companies, in line with ALPHA's slogan 'one solution for one problem'.

Taken together, the exploratory findings suggest that the impact of IT governance goes beyond the infrastructure and application landscape of corporations, as suggested by Proposition P1a. In a second step, a well designed IT governance framework has an impact on the business processes of corporations. The observations further suggest that a common IT landscape is a basis for such an ITG-driven business process redesign. Therefore, the following Proposition P1a and Proposition P2 are suggested. The applied constructs and a theoretical positioning of Proposition P1a and Proposition P2 are discussed subsequently.

Proposition P1b: The higher the maturity of IT governance processes, structures and relational mechanisms, the higher the business process relatedness.

Proposition P2: The higher the IT relatedness, the stronger the proposed positive effect between IT governance maturity and business process relatedness.

4.3.2.2 Business process relatedness and IT governance maturity – deduction and refinement of constructs

Business process relatedness

Following the previously described approach, the analysis of the exploratory findings was conducted involving close feedback from extant literature. The goal was to understand the effects of IT governance and to develop an exploratory model based on empirical data as well as a rigorous theoretical background. However, the above introduced findings in relation to business process could not be mapped entirely with an existing construct. Therefore, the meta-construct of resource relatedness (Davis and Thomas

1993), as introduced in Chapter 4.3.1.3, was chosen as a basis for the definition of the construct *business process relatedness* as: *usage of common business processes and managerial practices across business units*.

The construct builds on previous works in the area of relatedness (Chatterjee and Wernerfelt 1991; Davis and Thomas 1993; Farjoun 1994; Ilinitch and Zeithaml 1995; John and Harrison 1999; Prahalad and Bettis 1986; Tanriverdi 2005; Tanriverdi 2006; Tanriverdi and Venkatraman 2005) and is based on the theoretical foundations of the resource-based view. Following Barney (1991) business processes and managerial practices are basic organisational resources that enable the firm to increase efficiency and effectiveness. Again, this study refrained from applying standardisation-based constructs (Manrodt and Vitasek 2004; Wüllenweber et al. 2008) in this context, as these would not be able to precisely map the observations of the exploratory cases. Meanwhile, scholars in the field of relatedness provided a good spadework for defining the construct of business process relatedness.

In consequence, business process relatedness was chosen in this study to model the observed findings related to the achieved harmonisation of business processes and managerial practices in the exploratory case studies.

IT governance maturity

The cases of ALPHA, BETA and EPSILON were extremely insightful for an improved understanding of the complex concept of IT governance maturity. What makes these three cases unlike the ones previously introduced (see Chapter 4.3.1) is a different objective of the ITG frameworks in place. IT governance of ALPHA, BETA and EPSILON is rather focused on a deliberate design of underlying business processes than on the implementation and operation of the infrastructure or basic application landscape itself. The latter two issues are regarded as solved to a satisfactory extent in these three case companies.

Consequently, the ITG in the cases of ALPHA, BETA and EPSILON has a strong service focus compared to the rather technical view in, e.g., the cases of DELTA or GAMMA. This managerial focus brought along a stronger penetration of non-IT staff by IT governance mechanisms. However, the interviewees at BETA and ALPHA stated that their ITG frameworks were developed and refined for almost two decades and that the current state of IT governance is building on achievements that were accomplished with a more technical view of ITG. They underlined the fact that the development of efficient and effective ITG is a process which involves many stakeholders and which requires time.

The observations further emphasised that the pure existence of a number of ITG mechanisms does not necessarily provide insights about the maturity of an ITG framework as a whole. While companies which are starting ITG initiatives often enact numerous guidelines for the implementation of hard- and software, ALPHA reported that various guidelines became obsolete after staff adapted the basic ideas behind them. EPSILON substantiated the impression that a close assessment of an ITG framework is necessary to gain understanding of its maturity. The interviewees at EPSILON made the experience that even a radical redesign of the organisational structure can stay without any impact if it happens only on paper, without actively involving the respective actors.

Summing up, the observations of the exploratory case studies in this chapter substantiate the good applicability and reasonableness of a maturity based concept of ITG as developed by De Haes and Van Grembergen (2009) (see Chapter 2.3.5.3). The insights furthermore accentuated the necessity of an in-depth assessment of each individual case site in order to gain a comprehensive picture of the state of the ITG maturity, based on the number of ITG processes, structures and relational mechanisms on one hand, and on a qualitative assessment of their effectiveness on the other.

4.3.2.3 Theoretical positioning of Proposition P1b and Proposition P2

Despite the varying organisational approaches of ALPHA, BETA and EPSILON, all three case companies came to the same conclusion, namely that the IT support of the organisation can be optimised only to a limited extent without an active redesign of the supported business processes. This meant in consequence that IT governance guidelines were expanded gradually towards non-IT departments. After this was accomplished successfully, i.e. after IT governance rose to a certain maturity, one could observe that the consolidation of infrastructure and the application landscape was followed by a harmonisation of the supported business processes on the baseline.

It is crucial to note that this did not mean that the IT department turned into a business-process hegemon in all cases. This would basically be equal to a highly centralised IT governance design, with extensive decision rights in the IT department. On the contrary, the cases suggest that the exact design of the IT governance is not pivotal, as all three case companies pursued varying approaches, while showing comparable results:

ITG at ALPHA is based on a hegemonic system where decision rights were cumulated in the IT, including the authority over business processes. On the contrary, EPSILON enacted ITG guidelines which strictly segregated the decision domains of the IT and the process design unit. However, ITG at EPSILON ensured that major decisions can only be made in cooperation between these two departments. BETA followed a similar, hybrid approach. While the decentral business units were disempowered to a large extent in relation to the design of business process, the respective decision rights were not transferred to the IT, but towards project specific multi-competence teams. These are composed of representatives from the IT, the respective business units and the central CIO department.

Summing up, the exploratory cases suggest that effective and efficient governance of IT is not ensured by one specific pattern of IT decision rights, but that the key is a purposeful design of IT governance which is matching the companies' specific characteristics. While IT governance is aiming at an efficient coordination of the different parties at BETA, it is designed to ensure the modular technology and process design at ALPHA or, in the case of EPSILON, IT governance is guaranteeing collaboration and positive friction between business and IT.

These observations are fully in line with Weill's (2004, p. 3) seminal study, where he states that effective IT governance is based on an *"actively designed [...] set of IT governance mechanisms (e.g., committees, budgeting processes, approvals, IT organisational structure, chargeback, etc.) that encourage behaviors consistent with the organization's mission, strategy, values, norms, and culture."*

However, prior research is confined to very general statements about the eventual consequences and value-add of mature IT governance. Weill (2004) claims that effective ITG leads to higher profitability and focuses on various patterns of decision rights. Doing so, he provides a collection of good practices, but remains unclear about the value generating impact: *"Good governance ensures that the right groups are making the key IT decisions so that those decisions enable the desired goals and behaviors of the enterprise. Good governance makes clear who can make decisions and how they are accountable for the enterprise goals."* (Weill 2004, p. 17). Other scholars hypothesise that maturity of ITG enhances business/ IT alignment (Csaszar and Clemons 2006; De Haes and Van Grembergen 2009; Liang et al. 2011; Luftman et al. 2008; Silva and Chaix 2008). While this hypothesis is promising, Chapter 2.3.6 highlights that it does not represent a significant gain of knowledge or an answer to the basic question of how ITG provides impacts the firm and how value is eventually created by mature ITG.

The findings of the 11 exploratory case studies suggest an answer to this gap in research. When comparing the introduced observations, a clear pattern can be observed: With rising ITG maturity of the firms, first, IT relatedness is rising (as suggested by Proposition P1a), before, second, a further increase in ITG maturity leads to rising business process relatedness (as suggested by Proposition P1b). The ITG-driven rise of business process relatedness is strongly promoted by a high relatedness of IT (as suggested by Proposition P2). These propositions are fully in line with the RBV as shown in the following.

The discussed insights suggest, seen from a more holistic perspective, that after an IT governance framework has reached a certain maturity, it encompasses various managerial topics which go beyond pure IT. This was observed particularly for the subject of business process design and related managerial practices. While in case sites with low ITG maturity this topic is mostly pursued feudally, case sites with high ITG maturity have enacted a collection of mechanisms, which ensure a transparent and collaborative design of business processes and related managerial practices. Since business processes and managerial practices are regarded as resource arrangements of a company (Barney 1991), this study ties in with the previous RBV-based line of argumentation, as presented in relation to Proposition P1a (see Section 4.3.1.4). Extant literature asserts that relatedness of resources is a major source of synergies (Davis and Thomas 1993) and, thus, performance gains (Robins and Wiersema 1995). Hence it is highly rational for the administration of a corporation to use the available instruments which are provided by a mature ITG framework and a highly streamlined IT landscape so as to increase business process relatedness and eventually enable a better exploitation of its resources (Barney 1991; Davis and Thomas 1993; Mata et al. 1995; Robins and Wiersema 1995). Proposition P1b and Proposition P2 are therefore in line with the prospects of the RBV.

4.4 Performance Effects of Relatedness

Chapter 4.2 introduced resource relatedness as the mediating construct between IT governance maturity and business performance in the explanatory model that is suggested to answer the research questions of this study (illustrated in Figure 7). The preceding section discussed the employed constructs of IT relatedness and business process relatedness in detail. The suggested propositions P1a, P1b and P2, which are linking ITG maturity to the constructs of IT relatedness and business process relatedness, were introduced with observations from the exploratory case studies and compared to extant literature.

The following section presents empirical evidence for the suggested propositions that are linking IT relatedness and business process relatedness to business performance.

4.4.1 IT Relatedness

Despite the fact that the positive impact of IT relatedness on business performance was shown by previous studies, the next section follows the introduced approach and begins with empirical evidence observed in the companies of the exploratory case study phase. Subsequently, the insights are compared to existing literature.

4.4.1.1 The positive impact of IT relatedness – empirical observations

Basically all analysed case companies reported strong performance gains from past projects which increased IT relatedness. In addition, insights into business cases of currently running or upcoming projects, together with expected value gains, were offered by some case companies.

Most interviewees described massive cost savings in relation to increased infrastructure relatedness and stated that the performance gains are relatively 'low hanging fruits'. To offer an example, the head of BETA's controlling asserted that hardware consolidation projects pay off very quickly and that these projects are rather simple to calculate:

> *"If I take for example our desktop solutions, I can immediately say 'since we introduced the standard workstation, we save each month the amount of X euro on each work space'. The desktop costs per user were cut by more than 50% after introducing a uniform solution."*

ALPHA, with more than 200,000 standardised workstations, reported similar savings through harmonisation projects for end-user computing and, for example, data centres or communication infrastructure, as described before.

But not only cost considerations were driving consolidation efforts for infrastructure or hardware. DELTA and GAMMA, both in the process of infrastructure harmonisation explicated that a common IT infrastructure is the basis for all further strategic considerations in relation to information technology. This view was shared by virtually all case companies. The CIO of DELTA explains:

> *"Now we are at the beginning of the technological consolidation, [...] thereafter, we will tackle the application landscape. The final step is [involvement in] process design."*

While the prospects of infrastructure consolidation were regarded quite similarly among the case companies, a rather diverse picture was offered by the exploratory findings in relation to performance effects of a harmonised application landscape. In the following, various examples are provided.

Again, costs were mentioned by many interviewees, but in most cases other effects were regarded as extremely relevant in addition. The CIO of ALPHA reported, for example, that the main customers, large OEMs, provide proprietary EDI ports which need to be linked to each of the systems in use. With multiple systems in-house, the effort of linking the systems rises enormously:

> *"Our customers are large OEMs that are very self-confident [...]. If OEM X says he wants the data in the format of CAD system Y, we have to implement it, and link it to our systems. [...] Each OEM has different systems and different tools with different ports. [...] As a consequence, we have a group of people which converts data back and forth."*

The interviewee at LAMBDA reported serious risk-management issues which will not be solved before the consolidation of the proprietary banking systems is completed:

> *"If I try to get numbers for the risk management, I have to compare apples to oranges due to the different databases in use."*

KAPPA reported time to market issues due to multiple core-banking systems that still are in use and which require attention when new products are introduced:

> *"Our traders often call the IT and say that they need a specific solution very rapidly [...] if we cannot provide the implementation in a certain time frame, the window of opportunity often closes, and the revenue is gone."*

Similar issues were reported by various other case-companies, where a harmonised application landscape was seen as a basis for agility and flexibility in a case of emerging requirements. Another example was presented by the interviewees at THETA, who reported that a harmonised application landscape provides new opportunities like seamless services for the customers:

> *"Our goal is to reduce barriers between our brands for our customers – the topic of seamless services."*

Such services are very hard to realise on a disparate application platform. The CIO at BETA reported as well customer relations issues, which are one of the many reasons for an ongoing ERP consolidation:

> *"Despite the fact that we are one company working under one main brand name, we still have to send our customers from department to department. This is due to the fact that our sales divisions are operating with different systems. Before the new ERP solution is up and running, we won't be able to offer our products through one single point of contact."*

The presented examples provide an insight into the observed downsides of disparate infrastructure and heterogeneous hard- and software solutions, and, vice versa, the various observed positive impacts of a harmonised IT landscape. The exploratory case studies offer evidence that high IT relatedness in fact penetrates most of the dimensions of business performance, which were suggested by Sabherwal and Chan (2001) for an evaluation of IT business value. Therefore, Proposition P3a is suggested in line with previous research (Tanriverdi 2006):

Proposition P3a: High IT relatedness has a positive impact on the business performance of a multibusiness firm.

4.4.1.2 Theoretical positioning of Proposition P3a

In the course of a large-scale quantitative study Tanriverdi (2006) presented evidence that IT relatedness positively impacts business performance. The author argues this to be the result of sustainable competitive advantages that are generated with synergies offered by high IT relatedness.

As introduced in Section 2.2.3.3, the concept of synergies is divided into sub-additive cost synergies and super-additive value synergies. Following Teece (1982), sub-additive cost synergies are generated if a firm uses common factors of production to reduce joint production costs. Super-additive value synergies arise if the joint value of two units of production is greater than the sum of their individual values. The major source of both types of synergies is regarded to be resource relatedness (Davis and Thomas 1993).

Examining the relation between IT relatedness and corporate performance, Tanriverdi (2006) can show that high relatedness of single IT resources leads to sub-additive costs synergies, while high relatedness of a complementary set of IT resources leads to (additional) super-additive value synergies. In other words, consolidating infrastructure or a confined set of applications in a detached manner will primarily lead to cost savings. On the contrary, if these harmonisation efforts are accomplished in an integrated manner, the corporation will achieve additional values that arise from effects of complementarity. This distinction is crucial for the understanding and classification of the business performance gains that can be achieved with high IT relatedness.

Based on the RBV and in line with previous research on resource relatedness and complementarities (Milgrom and Roberts 1995), Tanriverdi (2006) argues that values from sub-additive cost synergies can only provide a temporary competitive advantage. In consequence, only a limited (temporary) impact on the business performance (regarded in relation to competitors) can be expected (Farjoun 1994; Robins and Wiersema 1995). If a company, for example, achieves substantial cost cuts with standardised desktop-computers, competitors will implement similar solutions, which will eventually lead to competitive parity.

Super-additive value synergies arising from a complementary set of IT resources with high relatedness, on the contrary, are not only hard to imitate, but often even hard to observe by competitors (Tanriverdi and Venkatraman 2005). Even if such values are recognised and identified, it might be necessary to change the whole architecture of a firm in order to imitate and implement them. Hence, it might even not be sensible for a corporation to try copying a valuable complementary set of IT resources, as this might affect its own unique value providing methods (Milgrom and Roberts 1995). Based on these theoretical foundations, Tanriverdi (2006) argues that that super-additive value synergies arising from a complementary set of IT resources with high relatedness leads to sustained competitive advantages and hence to a higher business performance. In other words, a highly integrated and complementary infrastructure and application landscape can provide, for example, the access to new services or products, a lower time to market or a unique market position. Such benefits that can be guarded from imitation for a significant amount of time, thus, can provide sustainable competitive advantage (Tanriverdi 2006).

The empirical insights from the exploratory cases are congruent with Tanriverdi's (2006) observations. His theoretical reasoning provides groundwork for the explanation of positive impact of ITG on the business performance of a firm based on the prospects of the RBV.

4.4.2 Business Process Relatedness

After the previous section has discussed the positive impact of IT relatedness on business performance, the following chapter sheds light on the performance impact of business process relatedness.

4.4.2.1 The positive impact of business process relatedness – empirical observations

> *"Integrating infrastructure, that's relatively easy. There are synergies and almost all infrastructure projects are quite quickly economically beneficial. Harmonising applications, that is a bit harder and can take a few years. Generally spoken - if you start off with IT, that's fine, you will achieve synergies. However, you get the really big synergies if you look at business processes."*

This was reported by the CIO of ALPHA, where most business processes were growing over decades and got adapted in line with upcoming demands. Recurring business process reengineering was carried out successfully, but the gained optimisation remained often local, that is, confined to a certain production site or a specific product. After the IT harmonisation was conducted to a large fraction, the board of ALPHA posed the question why the corporation meets problems on the process level on different sites with different solutions, when the striving for a 'one best approach' works for the IT. According to the CIO, this local approach in the domain of process design was rooted in the historical development and, hence, the culture of ALPHA. He stated that departments did not look left or right, but only into their own past, trying to enhance the processes they had:

> *"Many of the business areas develop their business processes out of their history. [...] they try to adapt their existing processes to new demands, without doing a real step forwards."*

ALPHA realised that massive sub-additive cost synergies can be achieved with harmonised processes, because it was basically the heterogeneous process landscape that caused inefficiencies in the area of IT:

> *"The process owner has to talk to the IT, because if he doesn't he simply maps his processes to the IT. This is what was done in the past with our old SAP R/3 solution. The effect was that it consisted of 50% customising in the end. We eventually realized that this was financially not feasible anymore."*

But it is not only about costs. ALPHA went on to the next step in search for a collection of one-best solutions in the domain of its core processes, namely research and development as well as production. In doing so, ALPHA was able to allocate and promote the best process approaches to all departments that are working on similar products:

> *"Eventually the business areas should talk about processes with us, not about IT. We want to ensure that unified processes are used wherever similar problems can be found. [...] The benefit is that we now can offer many standard solutions for many business areas."*

Right now, ALPHA is working on the next step of process harmonisation and analyses which process can be harmonised on a meta-level. That is, if certain modules of production and business processes can be implemented in the same way, e.g., into the design and development of an engine system and the design and development of a truck headlight. In doing so, ALPHA is not only striving for the implementation of the best processes approaches; it is obvious that in some cases locally adapted processes certainly are more efficient. But ALPHA aims at finding a global optimum between local adaption and company-wide integration of business processes and production methods. This is not only valuable for ALPHA as it generates super-additive value effects which arise with complementarities in the course of the processes integration. The CIO of ALPHA stated that this as well leads to a comfortable market position:

> *"We develop many products in close collaboration with our customers, who often deal with six or seven ALPHA departments. These customers demand for the same processes when they deal with ALPHA."*

If ALPHA is able to offer similar or comparable processes to its customers, these can achieve large synergies in their own production cycles. This way, ALPHA becomes a more attractive partner in comparison to its competitors.

BETA also reported large cost-synergies that were achieved in the course of increased business process relatedness; especially in regard to a shared service centre for back-office solutions. Furthermore, according to the interviewees, very promising synergies were achieved in the course of a harmonisation of the supply chain and customer order processing:

> *"After an initial analysis, it was clear that we needed to get rid of the differences in these two processes, locally, regionally and globally [...] not for single product lines, but for BETA as a whole."*

Similarly to ALPHA, BETA was able to achieve super-additive value synergies with a harmonised integration of these processes on a global scale. Again, the values achieved were not only confined to BETA's internal value chain, but offered customers new possibilities to reap additional benefits in cooperation with BETA. This led to a better market positioning according to the interviewee. However, these two business processes represented only the beginning of a much larger process harmonisation campaign at BETA. The interviewees expect additional value, based on complementary effects, with every further process that is harmonised on a global scale.

In addition to the described benefits, BETA regards the ongoing process harmonisation campaign as essential to strategic considerations. BETA's industry sector is undergoing a major transformation for over a decade now. Furthermore, small and large mergers and acquisitions are expected by the interviewees, who consider a harmonised process landscape as a major strategic asset for a successful and profitable acquisition.

On the one hand, it is not surprising that effects from back-office harmonisation efforts were regarded relatively equally across all industries in the regarded case-sample. On the other hand, it is important to note that super-additive values arising from business processes relatedness were not confined to case companies that are active in manufacturing industries. Other examples were provided e.g. by THETA, where the increase of the cross-unit relatedness of the business processes procurement, catering, and in-flight-HR is already valuable in isolation as it provides sub-additive cost synergies. But these processes are highly interrelated and their commonality is mutually reinforcing, hence complementary. If THETA achieves commonality in one of these processes, it becomes more valuable to do so in the others as well. The use of the same sets of meals across the different THETA brands increases the purchase quantity of similar ingredients and, thus, the negotiation power of the procurement department. Simultaneously, it simplifies the harmonisation of the catering and in-flight service, and, consequently, the pooling and sharing of catering and in-flight staff.

Based on these empirical findings and on existing literature, this study suggests that business process relatedness influences the business performance of a firm. Proposition P3b is suggested accordingly and discussed subsequently.

Proposition P3b: High business processes relatedness has a positive impact on the business performance of a multibusiness firm.

4.4.2.2 Theoretical positioning of Proposition P3b

While previous research has shown that business process harmonisation leads to better performance (e.g. De Vries 1999; Lee and Kim 1999; Manrodt and Vitasek 2004; Wüllenweber et al. 2008), these studies are often focused on sub-additive costs which do not lead to sustainable competitive advantage. However, by combining these insights with the introduced empirical observations, the RBV (Barney 1991; Mata et al. 1995; Melville et al. 2004), the theory of complementarities (Milgrom and Roberts 1995) and the numerous works on relatedness (Chatterjee and Wernerfelt 1991; Davis and Thomas 1993; Farjoun 1994; Ilinitch and Zeithaml 1995; John and Harrison 1999; Prahalad and Bettis 1986; Tanriverdi 2005; Tanriverdi 2006; Tanriverdi and Venkatraman 2005), it becomes obvious that Tanriverdi's (2006) hypotheses in relation to the positive impact of IT relatedness can be transferred to the impact of business process relatedness, as suggested in Proposition P3b.

As a consequence, it is argued that values gained through high relatedness of singular, isolated business processes and managerial practices result in most cases only in sub-additive cost synergies, which are prone to imitation by competitors. Thus, only a temporary competitive advantage can be expected from high relatedness of singular (non-strategic) business processes, like, e.g., HR management or payroll management.

However, if an integrated complementary set of business processes and managerial practices with high relatedness is available, super-additive value synergies arise that are comparably safe from imitation. This is due to two basic facts:

First, due to causal ambiguity (Melville et al. 2004), which means that it is extremely hard for competitors to observe where and how value arises within a complex system of integrated processes. Second, due to the aforementioned fact that it might be impossible for competitors to reproduce a large set of processes without negatively affecting their own value providing process (Milgrom and Roberts 1995). The latter argument is even more applicable to business processes than to IT, as the former represent the core competence of a firm, while the latter is mostly representing a support function. Taken together, super-additive value synergies arising from a complementary set of business processes and managerial practices with high relatedness can generate sustainable competitive advantages. Thus, they have a positive impact on the business performance of a firm.

In summary, it is argued that the Proposition P3b, which was suggested on the basis of the presented empirical observations, is not only in line with the prospects of the RBV but also represents a valid and valuable expansion of previous theoretical work by Tanriverdi (2006).

4.4.3 Interacting Effects between IT Relatedness and Business Process Relatedness

The previous sections introduced subsequently the impact of IT relatedness and business process relatedness on business performance. It was possible to show that both relatedness types enable firms to generate values, which can be a source of sustainable competitive advantages based on effects previously shown by Tanriverdi (2006).

In addition, the exploratory case studies suggested interacting effects between the two constructs as well. These are introduced and discussed in the following.

4.4.3.1 The positive impact of interacting effects between IT relatedness and business process relatedness – empirical observations

Many of the elaborated effects of IT relatedness and business process relatedness, as introduced in the preceding sections, show, in addition to the presented positive impacts, significant logical interrelations.

ALPHA's 'one solution for one problem' initiative in the domain of business processes was boosted by the fact that it was possible to map the harmonised business processes onto an already consolidated IT infrastructure and application-landscape. The application landscape, on the other hand, rose in a guided modular way, offering more possibilities with every novel feature that was added on top. The CIO explicated:

> *"Even if someone [a department] has deviating processes, we have a unified IT platform which we can use, therefore we reflect on how we can map the process on it. It is like using LEGO stones. If it doesn't work, we try to adopt the processes first. If that does not work either, we are happy to build a new LEGO stone [i.e. a module that fits with the platform at hand]. [...] The positive thing is: this way we have a lot of standard solutions for various departments, which we can reuse; meaning that we come to solutions for various problems quickly."*

While this leads to large benefits for the business departments, with shorter time to market and lower costs of development, the value of the harmonised IT platform, in turn, is massively elevated when being used by multiple departments. With every business process that is delegated onto the harmonised platform, costs are sinking in two ways. First, the originally used proprietary solution is not needed anymore, and second, the costs per user on the new platform go down through economies of scale. The same applies to the linkages between ALPHA and its suppliers, where technology- and process-related harmonisations benefit highly from each other. When various departments follow the same procurement process, one technological channel can be instituted, as reported:

> *"Together with other players, we introduced TRADE, a marketplace where we can carry out many of our daily transactions. Many of our suppliers use it."*

This unified solution does not only save IT costs for ALPHA, while simplifying the procurement processes for all departments, it additionally offers ALPHA's suppliers a better service through a unique point of contact, which pushes their costs down as well.

The same effects holds true for BETA's supply-chain and customer relationship harmonisation initiative on one side, and the ongoing ERP project which aims on unification of 24 ERP solutions, on the other. Even though the integration between all sales departments and the respective ERP modules is not finished yet, BETA made more revenues through the new ERP module in 2009 than Amazon had sales worldwide, according to the interviewed head of controlling:

> *"I use this number to clarify to our staff how significant a good integration between our business processes and our IT is."*

The CIO of BETA added that effects of complementarities between high IT relatedness and high business process relatedness are best visible in the case of large acquisitions. The extremely successful technical and organisational integrations of competitors in the past were only achievable due to the fact that a set of harmonised business processes was rolled out and then mapped onto the available harmonised IT landscape in BETA.

Again, while these effects were best observable at BETA and ALPHA due to their high IT and business process relatedness, they are not limited to industrial organisations, but were reported as well on cases sites in the finance and service sector. KAPPA reported that a reinforcing effect between IT relatedness and business process relatedness was observed after regulation enforced consistent and compliant business processes in many areas. This harmonisation of business processes boosted in turn existing plans to implement a shared and consistent IT landscape to support these processes, which then again were easier to handle and control through one point of technical access. While THETA is focused on the integration of business processes for strategic reasons, as discussed before, the company expects operational synergies on its landscape as a positive side-effect.

Taken together, the empirical findings suggest that, besides the previously introduced positive impact of high IT relatedness and high business processes relatedness, additional value is provided by complementarity-based effects of interaction. Therefore, Proposition P4 is suggested as follows.

Proposition P4: Synergies arising from the interaction of a complementary set of high IT relatedness and high business process relatedness have a positive impact on the business performance of a multibusiness firm.

4.4.3.2 Theoretical positioning of Proposition P4

The collection of IT resources and IT management practises of a firm on one hand, and the collection of business processes and managerial practices on the other can be regarded as resource bundles of the firm according to the RBV (Barney 1991; Mata et al. 1995; Melville et al. 2004). Therefore, this study proposes that the previous RBV- and TOC-based line of argumentation is fully valid on a higher level, namely for the interaction of the concepts of IT relatedness and business processes relatedness as reasoned in the following.

As shown in the exploratory case studies, two above mentioned bundles of resources are highly interrelated, while their relatedness is complementary. This means that by increasing commonality in IT resources and IT management practices (i.e. by increasing IT relatedness), the value provided by the existing degree of commonality in business processes and managerial practices (i.e. the value provided by the existing degree of business process relatedness) rises as well. This causal relationship is also valid vice versa.

In other words, increasing IT relatedness provides value (P3a) and enhances in addition the value delivered by the extant degree of business process relatedness (P4). Vice versa, increasing business process relatedness provides value (P3b) and enhances in addition the value delivered by the extant degree of IT relatedness (P4). Proposition P4, thus, represents super-additive value synergies arising from the complementarity of the relatedness of IT and business processes.

If a corporation is able to generate a competitive advantage on the foundation of these complementarity-based super-additive value synergies, it is very probable that the advantage generated can be sustainable (Tanriverdi 2006). This is due to the fact that the values generated through the interaction of IT relatedness and business process relatedness are so deeply rooted in the corporation's organisational and operational structures, that an exact imitation of the whole interdependent value generating system is highly improbable.

4.5 Moderating Effect of Absorptive Capacity

Structured according to the explanatory model introduced in Chapter 4.2, the previous sections have discussed the suggested propositions that are deemed appropriate and valid for describing and explaining the value generating mechanisms of IT governance.

Moreover, the exploratory case studies offered insights into further, moderating effects that are discussed in the following.

4.5.1.1 The moderating effect of the absorptive capacity of the IT department – empirical observations

A major requirement for the successful execution of ITG-triggered harmonisation initiatives within the case companies was observed to be a high absorptive capacity of the IT departments. A few excerpts of the empirical observations are provided for illustration.

Most of the interviewees reported that IT acted in the past primarily as a pure service provider for the business. Hence it was often adequate to understand and implement the requirements of the business, without digging deep into the business logic itself. The CIO of ALPHA explained in the previously named examples that, especially in the beginning of harmonisation campaigns, resistance was encountered from business units. While the IT department was well aware that unified e-mail or office solutions were able to serve the needs of all the departments, the situation was more complex in other cases, especially in relation to business processes. In a reaction, ALPHA accumulated process knowledge in the IT department, according to the interviewee:

> *"Today, it is almost the other way around; we have built up such a high stack of process knowledge that we have to take care that the departments don't lean back [and expect IT to solve process issues]."*

BETA made similar experiences, e.g. in the course of the ongoing ERP harmonisation. When HR staff claims that processes generally cannot be aligned due to e.g. legal reasons, the IT needs to be able to talk with these departments on eye level and distinguish what can be done similarly and what needs to be kept separated. EPSILON and GAMMA reported comparable experiences with highly specialised units and processes, along with the resulting need for context-specific knowledge and absorptive capacity in the IT department that assures an ongoing accumulation of that kind of knowledge:

> *"In many departments, EPSILON staff is sitting all day in front of computers, programming. But not all of them are IT staff – some are molecular biologists who are doing research on genomes."*

The head of the CIO office at GAMMA summarised:

> *"I need people in my IT that are able to understand the highly specific processes we run. [...] If not, there is no need to have them in-house, [...] I can buy the run-business from IBM. [...] If you would have the idea to do an integration process with people that are technically qualified only, you are lost."*

Summing up, the exploratory case studies suggest that the more the ITG departments were pursuing relatedness projects, the more the IT had to actively gather and accumulate business-specific knowledge for a successful implementation. The success of relatedness projects is thus, in parts, dependent on the absorptive capacity of the IT departments. Propositions P5a and P5b are therefore suggested accordingly.

> *Proposition P5a: The higher the absorptive capacity of the IT department, the stronger the proposed positive effect between IT governance maturity and IT relatedness.*

> *Proposition P5b: The higher the absorptive capacity of the IT department, the stronger the proposed positive effect between IT governance maturity and business process relatedness.*

4.5.1.2 Theoretical positioning of Proposition P5a and Proposition P5b

As introduced in Chapter 2.2.3.2, knowledge is horizontally and vertically divided among staff (Jensen and Meckling 1995). IT departments, which possess primarily technology-specific knowledge, thus, have to recurrently acquire context-specific knowledge from BUs to successfully implement information systems that are deemed to support the BUs (Sabherwal and Becerra-Fernandez 2005). In other words, they have to utilise outside knowledge. This ability is referred to as absorptive capacity (AC) (Cohen and Levinthal 1990).

The exploratory findings suggest that high absorptive capacity of an IT department is in particular not substitutable for successful relatedness-projects due to the fact that relatedness projects are in many cases not fully supported by BUs. In other words, IT departments may have to acquire context-specific knowledge on their own initiative, even against the resistance of business units.

Absorptive capacity is highly tacit and deeply rooted in the specific social and organisational structures of a corporation. Consequently, AC of an IT department cannot be acquired on the market but has to be developed internally over years. AC is therefore rare and immobile. In terms of the KBV, AC is highly valuable, as it supports the firm to implement strategies that can lead to competitive advantage (as shown by the Propositions P1a-P4). As a consequence, a high absorptive capacity of an IT department is a possible source of sustained competitive advantage.

In summary, the propositions P5a and P5b, which suggest that the absorptive capacity is significant for the achievement of relatedness and hence a competitive advantage are not only in line with the observations made in the course of the exploratory case studies, but as well in line with the implications of the knowledge-based view.

4.6 Summary

This chapter presented the findings of the first empirical case study phase which constituted the basis of the explanatory model that was proposed in order to explain how IT governance and business performance are related. Building on insights from 11 exploratory case studies of large German corporations and theoretical work derived from extant literature, a number of constructs and relationships was identified that mediate and moderate the positive impact of ITG on the business performance of a firm.

The explanatory model, illustrated in Figure 7, conceptualises ITG with a maturity construct provided by previous research. It is suggested that the impact of ITG on business performance is mediated by the degree of IT relatedness and business process relatedness. The model proposes that the higher the maturity of IT governance in a firm is, the higher is its IT and business process relatedness (Proposition 1a and Proposition 1b). Moreover, it is proposed that the degree of IT relatedness moderates the impact of ITG maturity on business process relatedness (Proposition 2).

In line with extant literature, it is proposed that IT relatedness enhances business performance (P3a). Building on the same line of argumentation, it is furthermore suggested that business process relatedness enhances business performance (P3b) and that complementary effects of interaction between business process relatedness and IT relatedness enable additional values that, following previous literature, can be a basis for sustained competitive advantage (P4).

Moreover, the findings of the exploratory case study phase suggest that the absorptive capacity of the IT department has an essential impact on the success of ITG driven relatedness projects. As a consequence, a moderating effect of the absorptive capacity of the IT department on the impact of ITG maturity is proposed (Proposition P5a and Proposition P5b).

Building on this theoretical basis, the following chapter introduces the second empirical phase which was undertaken in order to substantiate and refine the developed empirical model.

5. Empirical Substantiation and Theory Corroboration

As discussed in the research design (see Chapter 3), this study follows a multiple stage approach in order to develop an explanatory model that is able to explain how IT governance influences the business performance of a firm. The first phase, exploratory in nature, was introduced in detail in the previous section. The presented results (see Figure 7) suggest that ITG maturity heavily influences the IT relatedness and business process relatedness of firms. Based on empirical evidence it was shown that resource relatedness, in turn, is able to provide values that, following extant studies, can be the basis for sustainable competitive advantages and, hence, an increase in business performance. What is more, the empirical observations suggest that the absorptive capacity of the IT department has a vital role for a successful implementation of relatedness projects that require a large portion of context-specific knowledge.

This chapter discusses the second empirical phase of this study, which aims at corroborating the developed mid-range theory. To do so, another set of case studies was conducted to analyse if the developed explanatory model holds when being applied to a second data sample.

The subsequent section introduces the analysed case companies and presents the data collection and analysis, which follows the procedure as discussed in section 3.5.

5.1 Data Selection and Analysis

The case sample of the refinement phase encompasses 10 corporations which are comparable in size and industry to the case companies of the first round. In order to avoid a selection bias and meet the requirements of the corroborating nature of the second data collection, the case samples of the exploratory and the corroborative empirical phases were kept disjoint. This way, the explanatory model was applied in the second phase to a novel context outside of the original data set. Following such an approach allows an analytical generalisation of findings.

Consequently, a collection of firms that were not part of the exploratory phase was approached. Table 9 provides an overview of the participating firms in the corroborative empirical phase together with their respective core businesses.

Case company	Core business	Turnover 2011	Bal. Sheet 2011
OMEGA	Manufacturing industry	>€ 2 bn	
PSI	Manufacturing industry	>€ 2 bn	
CHI	Manufacturing industry	>€ 2 bn	
PHI	Manufacturing industry	>€ 2 bn	
YPSILON	Manufacturing industry	>€ 15 bn	
TAU	Energy industry	>€ 15 bn	
SIGMA	Energy industry	>€ 15 bn	
RHO	Retail industry	>€ 15 bn	
PI	Financial industry		>€ 10 bn
OMIKRON	Financial industry		>€ 0.5 bn

Table 9: Case sample of the corroborative phase

Following the approach of the exploratory phase, the data in the corroborative empirical round was collected in the form of expert interviews, as well. Internal documentation and publicly available information of the case companies were applied for data triangulation, aiming at an increase of internal validity. Again, a top level view was pursued. Therefore, the highest ranking IT executive was interviewed, wherever possible. In cases where a CIO position was not implemented, or where an interview with the CIO was not feasible in the available timeframe, the head of IT or another knowledgeable member of top-management was interviewed. Table 10 provides an outline of the interview partners. Due to the fact that the interview guideline of the corroborative phase (see Appendix 2.2) was designed closely to the developed explanatory model of the first round, it is more structured in comparison to the exploratory round. In consequence, personal on-site visits were not regarded as obligatory and the interviewees were given the choice between a personal and a telephone interview. This led to a mixed approach.

Case company	Interview partner(s)
OMEGA	Head of services
PSI	Head of IT
CHI	Head of CIO office
PHI	CIO
YPSILON	Division CIO
TAU	Head of IT governance
SIGMA	Head of IT
RHO	Head of IT
PI	Head of IT strategy
OMIKRON	CIO

Table 10: Interview partners in the corroborative phase

All interviews were recorded on tape, fully transcribed and then sent to the interviewees for approval before the analysis was started. The interview transcripts add up to 60,000 words (approx. 120 pages) of qualitative data for the corroborative phase. The analysis procedure in the second round was held close to the constructs developed and applied in the explanatory model of the first round. Doing so, construct labels were assigned to the respective text passages in the transcripts using indicators developed in the first round. Table 11 offers an overview of the constructs that are forming the explanatory model of the first phase, together with exemplary indicators.

The next step constituted the writing of case stories for each analysed company. Following Miles and Huberman (1994), case stories are a good means to gain an in-depth understanding of each specific case and context. This is particularly important in this study in relation to the complexity of the ITG maturity construct which obligates an in-depth analysis.

Construct	Exemplary indicators
ITG Processes	Availability of portfolio management, charge-back arrangements, Service level agreements (SLAs), ITG frameworks, IT budget management, IT budget control & reporting, etc.
ITG Structures	Availability of IT strategy committees, IT architecture steering committees, IT project steering committees, established reporting structures, etc.
ITG Relational Mechanisms	Availability of informal meetings between business and IT, established business IT partnerships, business-IT account managers, etc.
ITG Maturity	The degree of availability and effective and efficient application of ITG processes, ITG structures and ITG relational mechanisms
IT Relatedness	Usage of common hardware/ infrastructure/ applications/ IT management processes across different business units
Business Process Relatedness	Usage of common HR/ logistics/ customer support/ procurement/ production processes across business units, etc.
Resource Relatedness	Degree of the interaction and concurrent availability of IT Relatedness and Business Process Relatedness
Business Performance	Cost savings, customer satisfaction, development of new business fields/ products, time to market, agility in mergers/ acquisitions or economic turmoil, etc.
Absorptive Capacity of IT Department	Acquisition & application of context-specific knowledge, like e.g. procurement processes, engineering procedures, regulatory requirements, etc.

Table 11: Identified constructs and exemplary indicators

Subsequent to the writing of the single-case stories, a cross-case analysis was conducted for corroboration of the proposed explanatory model. Doing so, each proposition was examined in the context of the second data sample. The eventual goal was to either substantiate or drop the suggested propositions that were developed in the exploratory case study phase and which provide an analytical generalisation of the study's findings.

The following section introduces the findings of the single-case analysis. Subsequently, the outcomes of the cross-case analysis are presented.

5.2 Single-Case Analysis

In the following, the insights gained in the corroborative case studies are presented consecutively. To do so, each case company is introduced briefly before the IT governance maturity, the resource relatedness and the reported business impacts are discussed. Appendix 4 provides detailed tables with an assessment of constructs and corresponding evidence for each case.

5.2.1 OMEGA

OMEGA is a typical industrial world market leader, with a market share of around 40% in its core business. The engineering company employs approximately 15,000 people with subsidiaries all around the globe (primarily for sales and support) and generates revenues of more than two billion euro annually. Despite successfully defending its strong position on the market, OMEGA has to deal with decreasing sales in consequence of a structural crisis.

IT governance maturity at OMEGA can be regarded as medium. Aiming at more efficiency, an ITG implementation project was started with the primary goal to govern and prioritise IT projects better. Consequently, ITG is regarded mainly on an IT strategy level and not yet penetrating all IT employees or a large non-IT group. The interviewee named an IT steering committee and an IT project steering committee as relevant ITG structures at OMEGA. ITG processes that are applied encompass charge back arrangements, IT budget and control processes as well as a portfolio management process and an IT balanced scorecard. A service catalogue is being planned. ITG relational mechanisms are not in place to a large extent yet, besides first attempts to enable structured communication between IT and business departments. Generally, knowledge sharing seems to be an issue at OMEGA. Most business departments do not have IT savvy staff at all and often underestimate the complexity of IT projects. The interviewee reported of recurrent cases where an outsourcing offer of 3€/ GB for an SAP environment was heatedly discussed by non-IT managers and repeatedly compared to hard drive prices from retail shops like ALDI. The interviewee claimed that the ITG is on a good way, that many instruments were implemented but that there is still a way to go. Following his estimations, ITG is penetrating less than half of the currently running IT projects. The goal is to implement further ITG mechanisms in order to cover 80-90% of the future IT projects and promote a better business/ IT knowledge sharing.

IT relatedness at OMEGA can be regarded as medium. IT infrastructure is globally consolidated, and IT processes are in many areas streamlined on an ITIL-basis. A service-catalogue consisting of SLAs is being developed. A standardised desktop-client is available globally. However, decisions about IT sourcing and the development of new applications are done locally. The respective business managers are the process owners and have extensive decision rights. Some applications for business processes were rolled out on a meta-level globally, like a sales and services template, but the local subsidies have customised it to an extent so as to map their existing process. While the central IT department is interested in the roll-out of stringent solutions, decentral business units use their extensive rights to veto such decisions in order to realise local customisations. Hence, applications that map processes remain harmonised only on a meta-level in most cases and are used as a basis for local adaption. While the interviewee reported some exceptions, like the CRM system or a mobile solution that promoted the harmonisation of on-site service, other ideas, like a harmonised HR process, were described by the interviewee as *"inexecutable"*. Consequently, business process relatedness can be regarded as medium.

When discussing performance impacts, the interviewee primarily mentioned sub-additive costs at OMEGA, since a required integration of information systems and business process is missing to reap more synergies. However, a few exceptions were provided by the interviewee, like e.g. the introduction of a mobile device that in combination with a harmonised CRM system and streamlined on-site support process generates super-additive value synergies.

5.2.2 PSI

PSI is an international industrial conglomerate which employs over 30,000 staff and generates revenues above two billion euro annually. The PSI management has propagated a decentralisation strategy for over a decade now, including all aspects of information technology. However, with the recent nomination of a new CIO, the IT started a tremendous change in strategy, including a large-scale infrastructure and application harmonisation initiative.

Despite the fact that the new CIO of PSI has initiated a complete reorientation of IT, including the development and enactment of a corporate-wide ITG framework, IT governance maturity is still low as the implementation just started. The only ITG structure in place is a steering committee for IT projects. All other ITG structure mechanisms are still in the phase of planning and development. The interviewee reported that comparable approaches were not usual in the past and that even an internal audit is not available at PSI. A similar situation was observed in relation to ITG processes. Only a charge back mechanism based on keys like e.g. number of users or transaction volume is in place. Most business projects are started without even considering or calculating IT costs. SLAs, reporting structures, performance measurements or frameworks like ITIL, ISO or COBIT are not considered at all in the domain of information technology. Even a deliberate portfolio management process or prioritisation of IT investments is missing. Again, the interviewee stated that the implementation of ITG processes started less than one year ago and that most of the planned actions are not beyond the stage of a blueprint yet. ITG relational mechanisms at PSI are on an initial level as well. The interviewee reported that first steps are done with informal meetings between CFOs and IT managers and that furthermore a process is enacted that ensures an interaction between business process owners and the IT department. However, the interviewee reported as well numerous conflicts between the business and the IT side which were escalated in the past. The interviewee summarised the status of ITG at PSI as follows:

> *"If ITG is regarded as a holistic frame, [...] we are plenty of miles behind a status of maturity. However, we are on a good way."*

IT relatedness at PSI is medium. The big picture is in parts similar to the status of IT governance, that is, many projects are planned or in execution, but only a small fraction is already accomplished. Less than one year ago, a standardised e-mail system and a web portal were introduced. IT infrastructure is almost consolidated, as well as the implemented CRM applications. The procurement of Microsoft and SAP licenses is done centrally now. However, the harmonisation of the SAP environment just started and will go on for at least two years. Production critical systems are not on the roadmap at all, yet. The interviewee explicated that IT staff since years is living with the challenge to map and optimise existing processes on diverse architectures in cooperation with the BUs. According to the interviewee, performance measurements are not established yet:

> *"The transparency in terms of costs is difficult to obtain, since the issues were aggregated last year for the first time. In the past, such costs were not calculated; therefore, a benchmark is not available. However, we started with over 20 distinct ERP solutions [...]. In a few years, there will be only one. This fact speaks for itself."*

Business process relatedness is low at PSI. This was reported to be a consequence of the strategic positioning in the past. Each division or even each department had a maximum of freedom when designing its processes. For the started ITG initiatives, which eventually aim at rolling out harmonised applications that determine business processes, this is a major issue; especially in combination with the diversified structure of PSI. The interviewee explained that a few years ago, every department at each location was free to design its IT strategy, its HR strategy or the way procurement was done. While many things in the context of IT are being adapted, the interviewee was not able to give a clear statement about what is expected in relation to business processes planning and design in future.

5.2.3 CHI

CHI is among the world's leading suppliers in the automotive industry. The company generates total revenues of more than two billion euro annually and employs approximately 15,000 people in 25 countries.

The case of CHI is particularly interesting as it shows a successful IT strategy turnaround. The interviewee explicated that the IT department in general has a tough standing in the corporation:

> *"IT is regarded [by the board and the owners] as a necessary evil and the IT department as a luxury good. Transferred to electricity, the attitude is comparable to saying 'we don't need power plants, because electricity comes out of the wall'."*

Nevertheless, the CIO department at CHI managed to realise a major turnaround in the area of information technology, which was accomplished in a collaborative way with the business side. The success of this project was not only acknowledged internally, but also won the company a well known IT strategy prize.

CHI started a major revision of its IT governance six years ago and disposes today, after various enhancements, over a very efficient and effective set of diverse ITG mechanisms. ITG maturity at CHI is regarded as high. A number of committees and ITG processes are not only enacted, but the interviewee was able to describe in detail how efficiently these processes work, and how well they are embedded in the whole organisation. The best sign for this fact is that the ITG structures and processes in place are applied as a reference model for the companies' future process governance. After first antagonism from the business side, most managers have accepted the enacted ITG measures and acknowledge their benefits. The interviewee stated that the well designed ITG relational mechanisms were of vital significance in the process of redesigning decision rights and accountabilities. Numerous informal meetings, special business-account management positions, well developed communication structures between IT and business and, most important, a good relationship between IT and business managers enabled a cooperative partnership.

IT relatedness is high at CHI. IT infrastructure consolidation was done years ago. CHI runs one central data centre with two local branches overseas for better performance. Standardised workplaces and harmonised ERP solutions are available world-wide. The interviewee claims that 85% of all IT processes are standardised and operating efficiently. IT sourcing is coordinated centrally. Hand in hand with a rising IT relatedness, CHI enhanced as well business process relatedness. While the business processes are still fully owned by the BUs, an ITG process ensures that the IT department is fully involved in the design of each business process that needs to be supported by information technology later on. The head of the CIO office stated that IT staff has a high portion of context-specific knowledge and that the IT department is regarded as a valuable partner in the design and optimisation of business processes. CHI uses job-rotation for knowledge transfer between IT and business units.

Despite the fact that IT does not generate new business fields or higher sales for CHI, the company realised that IT and good governance of that resource provide tremendous value to the corporation as a whole. The interviewee summarised:

> *"The value delivered by IT is the provision of a platform enabling the firm to operate on a global level with regard to business processes like e.g. logistics or procurement. [...] ITG is the basic requirement for any kind of process-harmonisation and thus for the realisation of global synergies. [...] In the long term, the relatively strict ITG will be accepted as a reference model for [business processes in] many areas."*

5.2.4 PHI

PHI is an engineering company that manufactures machines that are used in various industries. With more than 12,000 employees, PHI generates annual sales above two billion euro. The case study at PHI showed how ITG can lead to process innovations and even generate entirely new business for a classic industrial manufacturer.

ITG maturity is medium at PHI. The initiation of an ITG framework goes back to serious difficulties and conflicts that arose four years prior to the interview between the IT department and the business side in the course of various projects. Due to the fact that no clear decision rights or accountabilities were defined in relation to IT-specific questions, the top-management decided to instantiate a clear set of rules. Compared to recommendations from literature, PHI emphasises primarily ITG processes, while ITG structures are relatively underdeveloped. Only one mechanism is in place that is classified as an ITG structure, namely a project steering committee. However, ITG processes are highly specified. PHI works with charge back arrangements, a well developed portfolio and performance management and ISO standards in the IT domain. Furthermore, IT project governance, budget reporting and budget controls are highly developed. The CIO explained that many of these instruments were adapted and refined repeatedly in the last few years. The charge back methods, for example, were changed from a very precise calculation on the basis of CPU seconds towards a flat rate. The CIO stated that sometimes simpler is better. These adaptations show that the ITG framework at PHI is being actively aligned with the corporation and its endogenous processes. The CIO of PHI emphasised the value and importance of relational mechanisms, such as informal meetings, job rotations and a well developed internal communication.

It is instructive to see that PHI has, despite widely missing ITG structures, an exceptionally high IT relatedness and medium business process relatedness. IT relatedness was immensely increased in the course of the implementation of ISO 20,000. The CIO said that he promoted the unification and harmonisation of approaches not only for cost reasons:

> *"In Asia we have a few small subsidies and the baseline was always 'we don't need SAP there, that is too expensive', but I think that a global standard brings immense values, even if you have to put your hands deeper into your pockets to realise it."*

Today the application landscape is harmonised to the largest extent on an SAP basis, covering ERP, supplier relationship management (SRM), CRM, BI and HR modules. Most IT services are rolled out consistently across the firm. Simultaneously to the IT harmonisation, PHI aligned many business processes. However, the CIO stated in the interview that this process is by far not at the end:

> *"The implementation of cross-divisional processes is a permanent issue in the search for synergies. For that purpose, we must not only implement optimal IT processes, but also define the necessary organisational structures and processes."*

According to its CIO, PHI achieved in past projects massive super-additive synergies based on the harmonisation of information technology and corresponding business processes. In many of these projects, the IT staff was the driver and improved existing business processes essentially. The interviewee explicated that the absorptive capacity of the IT department proved to be very high in these projects. Harmonisation of IT in a first step reduced costs and allowed, in a second step, an integration of the application landscape which offered for the first time a unified picture on PHI's own production, customers and service processes. This in turn led to numerous super-additive value synergies. Subsequently, a harmonisation of business process was conducted. Eventually, interacting effects of IT relatedness and business process relatedness generated completely new service products in the area of customer support. These provided on-top revenues and a unique market position to the firm.

5.2.5 YPSILON

The parent company of YPSILON, an automotive producer, is one of Germany's largest corporations. Revenues beyond 15 billion euro are generated with more than 100,000 employees. YPSILON represents one major sub-division that employs more than 40,000 staff and which is responsible for approximately one quarter of the aggregated revenue of the holding.

Generally spoken, ITG, as understood in this study, has not been a significant topic for YPSILON yet. The company does have a few mechanisms in place that can be classified as ITG mechanisms, but there is no 'big picture' of IT governance. Basically, no strategy is in place for the IT as a whole in the moment. Enacted instruments which can be classified as IT governance mechanisms, such as IT steering committees, IT project committees or portfolio and performance measurement techniques do not form a coherent system, as a basis is missing. The IT department officially has authority over the entire IT staff at YPSILON, but the reality is different. Several business units are still running their own IT infrastructure and applications with own staff. While a strategy for the IT department was developed a few years ago, the division CIO explained that this strategy does not suit the requirements of the company anymore. According to the interviewee, the internal management structure is being revised and many resolutions are not brought to life yet. Summing up, YPSILON is currently in the centre of a managerial reorganisation with very low ITG maturity.

IT relatedness is low at YPSILON, as well. While the infrastructure is harmonised to a certain level due to a sourcing solution, the application landscape is completely disparate. Most projects are approached individually and independently of each other. While the IT department works on an SAP solution for logistics and order management on the one hand, business units like HR, finance and controlling work on own approaches and solutions on the other hand. What makes the case study at YPSILON interesting is that the observed decentral state of IT was not an intentionally organised approach, but rather an undesired heritage of decentral structures. This inheritance is due to a missing vision not fully under control, yet.

When discussing business process relatedness, the division CIO stated that the IT department would fully support the idea of harmonising processes across divisions and departments. However, the current organisational setting does not offer opportunities for such endeavours.

5.2.6 TAU

TAU is a large player in the energy & utilities industry in Germany and Europe and generates turnovers of over 15 billion euro annually. The company employs people in numerous subsidiaries along the entire value chain of energy production, transport and delivery. Due to a significant change in regulation, requiring a legal and operational spin-off of the energy transmission system, TAU is currently facing a major organisational challenge, including far-reaching consequences for the corporate IT.

In reaction to recurring issues and conflicts about decision rights, TAU has introduced an IT governance board and various corporate-wide guidelines which determine IT decision making across the corporation. ITG structures are traditionally well developed at TAU. In parts, this goes back to regulatory requirements. The IT governance board basically represents the IT steering committee and is composed of the CIO office and the so-called information managers. The latter are IT representatives that are located in the business units. Below the IT governance board, several layers of working groups are established. These deal with specific topics and projects. IT architecture committees as well as IT project steering committees are in place and were reported to be operating efficiently. ITG processes are regarded to be on a medium maturity level at TAU. On the one hand, some processes are extremely well developed, such as SLAs, charge back arrangements or project prioritisation. On the other hand, effective performance measurement or efficient IT reporting structures are missing. Frameworks like COBIT, ITIL or ISO are not applied in the domain of information technology. According to the interviewee, such frameworks would entail too much formalism. However, particular organisational structures at TAU are designed according to COBIT recommendations. Relational mechanisms are developed well at TAU. Beyond informal meetings and a good internal communication, the aforementioned information managers form the backbone of cross departmental/ functional communication. The interviewee explicated furthermore that due to partly decentral organisational structures, the central IT department has not full authority over a collection of IT departments. Especially in these cases, a constructive and close dialogue is crucial and, according to the interviewee, in place. However, there are weaknesses in relation to business process design as the respective business units often start projects without informing the IT. Summing up, ITG maturity at TAU is on a medium level. While many effective as well as efficient mechanisms are in place, the interviewee reported that decisions are often made in contradiction to the governance guidelines. Nevertheless, the major problem at TAU is not a weak ITG framework, but an uncertain organisational structure that is currently under redesign.

The assessment of IT relatedness at TAU offered a mixed picture. After a harmonisation campaign was started a few years ago, the infrastructure of the headquarters and the largest subsidiaries got consolidated. However, small subsidiaries and recently acquired firms are still running their own infrastructure. The interviewee states that rigorous harmonisation of infrastructure shall and will go on, as it proved to be the right strategy. The IT unit offers two SAP systems for HR, reporting and alike applications. While this system provides a good basis, the CIO at TAU proposes enormous potential for further synergies in a possible harmonisation of over 1,700 distinct applications that are currently running. However, the interviewee stated:

> *"The responsible business managers have to be convinced in painful legwork with business cases in order to centralise their applications."*

In other cases, a corporate-wide harmonisation of applications is not regarded as the right way since the business logic of the respective functions is too diverse. In summary, the IT relatedness of TAU is medium.

Beyond some exceptions, comparable business processes are not rolled out across different departments and subsidiaries at TAU. Again, the interviewee stated that the requirements are too industry-specific. Nevertheless, the IT complains that the BUs conceptualise and optimise their business processes without a structured involvement of IT experts. This happens despite the fact that many IT employees have a lot of context-specific knowledge as they work for many years with specific business processes. Thus, a better collaboration in the course of process design and optimisation would benefit both parties.

In addition to sinking costs in the course of infrastructure harmonisation, TAU reported better processes, which provide operational synergies, as a major result of relatedness projects. An example named was a new accounting system in EUROCOUNTRY. In other cases an integrated system of IT and business processes provided new business opportunities like smart metering. However, such cases represent rather an exception as a corporate-wide integration of IT and business processes is absent. Especially in relation to business processes, the interviewee stated that the late involvement of the IT department is a major hurdle on the way to more synergies.

5.2.7 SIGMA

SIGMA is, similar to TAU, among the major corporations in the energy and utilities industry in Germany and Europe. The firm generates annual turnovers over 15 billion euro and employs people in the entire value chain of energy production, transport, and delivery. Similar to TAU, SIGMA went through a major organisational restructuring in the course of regulatory amendments concerned with the energy transmission system.

The case study conducted at SIGMA is particularly instructive, as ITG at SIGMA is decentralised, but of high maturity. ITG structures are divided into central and decentral systems. The former encompass an IT steering committee and an architecture board as well as a central reporting system. The latter includes project steering committees. A similar divide is found in relation to ITG processes. Charge back arrangements and numerous SLAs are governed centrally, while the project portfolios, budget planning and IT reporting are governed decentrally. ITIL and parts of CMM are rolled out and various ISO standards are being prepared for certification. The interviewee summarised:

> *"The decision for such [decentralised IT] governance has been made since flexibility and velocity in adaptation were favoured over central and cost-optimised standardisation within the period of market liberalisation. However, the rising cost pressures caused by CO2 certifications, the nuclear fuel-rod tax and the nuclear power phase-out can lead to a change in the governance [mode]. We are in a process of reassessing the IT governance in the current situation and I believe that a further centralisation of governance is necessary. Cutting costs is only possible if a mode of governance is applied that is centralised further."*

ITG relational mechanisms are well developed, too. Formal and informal meetings between IT and business managers are scheduled regularly. Key account managers have an important role. The interviewee stressed, moreover, that in the course of IT projects, an allocation of IT staff in business departments proved to be extremely valuable for an exchange of knowledge. According to the interviewee, the relationship between IT and business is very good; despite being characterised as a customer-supplier relation rather than a partnership.

IT relatedness is high across the largest fraction of SIGMA, despite the decentral mode of ITG. Data centres are consolidated and IT services are delivered by one source. Exceptions are found in a few small and regional subsidiaries which are not integrated yet. A similar situation is evident in relation to the application landscape that is largely based on an SAP solution for the utilities industry. However, besides some financial topics, business process relatedness is still very low at SIGMA due to the decentralised structure. The interviewee stated:

> *"For instance, there is no reason at all that HR acquisition, mentoring and development is not standardised, since these processes reflect a similar logic across all departments. The reality, however, outlines another picture. Subsidiaries, instead, have their own HR departments supported by their own HR processes with their own systems in the background. Nevertheless, we succeeded with the enterprise-wide deployment of employee self services. Even subsidiaries, which are strongly independent, acknowledge the value of that project."*

When discussing about performance impacts of IT and IT-related projects, the interviewee drew a very clear picture. According to him, high IT costs are caused by the decentralised structure of the corporation. In order to achieve synergies, business processes need to be recentralised and harmonised. This would lead to positive performance effects within the observed business process and simultaneously push IT costs down due to large-scale synergies. The interviewee provided an example where a project was started in order to bring IT costs in accounting down to benchmarks:

> *"The subsidiary eventually acknowledged that the business processes was actually the issue, so the scope of the whole project changed. After redesigning the particular business processes in accounting, it was possible to migrate the process to the platform provided by the IT and eventually realise extensive cost savings."*

5.2.8 RHO

With more than 40,000 employees and annual turnovers of more than 15 billion euro, RHO is a market leader in its commercial branch. The company looks back at rapid growth over the last 10 years, which had significant influence on the IT department of the corporation, growing from 80 to over 400 in staff.

ITG at RHO was virtually nonexistent up until a few months prior to the interview. The head of IT, who was recently employed with the goal to realign IT with business, explicated that this is not only due to decentral structures of the firm, but as well due to IT management failures. It is important to emphasise that RHO did not consciously pursue a decentralised mode of IT governance, but that IT grew into anarchy in an environment of decentral business strategy and absent governance of IT. While the number of employees in the central IT department grew constantly, managerial structures were not adapted. The 'hey-Joe-principle' got established over the years according to the interviewee and a vast number of hard- and software solutions were implemented side by side, without considering the consequences. The head of IT at RHO stated that IT relatedness is in consequence *"near to zero"*, which as well applies to business process relatedness.

While RHO is growing further and aiming at a diversification of its distribution channels, the board decided on a complete 'reset' of the firm's information technology three months prior to the interview. In reaction to rising costs and recurring operational and managerial difficulties in the IT, a strategic reorientation was regarded as essential.

The interviewee stated that the idea is a green-field approach. While a deliberate ITG framework is developed and appropriate experts are recruited. Meanwhile, a shared and harmonised infrastructure landscape is implemented with an external partner. The company contrives, thereafter, to develop a new application landscape in a collaborative approach with the business departments. The eventual goal is to simultaneously increase IT relatedness and business process relatedness. Therefore, a large knowledge-transfer initiative is started as well. IT staff is sent to various business departments and branches of the company to learn about the processes in place. The interviewee summarised:

> *"We start from zero, therefore, I want the IT staff first to go out and see how the firm works and functions; they even have to spend a week at a checkout counter. Normally, it's 'IT follows business', but we try to do something different here and strive to redesign our IT and business process landscape together, from scratch. The IT was a mess, but to meet future market challenges, a realignment of our business processes is essential as well. Right now, we have a one-time opportunity to kill two birds with one stone."*

5.2.9 PI

Despite not being among the largest players in the financial industry, PI can offer the full range of financial services to its customers. The firm employs over 3,000 staff and is responsible for a double figure billion euro asset value, all along with a balance sheet of roughly one billion euro.

PI has started a complete redesign of its IT governance and IT landscape over a decade ago. The project was reported as very successful. Primary original drivers were cost considerations, but once initiated, the company realised many additional synergies. PI has a deliberate and effective set of ITG structures in place, which in parts go back to regulatory requirements. Among those are an IT strategy committee, an IT architecture committee and an IT project steering committee. The ITG processes at PI are well developed but stay behind the ITG structures in maturity. Project governance and an IT budget control system is in place as well as charge back arrangements and a portfolio management. However, the interviewee claimed that PI still has some potential for optimisation of its ITG processes. A system of SLAs is currently under development; the introduction is planned for 2012. The interviewee, furthermore, claimed that the calculation of the total costs of ownership (TCO) is not satisfying yet. The same applies to the performance measurement. The relational mechanisms were reported to be traditionally very well developed at PI. Informal meetings, a very good internal communication and a project management office, which is used as a basis for a collaborative partnership, are valued by the IT department as well as the business side. The interviewee explicated that ITG is generally seen quite positively among staff, which in his opinion has to do with the good relationship between business and the IT. Summing up, ITG maturity at PI is high. ITG processes need to be developed further; however, the ITG framework as a whole works effectively and efficiently and is valued and respected by IT and non-IT staff.

IT relatedness is very high at PI. This goes back in a first step to the aforementioned harmonisation initiative a decade ago. Building on consolidated hardware, the application landscape was continuously optimised for over a decade now. Starting with a first implementation of SAP R/3 in 1999, more modules were introduced and rolled out across the corporation, such as Enterprise Portal, Internet Communication Manager, SAP CRM or SAP Process Integration. The need for flexibility, risk mitigation and a focus on core competencies have replaced costs as main drivers for the move towards a standard platform and a focus on business processes.

Closely related to the increase in IT relatedness, PI amplified business process relatedness as well. Not only in the headquarters of the firm, but also in relation to front-office processes, such as acquisition of customers, consulting and contracting. However, it is important to note that, despite numerous branches, all core-processes at PI are running primarily in one location at the headquarters. This fact emphasises that achieving high business process relatedness at PI is less complex than in many of the aforementioned case companies.

5.2.10 OMIKRON

OMIKRON looks back at a long history and offers the full range of insurance services for individuals, communities and municipalities. The firm has a balance sheet of around 0.5 billion euro and obtains yearly insurance premiums of around 250 million euro.

ITG moved into the focus of OMIKRON in 2006 with the naming of a new CIO, who is a member of the company's board. While some ITG mechanisms were already in place, the new CIO redesigned the IT strategy, implemented new ITG mechanisms and promoted the topic of IT governance internally. The CIO stated that much development was done successfully, but that the goals are not fully achieved yet.

ITG structures encompass an IT strategy and an IT steering committee. These are supported by a project office since 2006. However, the interviewee emphasised that in his opinion, the ITG processes are even more essential for an efficient IT governance framework. OMIKRON refined and implemented various ITG processes since the new CIO was named. Among those are well developed charge-back arrangements, COBIT-like processes, a structured portfolio management, documented project governance procedures, effective budget controls and, for a few years now, an ex-post benchmarking of IT projects. The CIO explained that most of the processes grew organically, without being developed according to specific recommendations of frameworks. However, after a certain maturity was achieved, the CIO office compared the mechanisms in place with best-practices such as COBIT or ITIL to gain inspiration and refine the frameworks further. SLAs are not implemented yet. Summing up, ITG structures are of medium and ITG processes of high maturity at OMIKRON. Regarding ITG relational mechanisms, OMIKRON is well positioned, too. Formal and informal meetings are scheduled regularly. For several years now, business/ IT account managers are assigned. The CIO stated that even small gestures, like the removing of the security doors between the IT department and the rest of the corporation, had an important impact for the development of a collaborative atmosphere of partnership.

IT relatedness at OMIKRON is medium. Infrastructure, including the entire data centre and telecommunication hardware was rebuilt in a harmonised fashion from scratch in 2008. However, the application landscape still represents a fractured collection of different systems, proprietary solutions and recently implemented SAP modules. The CIO stated that the current IT strategy clearly aims at the replacement of custom-developed applications with SAP modules.

The business process relatedness at OMIKRON is closely related to the application landscape. The interviewee claims that the *"insurance factory of the company is the IT"*, meaning that the business processes can only be as integrated and harmonised as the underlying technology. It is important to add that at OMIKRON, comparable to PI, most core processes are running only once at the headquarters. The primary focus of the CIO is, therefore, the integration of the business processes and corresponding systems in place, in order to avoid duplication of work and overlapping of tasks. While many business processes were recently redesigned, OMIKRON still has some way to go in order to catch up with some major competitors. According to the interviewee, some of these already run many business processes without any staff, while OMIKRON still needs to handle numerous internal interfaces manually.

The interviewee explained that the effects of increased relatedness led to massive cost savings of around 5-10% of the annual IT budget. He further added that a reduced time to market was achieved, which clearly represents super-additive value synergies. However, the achievement of further super-additive value synergies is hindered by the confined integration of business processes relatedness, which goes back to the medium degree of application relatedness.

5.2.11 Summary

The observed case companies differ significantly in IT governance maturity as well as in resource relatedness. While CHI, SIGMA and PI have a mature IT governance, OMIKRON, TAU, PHI and OMEGA dispose over an ITG with medium maturity. PSI, RHO and YPSILON have rather underdeveloped ITG frameworks. A similar variance was observed in regard to the IT relatedness among the case companies. The analysis of the business processes offered a more homogeneous picture, with most of the case companies having low or medium business process relatedness. Based on the coding scheme provided in Appendix 3, Appendix 4 provides a detailed assessment of the singular constructs of each case company.

Based on the explanatory model and the underlying propositions developed in the exploratory phase, the following chapter offers a cross-case analysis and discusses commonalities and differences of the observed corporations. Doing so, the suggested propositions are either corroborated or dropped, leading to a refined explanatory model.

5.3 Cross-Case Analysis

After the conducted case-studies of the corroborative phase were discussed individually in the previous section, this chapter offers an aggregated analysis of the second case sample. The goal is to examine if the explanatory model, as suggested in the exploratory phase of the study, is able to explain commonalities and differences in the second case sample. Doing so, an analytical generalisation is aimed for.

The following sections are organised according to the explanatory model, starting with the impact of IT governance, before the performance impacts of relatedness and the moderating role of the absorptive capacity are discussed.

5.3.1 The Impact of IT Governance

The findings of the exploratory empirical phase suggested that IT governance maturity has a substantial positive impact on the IT relatedness and business process relatedness of corporations. Appendix 3 provides the applied coding scheme for the analysis of the observed ITG maturity and relatedness values, while Appendix 4 provides an overview of the singular construct ratings for each case.

5.3.1.1 The impact of IT governance maturity on IT relatedness

Corroborating the findings of the exploratory case study phase, the introduced single-case analysis of the second case sample showed a strong relation between IT governance maturity and IT relatedness in almost all case sites. Figure 8 compares the IT governance maturity of the firms of the second case study round with the observed degree of IT relatedness.

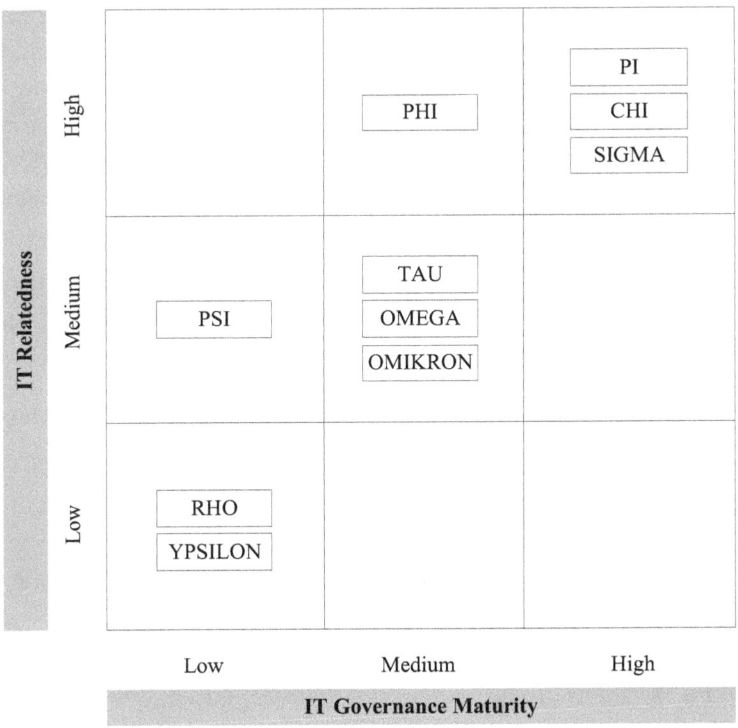

Figure 8: Assessment of IT governance maturity and IT relatedness

In addition to the observed pattern that clearly suggests a link between ITG maturity and IT relatedness, the qualitative data of the observed firms allows a close look at this relationship. Drawing on the single-case analysis, a few examples are provided.

The interviewee at CHI stated that the primary incentive for the redesign of ITG was the *"development of guidelines and the definition of [...] standards, since only those means allow governing the organisation in a way that ensures synergies"*. At PHI, ITG initiatives were followed by the successful consolidation of the application landscape towards SAP and Microsoft products, encompassing ERP, SRM or CRM.

At OMEGA, IT infrastructure and process consolidation was brought forward after a redesigned ITG was implemented. After introducing SAP R/3 in 1999, SIGMA was able to enforce a single-vendor strategy with effective ITG, allowing a company-wide replacement of legacy solutions with standard SAP modules, such as SAP Enterprise Portal, SAP CRM or SAP Process Integration between 2000 and 2008. YPSILON and RHO, with low ITG maturity, corroborated the proposed relationship with low IT relatedness. PSI, with low ITG maturity and medium IT relatedness, does not deviate from the explanatory model either. The firm has started its IT harmonisation projects shortly after initiating a redesign of the ITG framework. While the ITG is still immature, it provided the necessary decision rights for an increase in IT relatedness.

To sum up, the aggregated cross- and single-case analysis of the case companies in the second data collection substantiate Proposition P1a as developed and theoretically grounded in the empirical exploration.

5.3.1.2 The impact of IT governance maturity on business process relatedness

Even though business process relatedness was generally lower than IT relatedness throughout most of the analysed companies, the assessment as shown in Figure 9 supports the suggested relationship between IT governance maturity and business process relatedness. Exemplary excerpts from the single-case analysis are provided in the following, elucidating the proposition.

PHI established an ITG process which ensures that business processes that are to be supported by IT are developed based on best practices only once, in one pilot region. These processes are thereafter rolled out to Europe consistently and thereafter worldwide. This ITG design led to an increase in business process relatedness. The central IT department of CHI was the first department in the company to really go global with consistent work-practices and processes; these were ensured and enforced with ITG initiatives. Due to its great success, this project is now used as a reference model for consolidating IT-supported structures and process, especially within HR, controlling and R&D. In other words, the mature ITG framework at CHI increased in a first step IT relatedness, and, in a second, business process relatedness. OMEGA, with a medium mature ITG, took the first step towards ITG-driven increase of business process relatedness with the establishment of a unified sales and service template, which had to be employed globally so as to ensure a consistent database. Even though the singular subsidiaries are free to align their sales and service process according to their local needs, the uniform data template guarantees that the data and, thus, back-office processes remain globally consistent.

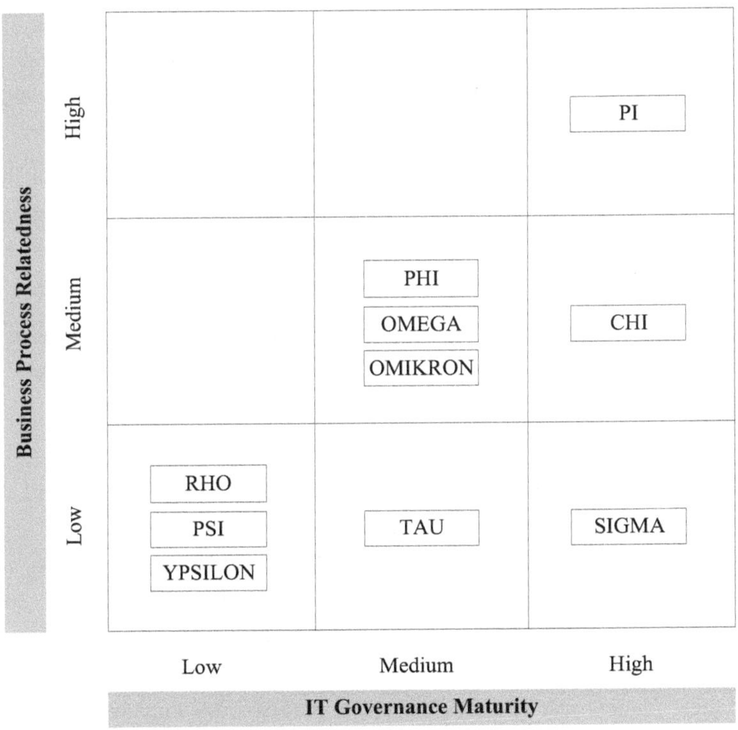

Figure 9: Assessment of IT governance maturity and business process relatedness

SIGMA has a low business process relatedness despite a mature ITG framework. However, as described in the single-case analysis, this goes back to specific circumstances in a phase of market liberalisation. The interviewee at SIGMA, furthermore, expects an increase in business process relatedness in the course of cost pressures as described in Chapter 5.2.7. Moreover, first ITG-driven achievements with employee self services provided evidence that business process harmonisations across departments and subsidiaries are sensible and possible. RHO, PSI, YPSILON and PI offer extreme cases which are in line with the model.

In summary, the aggregated cross- and single-case analysis of the case companies in the second data collection substantiate Proposition P1b as developed and theoretically grounded in the empirical exploration.

5.3.1.3 The moderating effect of IT relatedness

The explanatory model developed in the exploratory phase furthermore suggested a moderating role of IT relatedness associated with Proposition P1b.

Figure 10 compares IT relatedness and business process relatedness of the firms analysed in the corroborative phase. Only firms with medium or high IT relatedness show medium or high business process relatedness, but the relationship is evidently weaker than between ITG maturity and business process relatedness.

The qualitative data of the presented single-case analyses (see Appendix 4) supports the suggested proposition that high IT relatedness does not lead directly to increased business process relatedness, but that it positively moderates the aforementioned impact of ITG maturity on business process relatedness.

SIGMA or PSI offer examples where a (highly) streamlined IT landscape does not lead to enhanced business process relatedness, due to missing governance guidelines that have impact on business process design. CHI reported that the campaign for the harmonisation of business process benefitted from a harmonised landscape, but that it was an ITG campaign that promoted the process harmonisation. Similarly, PHI reported that a streamlined application landscape provided a basis for process harmonisations, but that the eventual cause of a rise in business process relatedness was an ITG specification enacted to regulate process design. OMEGA explicated that high IT relatedness offers new possibilities for harmonisation of processes, but that the latter is inexecutable when not initiated and accompanied by a governance initiative.

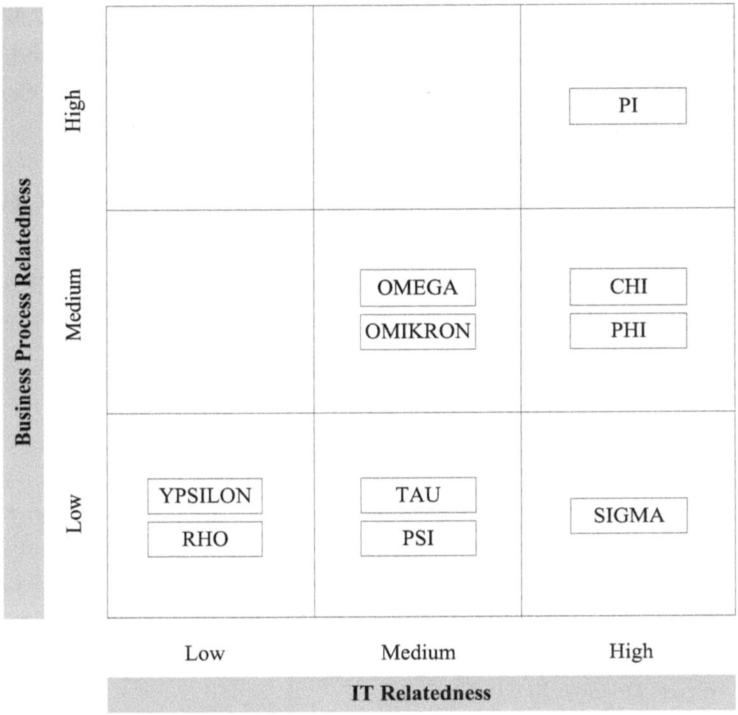

Figure 10: Assessment of IT relatedness and business process relatedness

In summary, the aggregated cross- and single-case analysis of the case companies in the second data collection substantiate Proposition P2 as developed and theoretically grounded in the empirical exploration.

5.3.2 Performance Effects of Relatedness

The previous section discussed and substantiated the proposed relationships between IT governance maturity and resource relatedness on the basis of the second case sample. This chapter examines if the suggested performance impacts of IT relatedness and business process relatedness can be observed in the second data collection as well.

Assessing the effects of relatedness based on a comparison of financial figures of the 10 case companies is not suitable in this study. The dataset is, especially with regard to the different industries the observed firms are active in, too small. As a consequence, the data was analysed in a way that the singular performance indicators, as presented in Table 11, were assessed and, thereafter, related to the specific IT- or IT-supported business-projects that caused them (see also Chapter 2.2.5). This way it was possible to contrast the observed business performance impacts in the case companies with the respective IT relatedness and business process relatedness, allowing an assessment of the synergy effects proposed by the explanatory model that was derived in the exploratory phase.

Appendix 3 provides the applied coding scheme for the analysis of the observed relatedness values and business performance impacts. Based on the coding scheme, Appendix 4 provides an overview of the singular construct ratings for each case, based on empirical evidence.

5.3.2.1 The impact of IT relatedness on business performance

The proposed positive impact of IT relatedness on business performance in the explanatory model of the first phase, that is Proposition P3a, was suggested building on extant literature providing quantitative evidence for this proposition (Tanriverdi 2006) altogether with evidence from the exploratory findings. Therefore, it is not surprising that the findings of the case studies in the corroborative phase are in line with Proposition P3a, as discussed in the following.

The firms with medium IT relatedness, OMIKRON, PSI, OMEGA and TAU, primarily reported sub-additive costs that were achieved in the course of infrastructure harmonisation. The head of IT at PSI clearly stated that the consolidation of 23 ERP systems towards one is expected to bring various synergies, but that for now not even the cost savings of the hardware harmonisation are transparent, since no information about costs was gathered in the previous years. OMIKRON reported that massive savings were achieved with the harmonisation of infrastructure (5-10% of the run-costs annually), but that the dismembered application landscape and numerous interfaces deter the company from achieving super-additive synergies, like observed in competing companies. The insights from TAU were comparable. The corporation has a widely harmonised infrastructure, but is running 1,700 distinct applications that obstruct the firm from reaping super-additive benefits that were observed in some pilot cases, like unified accounting systems in EUROCOUNTRY.

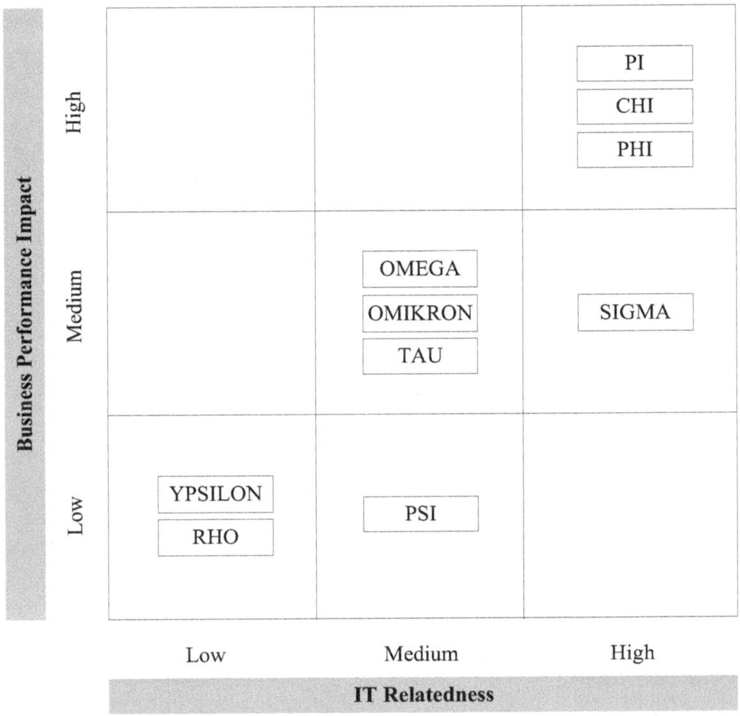

Figure 11: Assessment of IT relatedness and business performance impact

However, firms with high IT relatedness, that is PHI, PI, CHI and SIGMA, reported that both sub-additive cost synergies as well as super-additive value synergies are generated with high IT relatedness. While PI can be regarded as a specific case due to the fact that IT processes simultaneously are core business processes to a large extent, CHI, PHI or SIGMA allow a more differentiated observation. CHI reported that the combined worldwide harmonisation of ERP systems and infrastructure provided the basis for a new way of operating on a global level. Especially in relation to logistics and procurement synergies that were not accessible before, were reaped. The CIO of PHI reported that the impacts of the consolidation of infrastructure, hardware, software and IT processes went far beyond cost savings and offered the firm for the first time a unified picture of its own production, customers and service processes. This in turn was applied to refine ERP, CRM and production systems. As discussed in the single-case analysis, SIGMA offered a specific picture with a heavily disparate business process landscape that impedes obtaining the full benefits of high IT relatedness. Nevertheless, whenever organisational boundaries are overcome, like in the introduced examples of employee self services or accounting systems, super-additive value synergies based on unified infrastructure, databases and operational systems come to light. Figure 11 contrasts the IT relatedness values of the observed firms with the reported business performance impacts of current and past IT and IT-related projects.

Summing up, the aggregated cross- and single-case analysis of the case companies in the second data collection substantiate Proposition P3a as developed and theoretically grounded in the empirical exploration.

5.3.2.2 The impact of business process relatedness on business performance

Building on the theoretical basis of the previously discussed Proposition P3a and insights from the exploratory case studies, the explanatory model introduced in Chapter 4.2 suggests furthermore a positive impact of business process relatedness on the performance of a firm, that is, Proposition P3b.

In particular, data from CHI, PI, OMIKRON and PHI (see Appendix 4) provides support for Proposition P3b. OMIKRON explicated that high business process relatedness is crucial to stay on eyelevel with competitors, which partly proceeded towards an advanced cross-integration of business processes, providing them cost advantages and a lower time to market. PI reported that through a high integration of business processes many core functions of the firm are fully automated. CHI, where the harmonisation of IT processes was a big success, applies, as described earlier, the IT governance principles now as a reference for corporate governance, with the goal to globally harmonise business processes. According to the interviewee, the company not only aims at cost-savings through synergies, but also expects to strengthen its position in the market once higher business process relatedness and closer collaboration, e.g. in logistics and R&D, is achieved. Eventually PHI pointed out that the implementation of harmonised cross-divisional processes is a permanent source of synergies. PHI provided data from user satisfaction surveys, trying to measure the general value add of IT. The surveys indicate that much value was created through the provision of cross-business process harmonisation, and, thus, support Proposition P3b.

What is more, SIGMA, OMEGA, RHO or OMIKRON in unison reported that the low/ medium business process relatedness significantly hinders the firm from generating evident super-additive synergies that would be achievable on the basis of further harmonised business processes. This was reported to be especially frustrating if comparable integrated business processes were observed in competing companies. Figure 12 contrasts the business process relatedness values of the observed firms with the reported business performance impacts of current and past IT and IT-related projects.

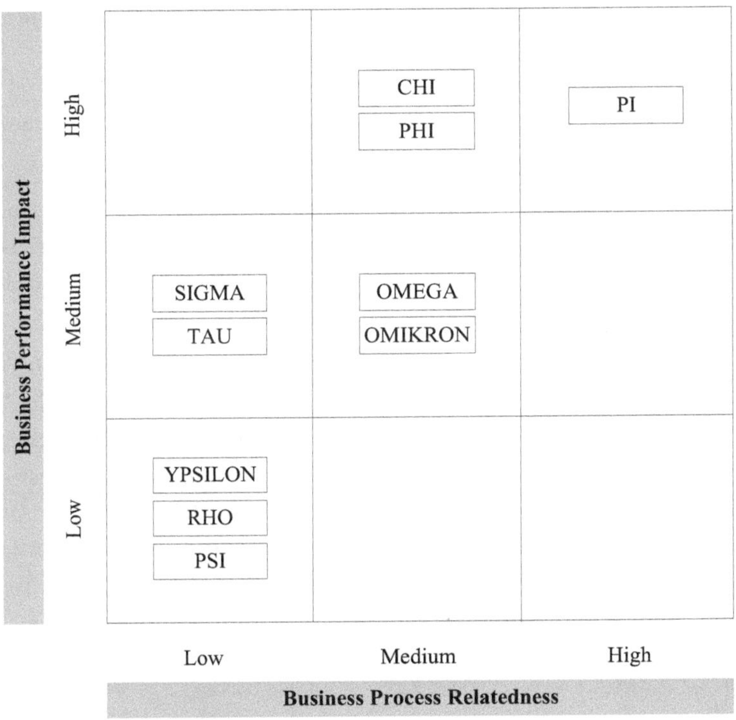

Figure 12: Assessment of business process relatedness and business performance impact

Summing up, the aggregated cross- and single-case analysis of the case companies in the second data collection provide evidence that substantiates Proposition P3b. Due to the nature of this proposition, it is not trivial to collect information from the IT side, with the proposition-specific data and business cases mostly being in the hands of business units. However, the conducted case studies in the corroborative phase indicate support for Proposition P3b as developed and theoretically grounded in the empirical exploration.

5.3.3 Interacting Effects between IT Relatedness and Business Process Relatedness

The explanatory model developed in the exploratory case study phase proposed beyond the singular positive effects of IT relatedness and business process relatedness additional interacting effects, Proposition P4.

Assessing these interacting effects, the conducted case studies of the second round substantiate Proposition P4 and provide great evidence (see Appendix 4 for respective quotes) for the suggested super-additive value synergies that can be generated if IT relatedness and business process relatedness are available in combination.

OMEGA reported that with the introduction of a unified CRM and the harmonisation of support-processes across business units, it was possible to redevelop in-field services and provide the service staff with a custom-developed mobile device. The field-workers now dispose over entirely new possibilities to work customer-oriented and provide support for products which were produced by different units of OMEGA. The technicians can check on-site every past support-process and provide assistance for different divisions much quicker and more efficiently. In addition to the improved customer satisfaction, the sales department can now extract data centrally from all support departments, see weaknesses of the customers' production facilities and improve goal-oriented cross-selling.

PHI reported of an even more expressive case, where concurrently increased business process relatedness and IT relatedness enabled an entirely new line of business. PHI, as reported in the single-case analysis, manufactures machines for assembly lines and production facilities. Due to the high number of product-variations, customers, who run up to a three digit number of PHI products in different production plants, had to deal with various PHI divisions for service and support. When the IT unit of PHI started merging all databases across divisions and eventually installed a unified CRM, the firm realised that it possesses data precisely showing which customer runs which product at which plant. Using all that information and unifying the support process across all divisions, PHI can now offer a completely new service to its clients. Today, PHI is able to remotely monitor all devices at the customers' plants, not only ensuring an immediate replacement of the correct device in the case of failure (one assembly line can utilise dozens of PHI products), but even providing accurate estimations on how long a certain device can run before breaking down. Doing so, downtimes of production facilities can be reduced immensely. In consequence, customer satisfaction and device sales went up, with PHI saving money by streamlining and accelerating support processes. But what is more, the combined increase of business process relatedness and IT relatedness facilitated an entirely new service-product, providing on-top sales and a unique market position that is grounded in an integrated system of information technology, production and business process that is very hard to imitate.

The described cases do not only provide support for Proposition P4 but are as well fully in line with the theoretical grounding of the proposition as described in the empirical exploration and theory building. The increase of business process relatedness and IT relatedness are complementary to each other in the sense that the increase of business process relatedness makes an increase of IT relatedness more valuable and vice versa. Consequently, concurrently increased business process relatedness and IT relatedness can provide super-additive value synergies which are not only hard to copy, but even hard to observe, as they are deeply rooted in the corporations' technical, organisational and cultural architectures. When exploiting these synergies, companies can achieve sustainable competitive advantages.

Therefore, the aggregated cross- and single-case analysis of the case companies in the second data collection substantiate Proposition P4 as developed and theoretically grounded in the empirical exploration.

5.3.4 Moderating Role of Absorptive Capacity

The previous sections discussed and substantiated the relationships between IT governance maturity, the mediating construct resource relatedness and the business performance of a firm, as suggested by the explanatory model that was developed in the exploratory phase of this study.

The exploratory findings further suggested a moderating impact of the absorptive capacity of the IT department on the Propositions P1a and P1b, that is, on the positive impact of IT governance maturity on IT relatedness (Proposition P5a) and business process relatedness (Proposition P5b).

5.3.4.1 The moderating role of the absorptive capacity of the IT department in relation to the impact of ITG maturity on IT relatedness

Closely analysing the data of the second case sample, it was not possible to substantiate Proposition P5a, that is, finding evidence for a moderating effect of the absorptive capacity of the IT department on the impact of IT governance maturity on the IT relatedness of a firm.

Despite emphasising the importance of context-specific knowledge and absorptive capacity of the respective IT departments in general, the enhancement of IT relatedness was regarded in wide parts detached to it.

The deviation from the assessment of the first case studies can be explained due to the exploratory nature of the first empirical round. The data of the first round was not rich enough to allow a clear perimeter of the moderating impact of absorptive capacity on relatedness-projects. Consequently, a moderating effect for the ITG-driven increase in IT relatedness (Proposition P5a) and business process relatedness (Proposition P5b) was proposed.

The data of the second round is based on a more detailed and structured interview guideline which was focused on the substantiation of the model. Thus, a more detailed inquiry of the effect of absorptive capacity and an isolation of its impact was possible. While this led to dropping of Proposition P5a, support was found for the suggested Proposition P5b, as presented in the subsequent section.

5.3.4.2 The moderating role of the absorptive capacity of the IT department in relation to the impact of ITG maturity on business process relatedness

Projects that aimed at the increase of business process relatedness in the second case sample were reported to be heavily dependent on the collaboration between business and IT and, as proposed in the explanatory model, knowledge absorption from the IT side (the respective quotes are provided in Appendix 4).

A good example for the moderating effect of absorptive capacity is provided by PHI. The CIO reported that high absorptive capacity of the IT staff enabled PHI to accelerate the ITG-driven business process harmonisation. Instead of only publishing guidelines that aim at business process harmonisation, the IT was able to offer possible solutions, as in the introduced case of customer support. YPSILON offered an extreme example where a harmonisation of three processes was only possible because IT disposed over staff that was able to understand the highly specific business process and enforce a compromise between the conflicting business parties. The CIO summarised: *"As a pure IT worker you would have no chance; you would not even understand the technical terms"*. In both case companies that were active in the financial industry, PI and OMIKRON, the interviewees explicated that the business processes are very close to the IT. This leads in turn led to a situation, where ITG penetrates business process relatedness quite directly. However, the speed and degree of the implementation of business relatedness projects is highly dependent on IT's ability IT to understand and structure the business processes.

In summary, the aggregated cross- and single-case analysis of the case companies in the second data collection did not provide support for Proposition P5a but offered evidence that substantiated Proposition P5b, as developed and theoretically grounded in the empirical exploration. Consequently, the former Proposition P5a is dropped, while the former Proposition P5b is renamed towards Proposition P5.

5.3.5 Summary

In an effort to substantiate and refine the theoretical model which explains the positive impact of IT governance on business performance and which was developed using 11 exploratory case studies, a second dataset was collected in order to avoid a selection bias. Analysing 10 case studies in detail, each proposition was closely assessed. It was possible to substantiate the original propositions P1a, P1b, P2, P3a, P3b, P4 and P5b as suggested in the exploratory phase of the research effort.

The original Proposition P5a could not be substantiated and is dropped consequently from the theoretical model. Thus, the original Proposition P5b is renamed to Proposition P5 in the substantiated and refined theoretical model as shown in Figure 13. All other propositions and constructs remain unmodified as introduced and defined in the empirical exploration and theory building.

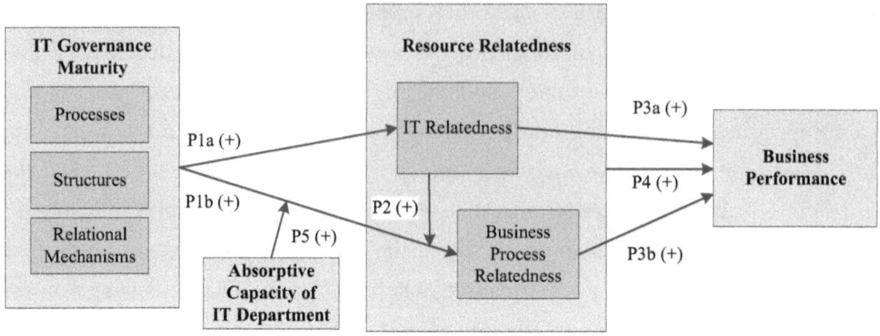

Figure 13: Revised model of the impact of IT governance on the business performance of a firm

6. Discussion of Findings

The intention of this research project was to enhance the understanding of the value contribution of IT governance. While the passage of the Sarbanes-Oxley Act in 2002 incited many organisations to establish deliberated IT governance frameworks, academic research in this area is still in its early stages. Although ITG best practices and descriptive frameworks have been available for years, theoretical models explaining the impact of ITG on business performance are missing (De Haes and Van Grembergen 2009). Extant literature on the topic of IT governance claims that ITG provides value to the firm (Weill 2004) and even offers guidelines on how to design ITG in order to achieve value gains (Weill and Ross 2004). However, the theoretical perspective on the mechanisms behind the relationship of ITG and business performance remained to a large extent unexplored (Lazic et al. 2011b) or was based on the assumption that ITG enhances business/ IT alignment (De Haes and Van Grembergen 2009; Lazic et al. 2011b; Liang et al. 2011), which was shown to be unsatisfying and in parts tautological.

In face of this significant lack of research, this study examines the theoretical perspective on the mechanisms behind the impact of IT governance on the business performance of a firm without employing the problematic construct of business/ IT alignment as a mediator (Lazic et al. 2011a; Lazic et al. 2011b). Moreover, this study is the first IT governance study to build on extant theory, namely the resource-based view (Barney 1991; Melville et al. 2004) and related theoretical work on the knowledge-based view (Grant 1996b; Nonaka 1994), complementarities (Milgrom and Roberts 1995), synergies (Davis and Thomas 1993; Teece 1982) and relatedness (Tanriverdi 2006).

This research project comes to the conclusion that resource relatedness is a major mediator of the impact of IT governance on the business performance of a firm. Doing so, the study provides significant contributions to theory and offers numerous managerial implications. After discussing the theoretical contributions in detail, this chapter presents the managerial implications and discusses the limitations of this study. Eventually, suggestions for future research are given.

6.1 Theoretical Implications

Building on the theoretical foundations as presented in Chapter 2 and Chapter 4, this section discusses theoretical contributions that are provided by this study within the following two domains: first, the body of knowledge on IT governance and second, the applied theoretical lens itself, the resource-based perspective on IT business value creation.

The central contribution of this study is the provision of an explanation of the positive impact of IT governance on the business performance of the firm. Previous literature on IT governance first analysed organisational modes and contingency factors of IT governance, before focusing on best practices that were proposed to have a positive impact on the business performance of the firm. A satisfying assessment of the ITG value creation process itself was to date not available. Building on this previous literature and profound theories from adjacent fields, this study provides an explanation of the positive impact of IT governance and thus makes a major contribution to the knowledge of IT governance and the applied theoretical lenses, as discussed in the following.

Assessing previous explanations of the positive impact of IT governance on the business performance of a firm

This study provides a first contribution to theory by showing that previous explanations of the positive impact of IT governance on business performance are inadequate and insufficient.

IT governance has been regarded over decades as a (tripartite) allocation of decision rights, which may fit or misfit contextual factors. These early studies did not query the existence or the quality of IT governance, but assessed the available structures of IT governance and, thereafter, contingencies which influenced the choice of the respective IT governance mode (Sambamurthy and Zmud 1999). Building on this research, more recent studies (Weill 2004) modified the basic assumption of the construct of IT governance and proposed that ITG is more than a label for an immaterial ever-existing object, i.e. the distribution of specific decision rights. Those scholars (among others Weill and Ross 2004) proposed that ITG, inter alia, encompasses a conscious act of designing and shaping an artefact that represents an explicit specification of decision rights and accountabilities that encourage desirable behaviour in the use of IT. Both, the act of designing such an artefact and the artefact itself, can be of high or low quality. Thus, by modifying this basic assumption of ITG, an assessment of the quality or even the existence of ITG became feasible. Weill (2004) thereupon speaks of 'effective' and 'above-average' IT governance. Based on numerous research projects and empirical data from more than 300 corporations worldwide, the author claims that firms with above-average ITG can achieve up to 20% higher profitability than their competitors. His study concludes that effective (/ above-average) IT governance is determinated by the presence of an actively designed set of IT governance mechanisms (Weill 2004). It is essential to note that this previous study does not offer an explanation on what exactly provides value to the firm after such an (effective) set of ITG mechanisms is enacted. In other words, while previous literature offers evidence for a positive impact of ITG, it does not provide an explanation for this assumption.

Building upon Weill's (2004) findings and other work on ITG mechanisms (Peterson 2004a; Van Grembergen 2004), De Haes and Van Grembergen (2009) develop the concept of IT governance further and consolidate previous findings into a maturity construct of IT governance. Applying this concept, De Haes and Van Grembergen (2009) as well as Liang et al. (2011) try to explain the positive impact of ITG on business performance as mediated by the concept of business/ IT alignment.

The study at hand provides a first contribution by showing that this explanation is inadequate and not satisfying for various reasons. The proposition that mature ITG enhances BITA, does not provide an explanation of the positive impact of ITG, but merely shifts the research question to the area of BITA. Yet, the notion of BITA is a field-driven concept that is not clearly defined, despite being discussed for more than two decades in over 150 publications (Chan and Reich 2007). Furthermore, as shown in Chapter 2.3.6, the formative indicators of BITA are overlapping with aspects regarded as indicators of mature IT governance (see also Lazic et al. 2011a; Lazic et al. 2011b), making the relation between ITG and BITA in parts tautological. In addition, some scholars point out that pursuing and achieving alignment as an exclusive goal can be contra productive from an IT governance point of view. This is the case when business strategy is not clear or in a process of change. If business processes are internally not consistent or left unmaintained over years, achieving alignment can lead to pathologies and IT stagnation. In other words, this study provides a first contribution by showing that previous research and the suggested models of De Haes and Van Grembergen (2009) as well as Liang et al. (2011) do not explain the positive impact of IT governance on business performance in a satisfactory manner.

Explaining the impact of IT governance on the business performance of a firm and questioning the non-ambiguity of the 'IT follows business'-principle

While building on previous findings and addressing shortcoming of existing research, this study provides its second and major theoretical contribution to theory with a model that is the first to analyse and explain the relationship between ITG and business performance in detail. Doing so, this study was able to show that the positive impact of IT governance on the business performance of a firm is mediated by the construct of resource relatedness. In particular, this study shows that rising IT governance maturity primarily impacts IT relatedness and business process relatedness of a firm. IT relatedness and business process relatedness, in turn, are the major source of sub-additive cost synergies and super-additive value synergies, and thus, an increase in business performance.

The empirical findings of both conducted multiple-case studies clearly suggest that rising maturity in ITG leads to the harmonisation of infrastructure and to a consolidation of the IT application landscape. This is accompanied or closely followed by the implementation of shared IT services and similar IT managerial practices across departments and subsidiaries.

A novel contribution to the basic understanding of IT and IT governance is provided by this study in showing that in a second step mature ITG leads to an increase in business process relatedness. That is, an increase in the usage of common business processes and managerial practices across business units. While IT governance was regarded as exclusively concerned with information technology in the past, the findings of this study suggest that especially mature IT governance is closely concerned with the design and governance of business processes.

In other words, besides explaining the impact of ITG, this study contributes to previous knowledge on information technology by offering evidence that one of the former basic assumptions of enterprise architecture namely the 'IT follows business'-principle (Winter and Fischer 2007) is to question in its pure non-ambiguous form. This is the third contribution of this study.

Application and extension of the resource-based view within the boundary of IT governance

Previous research on IT governance and ITG impact, including the seminal works done by Weill (2004), Peterson (2004a), Van Grembergen (2004), De Haes & Van Grembergen (2009) in unison abstain from applying theoretical concepts as a basis for their studies. Doing so, these findings are not of explanatory but of descriptive and, by providing recommendations on best practices, prescriptive nature.

The fourth contribution of this study lies, therefore, in the application of the resource- and knowledge-based paradigm as a basis for the explanation of the impact of ITG. The provided theoretical groundwork makes this study unique in the field of IT governance research.

This research endeavour shows that the RBV is particularly well suited as a basis for an analysis of the impact of IT governance on the business performance of a firm. The findings explicate that IT governance represents complex social relationships within the boundaries of a firm that eventually influence the varying success of the exploitation of its technological systems. In other words, research on IT governance is research on internal resources linkages of a firm. The resource-based view clearly addresses this kind of internal linkages as possible origins of varying performance, while the market-based perspective is not focused on or even neglects those as a possible source of improved business performance.

The RBV further suggests that only managerial IT skills can lead to sustainable IT-based competitive advantages, while e.g. access to capital, technical IT skills or proprietary technology are prone to imitation by competitors (Melville et al. 2004). The findings of this study strongly underline this reasoning. Immature ITG does not require a large portion of managerial IT skills and can only lead to technological innovations like a harmonised IT infrastructure. Such innovations, in line with the propositions of the RBV, primarily lead to sub-additive costs that can be imitated by competitors without substantial difficulties. This study shows that on the contrary mature ITG is highly dependent and based on excellent managerial IT skills. The empirical findings demonstrate that mature ITG leads to the development of a complementary system of IT and business processes with high relatedness. This systems offer values that are rare and hard to imitate and hence a basis for sustainable competitive advantages, which again is fully in line with the propositions of the resource-based view.

Application and extension of the knowledge-based view within the boundary of IT governance

In addition, this research emphasises insights from the knowledge-based view, where services rendered by tangible resources are seen as dependent on the way of their combination and application, which in turn is a function of the firm's know-how (Alavi and Leidner 2001). This know-how, or in other words, this knowledge, is embedded and carried within tangible and intangible entities of an organisation. Due to the complex nature of knowledge, especially if embedded within a social and organisational setting, knowledge-based resources are regarded as difficult to imitate and thus as a possible basis of long-term sustainable competitive advantage (Grant 1996a; Grant 1996b). Following the KBV, not only knowledge-assets themselves are unequally distributed among corporations and hard to imitate, but as well the capabilities to absorb and use knowledge (Cohen and Levinthal 1990). The fact that the absorptive capacity of an IT department is even less tangible and deeper rooted in the social and organisational setting than the knowledge assets themselves makes it even less mobile, and hence, following the KBV, more valuable and apt to generate sustainable competitive advantage.

The findings of this study are in line and substantiating these propositions of the KBV, as the empirical data suggests that the success of the impact of IT governance on business process relatedness is highly dependent on the absorptive capacity of the IT department.

By drawing on profound theories from reference disciplines, this study provides its fourth prominent contribution as it lays the basis for the formulation of a generalisable body of knowledge concerned with value creation through ITG. The theoretical model, which is fully falsifiable, is made amenable to quantitative theory testing. All constructs are precisely defined and the respective indicators have been developed; a translation into variables and hypotheses is at hand.

Refining the concept of resource relatedness

By adding knowledge to previous work on the concept of resource relatedness and synergies, the fifth contribution of this study is provided.

As introduced in Chapter 2.2.3.3, extant literature offers the construct of resource relatedness, which refers to the presence of shared resources and similar activities across business units of the firm (Davis and Thomas 1993). The construct of relatedness was applied and adapted to several organisational functions and resources as shown by Tanriverdi and Venkatraman (2005), such as product relatedness (Rumelt 1974), manufacturing relatedness (John and Harrison 1999), technological relatedness (Robins and Wiersema 1995; Silverman 1999), R&D relatedness (Chatterjee and Wernerfelt 1991), marketing relatedness (Capron and Hulland 1999), advertising relatedness (Chatterjee and Wernerfelt 1991), managerial relatedness (Ilinitch and Zeithaml 1995; Prahalad and Bettis 1986), human resource relatedness (Farjoun 1994) and IT relatedness (Tanriverdi 2006).

While previous research provided evidence that IT relatedness has a positive impact on the business performance of a firm (Tanriverdi 2006), the empirical findings of this study, first, strongly underline this proposition and, second, show that IT governance maturity has a major impact on the degree of IT relatedness in a firm. Providing evidence for the antecedent of IT relatedness is a significant contribution to the literature on resource relatedness.

Building on extant work on the resource-based view and resource relatedness, this study provides a further contribution to theory by introducing the concept of business-process relatedness. In line with the RBV, business processes are seen as resources of the firm (Barney 1991). Therefore, it is possible to transfer the implications of previous research on resource relatedness towards business processes. Doing so, this study proposes that business process relatedness has a positive impact on the business performance of a firm. The empirical insights of both phases of the conducted case studies support this proposition. As discussed before, this study furthermore offers evidence that IT governance maturity is a significant antecedent of business process relatedness.

Explaining complementary effects between IT relatedness and business process relatedness

Melville et al. (2004) propose that the IT business value generation is closely associated with enhancement of business processes and that the IT value-added is dependent on the complementarity of organisational resources (Rivard et al. 2006). As discussed earlier, this study fully substantiates these propositions and explains in detail how information technology and IT governance are related to the enhancement of business processes.

But what is more, this research endeavour shows that effects of complementarity are not only existent for organisational resources but in addition for their relatedness as well. This forms the sixth theoretical contribution of this study which is adding knowledge to the applied theoretical lenses, the resource-based view and the theory of complementarities.

As introduced before, the collection of IT resources and IT management practises of a firm on one hand, and the collection of business processes and managerial practices on the other can be regarded as resource bundles of the firm, according to the RBV (Barney 1991; Mata et al. 1995; Melville et al. 2004). As shown in this study, these bundles of resources are highly interrelated, while their relatedness is complementary. This means that by increasing commonality in IT resources and IT management practices (i.e. by increasing IT relatedness), the value provided by the existing degree of commonality in business processes and managerial practices (i.e. the value provided by the existing degree of business process relatedness), rises. This causal relationship is also valid vice versa.

In other words, this study shows that increasing IT relatedness provides value to the firm and increases in addition the value provided by the extant degree of business process relatedness. Vice versa, increasing business process relatedness provides value to the firm and increases in addition the value provided by the extant degree of IT relatedness. The complementarity of the relatedness of IT and business processes thus generates super-additive value synergies for the firm.

If a corporation is able to generate a competitive advantage with these complementarity-based super-additive value synergies, it is very probable that the advantage generated will be sustainable, according to the RBV. This is due to the fact that the values generated through the interaction effects between IT relatedness and business process relatedness are deeply rooted in the corporation's organisational and operational structures. Thus, an exact imitation of the whole interdependent value generating system is highly improbable.

Suggestion of ITG as underlying mechanisms which assures that IT as a resource is applied to its best use

While Melville et al. (2004) state that the RBV is missing the necessary underlying mechanism which assures that IT as a resource is applied to its best use (Rivard et al., 2006), this study eventually proposes that this mechanism is evidently provided with mature IT governance.

6.2 Managerial Implications

The findings of this study have direct implications for managers in practice, where IT governance is a highly significant topic and thus on the agenda of every IT executive. By showing what generally can be achieved with mature IT governance and what is to be considered within every ITG campaign, the outcomes of this study can serve as a general frame for planning and implementing IT governance in organisations. Today, the latter happens based on best practices and intuition, as no explanatory model of ITG value creation was available before.

Clarifying the integral parts of IT governance

First, this study offers insights to managers on what integral parts of IT governance are. In the course of past economic turmoil and legal pressures, ITG became a fashionable term. On one hand various so-called 'ITG frameworks' got published by a range of organisations, on the other hand numerous consulting companies presented own perceptions of IT governance in the hope to generate additional revenues on the ITG bandwagon. While some of this practice-oriented literature offered orientation to executives, much of it was insufficiently grounded on theoretical and empirical investigation and added to existing uncertainty on the integral parts of IT governance.

Building on previous academic literature and empirical research (De Haes and Van Grembergen 2009; Weill 2004) this study offers a clear statement on what IT governance is:

IT governance defines a framework for decision rights and accountabilities to encourage desirable behaviour in the use of IT. IT governance is a combination of ITG structures, ITG processes and ITG relational mechanisms.

- IT governance structures are formal structural devices and mechanisms for connecting and enabling horizontal contacts between business and IT decision makers. This involves the existence of responsible functions as well as IT committees.
- IT governance processes are the formalisation and institutionalisation of strategic IT decision making or IT monitoring procedures.
- IT governance relational mechanisms ensure the active participation of, and collaborative relationship among, corporate executives, IT management and business management. They include business/ IT participation and partnerships, strategic dialogue and shared learning.

Providing guidance for the implementation procedure of IT governance

Second, this study offers a clear guiding frame for planning and implementing IT governance initiatives by providing insights on the effects and value contributions that can be expected from actively designed IT governance. Empirical evidence of this study suggests that with rising maturity, three distinct focus areas are traversed subsequently in the course of an IT governance implementation.

In a first focus area, the IT organisation, the IT delivery processes and the IT infrastructure, that is hard- and software without business logic, are in the focus of IT governance initiatives. Empirical findings of this study suggest that these elements are to a large extent under the control of IT executives, which diminishes friction losses. Thus, initial successes in the course of ITG initiatives are achieved comparatively easy, namely:

- Consolidation of IT infrastructure, which leads to a reduction of different and often redundant technologies, altogether with related technical interfaces.

- Harmonisation of IT delivery processes, which leads to enhanced efficiency in the course of IT development projects.

Accomplishing these goals allows firms, in line with the developed explanatory model, to reap sub-additive cost synergies from their IT infrastructure and IT operations processes. The empirical insights from this study suggest that consolidation of the IT infrastructure landscape constitutes an essential basis for further development of IT governance.

In a second focus area of IT governance, applications, the service portfolio and demand processes move into the centre of attention. The empirical insights of this study show that a close collaboration of the IT and business departments has to evolve in order to successfully:

- Consolidate the application landscape and IT service portfolio, and, thus reduce software interfaces and redundant business functionalities.
- Harmonise the IT demand processes and establish clear linkages between the IT department and the businesses departments with unambiguous roles and responsibilities.

Consolidating the IT application and IT service portfolio leads to a reduction of complexity. On the basis of a consolidated IT infrastructure, these actions provide corporations with a high level of IT relatedness, thus, with both, sub-additive cost synergies as well as super-additive value synergies, according to the developed explanatory model. While operating costs go down, firms report to achieve more agility in the response to changed business requirements. Moreover, a harmonised application landscape enables companies to provide better services to their customers and business partners according to this study's findings.

In a third focus area IT governance is primarily concerned with the business process of the firm. The insights of this study suggest that firms with a highly mature ITG framework eventually establish mechanisms that deter business units from mapping existing or newly designed processes onto IT requirements without input from IT professionals. Instead, IT governance ensures that business processes are designed by interdisciplinary teams, consisting of IT professionals and representatives of business units that possess sophisticated process knowledge. Only that way a further enhancement of the IT-support is possible in these firms. In consequence, mature IT governance leads to:

- Harmonisation of related IT-supported business processes throughout the company. The empirical insights of this study suggest that such a procedure typically starts with non-core processes, such as HR, finance or back-office processes, mostly on the basis of a shared ERP solution. Alternative starting points were observed involving processes that encompass the transition of physical goods throughout the corporation, such as procurement or supply chain activities. In a second step, the focus moves to core business functions, often on a meta-level.
- Overcoming of the 'IT follows business'-paradigm in certain cases. Firms with highly mature ITG frameworks have mechanisms in place that ensure a professional and collaborative partnership between IT staff and business process owners. This way the firm can aim for optimal global solutions without being subject to specific organisational dogmas.

Corporations that are able to accomplish the above named transitions eventually dispose over high IT relatedness and high business process relatedness. Following the introduced explanatory model of this study, such corporations are able to reap super-additive value synergies that are deeply rooted in the firm's technological, organisational and cultural architecture.

While values provided in the aforementioned first focus areas of ITG are prone to imitation to a large extent, values provided in the third focus area of IT governance implementation are not only hard to copy, but even hard to observe by competitors. Thus they provide a basis for sustainable competitive advantages.

Summing up, this study provides implications to managers on what integral parts of IT governance are and how mature IT governance can enhance business performance and lead to sustainable competitive advantages.

6.3 Limitations and Future Research

This study balances the advantages of an in-depth analysis of a set of 21 cases with the disadvantages of the limitations imposed by the applied research method. Hence, the following limitations have to be considered when interpreting and drawing conclusions from its results. The chapter at hand offers a discussion on these limitations and provides suggestions on how future research could address them. What is more, this chapter discusses numerous opportunities for future research offered by the findings at hand.

The presented model originates from a limited set of data, namely an exploratory study with 11 companies and a second corroborative study with 10 corporations. The analysed data set offers a good representation of the largest firms in Germany and results from a careful case sampling procedure derived from extant literature. However, some peculiarities of IT governance in large enterprises may not be reflected in the analysed case samples.

Furthermore, despite a theory-guided qualitative examination of the analysed constructs and an independent assessment of their levels by two different individuals, a personal bias cannot be excluded entirely. The data collection method applied in this research was in line with this study's goals to increase the number of cases while relying on a limited number of expert interviews. However, Kumar et al. (1993) explicate that depending on a low number of knowledgeable informants on each case site may lead to a key informant bias. This is of particular importance for this study, since the findings suggest that IT governance has a significant impact on two distinct parties of a corporation, namely IT professionals and non-IT professionals. Though, the chosen key informants were in unison IT professionals since extant literature suggests that the highest ranking IT professionals are the employees most knowledgeable on the subject of IT governance.

Being based on a top level view and data of the analysed firms, this study took a macro perspective, which implies limitations regarding the investigated constructs. While the maturity of IT governance was seen as a combination of the maturities of its sub-constructs, namely structures, processes and relational mechanisms, the available data did not allow a detailed analysis of the interaction of these sub-constructs. In a similar vein and based on previous literature, the relatedness of IT and business processes was examined on a macro level. This implied a focus on the analysis of the use of common or shared resources across business units, without decomposing the constructs further. While this approach offered satisfying insights, a closer look on the details and the composition of the relatedness constructs would have been beneficial. Based on more detailed micro level data, including more emphasis on qualitative dimensions of the maturity of IT governance and a detailed decomposition of the constructs IT relatedness and business process relatedness, these limitations should be addressed in future investigations.

In order to increase validity and corroborate this study's findings, a reasonable next step would be a large-scale quantitative test of the developed explanatory model. When doing so, paired questionnaire surveys for IT executives and business executives should be used. In other words, building on this study's qualitative exploratory findings, future research may aim at confirming the suggested explanatory model of IT governance impact quantitatively.

Perceived business performance values, as suggested by previous literature, proved to be well suited for the pursued exploratory theory building endeavour. Assessing the observed relatedness effects based on a comparison of objective performance values of the 10, respectively 11 case companies was not suitable in this study. The analysed dataset is, especially with regard to the different industries in which the observed firms are active in, too small. However, a large-scale quantitative test of the suggested explanatory model may employ objective quantitative measures to complement perceived business performance values.

In addition, future studies may gather longitudinal data that comprises the implementation or redesign of IT governance initiatives in corporations. Doing so would offer an alternative way to corroborate the findings of the explanatory model and shed more light on the maturity concept of IT governance. Based on the available data, this study describes the maturity of the observed ITG frameworks in linear way, but it is conceivable that ITG maturity varies in both directions with the organisational lifecycle. In other words, ITG maturity and it impact on business performance may not only increase over time, but as well decrease under certain circumstances. In addition, longitudinal data would allow a refinement of the presented findings on the implementation procedure of IT governance. These are of immense value, especially for managers in practice.

Moreover, IT governance is concerned with both, generation and preservation of values. Both objectives may influence the business performance of a firm. This research project analyses the effects of the value generating aspect of IT governance only. Thus, future studies may focus on value preserving practices of IT governance, such as e.g. risk management, to complement this study's findings.

This study was furthermore limited to corporations from Germany, which enabled reducing complexity. However, previous research has shown that frameworks for accountabilities and decision rights, thus organisational hierarchies in general, are heavily dependent on cultural variables. Future research may focus on a further generalisation of the presented explanatory model with regard to the cultural dimension. Previous research did not provide evidence that company size is a significant contingency factor related to IT governance. However, a generalisation of this study's findings towards smaller and medium sized firms would be desirable, since this research is based on data from large firms only.

This study was aiming at developing a theoretical model that is able to explain the positive impact of IT governance on the business performance of a firm independently of the industry the specific corporation is active in. In order to achieve this goal, various valuable industry-specific findings that were collected in the course of conducted case studies were excluded from the explanatory model. Future research may therefore tailor down the developed model towards specific industries, which may increase its explanatory power.

7. Summary and Conclusion

The goal of this study was to develop a mid-range theory that is able to explain the positive impact of information technology governance on the business performance of a firm. To do so, two subsequent empirical studies were conducted which encompassed 11 and respectively 10 qualitative multiple-case studies of large German corporations active in various industries.

The first chapter of this study offers an introduction encompassing the problem statement, an overview of the research objective and design and eventually the organisation of the study.

The second chapter provides the study's theoretical foundations. Starting with the basic terminology, a detailed discussion on information technology and business performance is offered. Thereafter, previous research on the topic of IT governance is discussed. Building on the presented literature, a preliminary research framework is introduced that guided the subsequent empirical research.

Thereafter, Chapter 3 discusses the research design of this study. After the ontological and epistemological stance is presented, the research strategy and the choice of a qualitative multiple-case study approach are justified. The chapter closes after the case sampling procedure and the collection and analysis of data are explicated.

The fourth chapter presents the findings of the first, exploratory case study round that was conducted according to the deduced preliminary research framework. After introducing the proposed explanatory model, Chapter 4 is organised according to the revealed theoretical links between IT governance, resource relatedness and business performance. Chapter 5 offers the findings of the second, corroborative case study round and is structured into a single-case and a cross-case analysis.

Chapter 6 provides a detailed discussion of this study's findings. Starting with theoretical implications, contributions to previous work on IT governance and the applied theoretical lens, the resource-based view, are presented. Thereafter, implications for practice are given before limitations are discussed and future research based on this study's findings is suggested.

The goal of this research endeavour was to answer two research questions. First, this study posed the question of how IT governance and business performance are related. Building on previous literature from the IS discipline and adjacent fields, as well as two rounds of empirical research, this study was able to substantiate the assumed positive relationship between IT governance and business performance. The results of the two multiple-case studies offered evidence that IT governance is related with business performance via the mediating construct of resource relatedness. More specifically, the results suggest that IT governance maturity positively impacts the IT relatedness and business process relatedness of a firm. As shown in previous research and corroborated in this study's empirical findings, resource relatedness is a major source of synergies, which in turn have a positive impact on business performance.

The second research question assessed in this study was how the assumed positive impact of IT governance on business performance could be explained. Building on the resource-based view, this study showed that IT governance has a major impact on two of the firm's most basic and valuable resources: information technology and its business processes. Drawing on previous theoretical work on synergies, complementarities and relatedness, it was possible to demonstrate and explain how mature IT governance affects IT relatedness and business process relatedness in a way that in addition to singular values, interacting effects of complementarity arise. Based on these effects, firms are able to generate super-additive value synergies which are deeply rooted in the corporation's organisational, operational and cultural structures. Following the resource-based view, an exact imitation of such an interdependent value-generating system is highly improbable due to causal ambiguity. Even if competitors are able to observe and identify such integrated vale-generating systems, it might be impossible for them to reproduce those without negatively affecting their own value providing process. Thus, following the RBV, values generated by mature IT governance can be a basis for sustained competitive advantages, which in turn are a basis for an increase in business performance.

Appendix

1. Attributes Used to Assess the Case Studies (based on Dubé and Paré 2003)

Research design	
Nature of own study	Explanatory study based on a first, exploratory and a second, corroboratory stage. Strongly realist ontology combined with an analysis more typical of interpretivist approaches (see also Kirsch 2004; Madill et al. 2000; Mingers et al. 2011; Ravishankar et al. 2011).
Clear research questions	Yes.
A priori specification of constructs	Following Eisenhardt (1989b) preliminary conceptualisations of the basic constructs framing the research questions were derived from existing literature.
Clean theoretical slate	No, basic proposition was formulated a priori due to explanatory nature.
Theory of interest	Resource-based view, theory of complementarities.
Rival theories included	No.
Multiple-case design	Yes, two rounds of case studies with 11 and 10 case companies respectively.
Replication logic	Theoretical replication logic.
Unit of analysis	The unit of analysis is at the organisational level. Due to the fact that ITG, the central concept, was endemic to large organisations, the entire blue chip stock-market and all firms of comparable size in Germany were approached for the study.
Pilot case	Yes, two pilot cases were conducted for the refinement of the interview guideline.

Research design	
Team-based research	Yes.
Different roles of investigators	The author was supported by team-members in the course of the interviews and during the coding procedure in order to ensure intercoder reliability.

Context description	
Detailed site description	Yes.
Case period	The case material was collected in a period of 18 months with numerous onsite visits and follow-up phone calls.
Longitudinal design	No, not applicable.
Time spent onsite by the researchers	All interviews of the first round were conducted on-site due to the exploratory nature. The second, corroboratory round was more structured in comparison to the first, exploratory one. Thus, personal on-site visits were not regarded as obligatory and the interviewees were given the choice between a personal and a telephone interview, which led to a mixed approach.
Nature of data collection	Retrospective.

Elucidation of data collection process	
Multiple data collection methods	Yes. Both case study phases were based on expert interviews as primary sources of information and secondary, where access was provided, on document analyses. The exploratory phase encompassed additionally a round table with researchers and members of various case companies where potential weaknesses and omissions of the developed explanatory model were discussed.
Qualitative and quantitative data	Qualitative only.
Data triangulation	Yes, for different stakeholders and sources.
Case study protocol	Yes.
Case study database	Yes, using the software package NVIVO.

Data collection methods applied	
Interviews	Yes.
Documentation	Yes.
Observation	No.
Questionnaires	Yes, in the form of interview guidelines.
Artifacts	In some cases IT governance documentations or quality management guidelines were provided by the interviewees.
Time series	No.
Sampling strategy	The entire blue chip stock market and companies comparable in size were approached in Germany. A purposeful sampling process (see Chapter 3.4) ensured that both samples offered the required heterogeneity. Only German sites were chosen to ensure comparability and avoid a cultural bias.

Elucidation of data analysis process	
Field notes	Yes.
Coding	Yes.
Data displays	Yes.
Flexible and opportunistic process	Yes.
Logical chain of evidence	Yes.
Empirical testing	No.
Explanation building	Yes.
Time series analysis	No.
Searching for cross-case patterns	Yes.
Use of natural controls	No.
Quotes (evidence)	Yes.
Project reviews	No.
Comparison with extant literature	Yes.

2. Interview Guidelines

2.1 Exploratory Phase

- Information regarding the interview partner and the case company
  - Interviewees position, educational background and career?
  - Organisations' main business area, structure, employees, revenues?
- IT in the organisation
  - Relevance of information technology for the corporation?
  - Size, structure and role of IT organisation? Allocation and distribution of tasks? Performance and reputation of IT organisation?
- IT strategy
  - Specific IT strategy in place? How often adapted in the past?
  - Responsibility for contents, goals and attainment of IT strategy?
- Corporate governance
  - Interviewee's and firm's understanding of corporate governance?
  - Relation between corporate governance and IT governance?
- IT governance
  - Interviewee's and firm's understanding of IT governance? ITG on the agenda? Since when? What were the drivers? Which barriers were observed during ITG rollout?
  - Who is responsible for ITG? Who has which IT decision and IT input rights?
  - Which ITG mechanisms are in place (structures, processes, relational mechanisms)?
  - Positive impacts of ITG? On IT? On strategic IT goals? On strategic corporate goals? On IT processes? On business processes?
  - Negative impacts of ITG?
  - Relation between ITG and risk management? Relation between ITG and compliance?

2.2 Corroborative Phase

- Information regarding the interview partner and the case company
  - Interviewees position, educational background and career?
  - Organisations' main business area, structure, employees, revenues?
- IT in the organisation
  - Relevance of information technology for the corporation?
  - Size, structure and role of IT organisation? Allocation and distribution of tasks? Performance and reputation of IT organisation?
  - Context-specific knowledge of the IT department?
  - Absorptive capacity of the IT department?
- ITG maturity
  - Which ITG structures are in place? Operating efficiently and effectively?
  - Which ITG processes are in place? Operating efficiently and effectively?
  - Which ITG relational mechanisms are in place? Operating efficiently and effectively?
  - Is ITG in a mature stage?
- IT relatedness
  - Degree of harmonisation of the IT and communication infrastructure? Shared IT demand and supply processes?
  - Degree of the relatedness of application landscape?
  - Shared IT management practices?
- Business process relatedness
  - Shared business processes?
  - Shared managerial practices?
- Business performance
  - Changes in profits or return on investments?
  - Changes in revenues or market shares?
  - Changes in quality or reputation?
  - New technological developments and/ or innovations in business operations?
  - Changed time to market?
  - For each of the above questions: If yes, related to IT/ a specific business process/ combination of business processes?

3. Coding Scheme for the Corroborative Phase (based on Guillemette and Paré 2012)

ITG Maturity

Construct	Values	Coding scheme
ITG Structures	High	Three or more committees classified as ITG Structures (see Table 8) in place and operational.
	Medium	Two committees classified as ITG Structures (see Table 8) in place and operational.
	Low	Less than two committees classified as ITG Structures (see Table 8) in place and operational.
ITG Processes	High	Six or more processes classified as ITG Processes (see Table 8) in place and operational.
	Medium	Four or five processes classified as ITG Processes (see Table 8) in place and operational.
	Low	Less than four processes classified as ITG Processes (see Table 8) in place and operational.
ITG Relational Mechanisms	High	Four or more mechanisms classified as ITG Relational Mechanisms (see Table 8) in place and operational.
	Medium	Three mechanisms classified as ITG Relational Mechanisms (see Table 8) in place and operational.
	Low	Less than three mechanisms classified as ITG Relational Mechanisms (see Table 8) in place and operational.
ITG Maturity	High	Average rating of ITG Structures, Processes and Relational Mechanisms is High, and interviewee perceives the overall ITG as highly mature.
	Medium	Average rating of ITG Structures, Processes and Relational Mechanisms is at least Medium and interviewee perceives the overall ITG Maturity at least as medium.
	Low	Average rating of ITG Structures, Processes and Relational Mechanisms is low or interviewee perceives the overall ITG Maturity as low.

Degree of Resource Relatedness		
Construct	Values	Coding scheme
IT Relatedness	High	The hard- and software stack of the corporation is highly streamlined and shared by the entire firm. Niche solutions are found only in exceptional cases. IT management and IT service processes are very well developed and documented and, whenever applicable, used similarly across the entire firm.
	Medium	The basic infrastructure and a confined part of the software stack are shared by different business units of the corporation. However, business units quite commonly run niche solutions or parallel solutions for similar problems, even on a parallel infrastructure. Some IT management and service process best practices are shared; however, this is not the rule.
	Low	The sharing of common or similar hard- or software across the firm is uncommon. IT management and IT service processes are mostly run differently for each business unit.
Business Process Relatedness	High	Back office and customer support processes are highly streamlined and shared across the entire firm. The same applies to processes which involve the handling of physical goods, like procurement or logistics. Wherever high process specificity is prevailing (e.g. in production), at least sharing of meta processes is pursued.
	Medium	Some business processes like e.g. payroll, HR, finance or procurement are shared across the firm. However, more common is a decentral business process design, especially where high process specificity is found.
	Low	Similar or related business process across the firm are uncommon and hardly found.

Effects of Absorptive Capacity		
Construct	Values	Coding scheme
Absorptive Capacity of the IT Department	High	The IT department has a high potential to gain and utilise knowledge situated in most of the business units and showed this ability in past and current projects. This mostly involves a large portion of context-specific knowledge related to running business processes, upcoming industry challenges and the ability to talk to business units at eye level about process design. IT staff pushes product or process innovations.
	Medium	The IT department is able to gain and utilise knowledge situated in some of the business units, but is dependent on active and repeated input from others. While the IT department is able to talk on eye-level with some units about current and upcoming industry challenges, it is not able to challenge the requirements of other departments, due to confined context-specific knowledge and ability to gain and utilise that knowledge. Process or product innovations coming from the IT department are rare.
	Low	The IT department has problems to gain and utilise knowledge from business departments. Thus it is dependent on active and repeated input from business departments when designing technical solutions for ongoing and upcoming business challenges. Process or product innovations coming from the IT are not observed.

Contribution to the Business Performance		
Construct	Values	Coding scheme
Business Performance Impact	High	Several of the eight dimensions defining business performance (see Table 8) are (directly or indirectly) positively penetrated by past and current projects that can be related to IT or IT-supported business process (for details see Chapter 2.2.5).
	Medium	Confined penetration (mainly based on cost-savings) of the eight dimensions defining business performance (see Table 8) by past and current projects that can be related to IT or IT-supported business processes (for details see Chapter 2.2.5).
	Low	The eight dimensions defining business performance (see Table 8) are hardly (directly or indirectly) penetrated by past and current projects that can be related to IT or IT-supported business process (for details see Chapter 2.2.5).

4. Assessment of Constructs for the Corroborative Phase

4.1 OMEGA

Construct	Rating	Evidence
ITG Structures	Medium	IT steering and IT project steering committee are in place and reported to be operating well for new projects. However, they are only applied to recently started projects.
ITG Processes	High	ITG processes are reported to be developed quite well. Charge back arrangements, portfolio management, some ITIL processes, detailed IT project governance, IT budget control, a balanced IT scorecard and a clear IT reporting structure were reported to be in place.
ITG Relational Mechanisms	Low	Relational mechanisms and knowledge transfer were reported to be weak. Only a request management portal and first attempts to instantiate a structured communication between IT and business were reported in the interviews.
ITG Maturity	Medium	- *"We started two years ago with active IT governance.", "IT governance is yet only on the strategic level. [...] Once we reach IT services, more people will be penetrated by IT governance.", "Right now we are working on the extension of the ITG impact towards enhancement projects.", "Eventually ITG shall encompass the definition of SLAs and the IT service landscape.";* - The interviewee reported that the first steps are done, but that the installed ITG mechanisms are penetrating a smaller portion of the entire IT budget.

Construct	Rating	Evidence
IT Relatedness	Medium	- *"We run a unified client in the third version.", "The infrastructure is consolidated worldwide.", "We are establishing unified ITIL processes [...]", "Service orientation is the keyword here, we are developing a service catalogue containing SLAs [...]. The services will be offered for the whole corporation", "The IT services offered to the main departments A, B and C are the same.";* - IT infrastructure and desktop-clients are globally consolidated; IT processes are in many areas streamlined on an ITIL basis. However, many applications cannot be rolled out consistently or get adapted locally.
Business Process Relatedness	Medium	- *"Some business processes get rolled out globally [...] using a process template, but the singular country organisations adapt the processes.", "The singular country organisations historically have much power", "The IT would of course want to roll out business processes completely consistently, but the singular country organisations want their specifications adopted.";* - It was reported to be hard to align process across different departments or subsidiaries. The interviewee reported that the idea of harmonising HR processes is *"inexecutable"*. However, some business processes were consolidated out of the IT/ ITG, such as on-site support processes that are supported by a mobile device or certain back-office processes relying on specific database templates.

Construct	Rating	Evidence
Absorptive Capacity of IT Department	Medium	- *"The IT does not develop the processes, they built up process knowledge and then optimise the processes.", "The IT people know the processes best in some areas.", "Process optimisation comes [...sometimes...] from IT's own initiative, aiming at stabilisation of the process.";* - Good context-specific knowledge in some processes and even process innovations from the IT department were reported. The IT staff was able to build up enough business process understanding *"on the fly"* to give instructive feedback and support in daily optimisation routines, but that was not enough to generate innovation in the IT. Therefore, various initiatives were started to enhance business process understanding and absorptive capacity of IT.
Business Performance Impact	Medium	- *"The IT infrastructure is on a very good level now.", "In 2000 a team in COUNTRY developed the idea of mobile device supporting the service technician at the customer place. [...] This solution is associated with numerous benefits [...].", "A big success was the introduction of a new portfolio management process [...].", "We introduced a system that triggers knowledge transfer [...].", "Without ITG, we could not secure that the IT budget is spent for the right projects.";* - Sub-additive costs were reported to be the primary performance impacts of past projects. The required integration of IT systems and business process is missing to reap more synergies. However, a few exceptions were provided by the interviewee, such as the introduction of a mobile device that in combination with a harmonised CRM system and streamlined on-site support process generates super-additive value synergies. Moreover, knowledge transfer was improved.

4.2 PSI

Construct	Rating	Evidence
ITG Structures	Low	Only a steering committee for IT projects is operational yet.
ITG Processes	Low	No ITG processes beyond simple charge-back mechanisms are implemented.
ITG Relational Mechanisms	Low	There are no ITG relational mechanisms in place besides informal meetings between the CIO and the CFO.
ITG Maturity	Low	- *"ITG came along with our new CIO. [...] The company is coming from an extreme decentral structure, not comparable with a large organisation.", "It is important to note that we just introduced [documented] IT processes a year ago, that is why we are with almost all topics at the very beginning.";* - Most ITG mechanisms are under development. The interviewee stated that ITG as a holistic frame is *"miles behind maturity"*.
IT Relatedness	Medium	- *"5 years ago we started an IT infrastructure harmonisation project, 4 years ago an SAP harmonisation project", "Infrastructure is harmonised, SAP will be harmonised in two years.", "Some applications are harmonised [...]";* - A large harmonisation initiative is ongoing. Infrastructure, desktop solutions and some applications are harmonised already. ERP will be under development for at least two more years before being rolled out. System-critical applications are not considered yet.

Construct	Rating	Evidence
Business Process Relatedness	Low	- *"There is an ongoing and heated discussion if we should coordinate sourcing globally, right now we only coordinate small procurement processes globally, like the procurement of USB sticks.", "It is not part of our culture, the corporation has no internal revision and no corporate governance either.", "We are coming from a landscape with more than 20 different ERP systems, including support and external assistance.";* - Business processes including IT implementation and support were being designed locally and decentrally for decades. The interviewee expects positive change in the course of the future roll out of a harmonised ERP.
Absorptive Capacity of IT Department	High	- *"The business process knowledge of the IT is very high, acquiring it is part of the strategy.", "Our knowledge of processes allows us to talk on eye-level with business. That is important to be able to decide what is necessary and what is not.", "We don't regard ourselves as provider of hard- and software, but as process enablers and optimisers.", "Our employees are mostly the IT process champions on the respective sites.";* - Absorptive capacity of the IT department has evolved over the years due to the collaborative working practices of the business departments. IT had to acquire process knowledge constantly.

Construct	Rating	Evidence
Business Performance Impact	Low	- *"We stopped supporting everything [end-user solutions]. Now hardware gets exchanged when it gets to a certain age. The standardisation strategy brought along positive effects of an up-to date infrastructure."*, *"For the first time we have one process that is used by all business units in Europe, namely a unified failure reporting portal." "It is important to note that we just introduced [documented] IT processes a year ago, that is why we are with almost all topics at the very beginning."*; - The future consolidation of the currently running 23 ERP systems towards one is expected to bring various synergies, but at this time the interviewee is not able to report any performance impacts in numbers due to missing measurements in the past. Yet sub-additive costs are expected to result from increased IT relatedness.

4.3 CHI

Construct	Rating	Evidence
ITG Structures	High	An IT strategy committee, an IT steering committee as well as a project steering committee were reported to be in place and working very efficiently.
ITG Processes	High	Almost all ITG processes recommended in literature can be found at CHI: Charge back arrangements, SLAs, performance measurement, ITIL, project governance, IT budget control and a deliberate IT reporting structure. ITG structures are regarded as a reference model for other business processes.
ITG Relational Mechanisms	High	The interviewee reported that the well developed ITG relational mechanisms are the basis of the success story at CHI. Informal meetings, dedicated account managers, job rotations and knowledge sharing mechanisms ensure a collaborative partnership between business and IT.
ITG Maturity	High	- *"Many staff realised that our organisation is the only truly global one in the firm.", "Other areas which are in front of large globalisation efforts, like R&D, parts of controlling or HR ask IT for information and support for designing their own mechanisms.", "After starting their own campaigns, they realise how far the IT with its global [governance] mechanisms is and regard us then as a positive example.";* - CHI disposes over a very well developed ITG framework based on a variety of effective mechanisms that are acknowledged and valued by the IT department and business divisions.

Construct	Rating	Evidence
IT Relatedness	High	- *"Infrastructure is completely consolidated with one global data centre in GERMANTOWN and two local data centres.", "The network is completely consolidated with a partner.", "85% of all IT processes are harmonised.", "Desktops are standardised.",* - Infrastructure consolidation was successfully accomplished several years ago. A central data centre, harmonised desktop solutions and a unified ERP solution are operational.
Business Process Relatedness	Medium	- *"Process harmonisation goes on with the harmonised ERP", "PLM is almost completely harmonised.", "We are coming from a decentral past.", "Some local managing directors lead their departments with distance to the headquarters, we have problems accomplishing harmonisation efforts there.";* - Business processes that are closely relying on the implemented ERP solution, such as logistics or procurement, are harmonised to a large extent and used as a reference model for HR, controlling and R&D processes. The fact that IT is involved in the design of business processes supports the increase in business process relatedness. However, based on the decentralised past, there is *"still quite a way to go"*, according to the interviewee.

Construct	Rating	Evidence
Absorptive Capacity of IT Department	Medium	- *"Process knowledge of IT staff is very good, as it is our vision to understand processes", "We do not have a dedicated process-unit, so eventually it is IT staff that has to deal with it.", "However, we have a lot of specialists on detailed topics, but we lack people with a broad understanding.";* - The interviewee stated that particular IT members have a high portion of context-specific knowledge regarding specific business departments and that this staff is able to quickly familiarise themselves with new tasks in these particular departments. However, the IT department misses staff with broad context knowledge across different business departments.
Business Performance Impact	High	- *"We realised huge synergies through global licensing, pooled procurement [...]. Achieving this synergies would have never been possible if the local departments.", "In the past, without ITG, we would not have been able to run harmonised business and logistic processes on a unified ERP, our strategy would have been decrepit.", "The value delivered [...] is the provision of a platform enabling the firm to operate on a global level with regard to business processes like e.g. logistics or procurement. [...] ITG is the basis for process harmonisation and the realisation of global synergies.";* - Beyond cost savings, high resource relatedness enabled the development of an integrated application and process landscape that provided new possibilities to the firm. The observed performance impacts of IT relatedness and business process relatedness thus go far beyond operational efficiencies and are seen on a strategic level by the firm.

4.4 PHI

Construct	Rating	Evidence
ITG Structures	Low	Only an IT project steering committee was reported to be in place.
ITG Processes	High	A large number of ITG mechanisms were reported to be operating efficiently: charge back arrangements, portfolio management, performance measurement, ISO frameworks, IT project governance, effective IT budget controls and deliberately developed reporting structures.
ITG Relational Mechanisms	High	The CIO reported that the relational mechanisms are very effective and represented by informal meetings, job rotations and an extremely well developed internal communication between the IT and the business side.
ITG Maturity	Medium	- *"ITG got enacted 2,5 years ago."*, *"[The impulse for ITG was given by] disruptions in the collaboration with business units. Let's call it sub-optimal projects ending in arguments. Based on these problems we used the opportunity to enact an actively designed and documented ITG"*, *"We are able to see improvements."*, *"The ITG in its current state does not deviate from an ideal state in my eyes."*; - ITG processes and ITG relational mechanisms were reported to be extraordinary well developed at PHI but the development of ITG structures is rather at the beginning.

Construct	Rating	Evidence
IT Relatedness	High	- *"IT infrastructure and IT processes are harmonised.", "We implement many virtualisation solutions.", "Diverse consolidation projects in the area of applications and IT services were implemented", "We rolled our SAP solutions, despite resistance from many sides, towards the last corner, even to a three man subsidiary in South-East Asia.", "We run a coordinated and controlled sourcing.";* - PHI has a highly streamlined IT infrastructure and application landscape on the basis of an integrated SAP solution that was eventually rolled out into every subsidiary.
Business Process Relatedness	Medium	- *"The implementation of cross-divisional processes is a permanent issue in the search for synergies. For that purpose, we must not only implement optimal IT processes, but also define the necessary organisational structures and processes.", "The corporation comes from a decentral culture, where sensible, we harmonise functions and processes"; "We have the goal to harmonise processes further.";* - Many business processes were streamlined in the course of the conducted SAP rollout. New processes are developed only once in one pilot region, before being rolled out globally. Nevertheless, PHI sees more potential to continue this process.

Construct	Rating	Evidence
Absorptive Capacity of IT Department	High	- *"[Customers] are missing the overview of [our products ...] we suddenly realise that we do have this data [...] IT became product. [...] The IT department is able to generate direct revenues for the firm [with inventions in the core business]", "It is our vision to understand every day more there [the area of business processes], and become better.";* - The CIO rates the context-specific knowledge of the IT department as well as the ability to accumulate it as high. According to him, various business process enhancements in the course of the harmonisation were coming directly out of the IT, along with direct inventions leading to new products and revenues in the core business.

Construct	Rating	Evidence
Business Performance Impact	High	- *"Synergies in Assembly and Logistics are great examples. We defined the processes together, looked for best practices, mapped those to our unified SAP and roll it out right now, worldwide.", "[With harmonised IT and harmonised business processes] it is all about connecting two inventions, like with trolleys. Someone invented the wheel a long time ago, someone else invented a suitcase. But it took a very long time to put a wheel on a suitcase and invent a trolley. Its similar here [with IT and business processes]. Car builders use our products a lot, but they are missing the overview of where they have them. [...] A massive problem for support and service [...]. Then we suddenly realise that we do have this data [... after] connecting different data warehouses. So we invented a product together with our support for condition monitoring systems [...]. It gives huge benefits to our customers, and to ourselves. IT generated a competitive advantage";* - The reported performance impacts of relatedness at PHI encompass sub-additive costs as well as super-additive values. Harmonisation of IT in a first step reduced costs and allowed, in a second step, an integration of the application landscape which offered for the first time a unified picture on PHI's own production, customers and service processes. This in turn led to numerous super-additive value synergies. Subsequently, a harmonisation of business process was conducted which was strongly valued by the staff. Eventually, interacting effects of IT relatedness and business process relatedness generated completely new service products in the area of customer support. These provided on-top revenues and a unique market position to the firm.

4.5 YPSILON

Construct	Rating	Evidence
ITG Structures	Low	An IT steering committee and an IT project steering committee are place. However, the necessary authority over IT staff, which is essential for an effective functioning of these committees, is missing.
ITG Processes	Medium	Despite not being regarded in relation to ITG at YPSILON, a few mechanisms are in place that can be classified as ITG processes according to literature, such as IT portfolio management, IT performance measurement, IT project governance and IT budget control.
ITG Relational Mechanisms	Low	The division CIO at YPSILON stated that the internal communication between the IT department and business units is friendly and based on a partnership, but officially enacted relational mechanisms, as discussed in ITG literature, are missing.

Construct	Rating	Evidence
ITG Maturity	Low	- *"We do have a strategy, but coming from the top, and so general, that you can't do anything with it. [...] Great slides, but what is the relation to what the people [IT staff] do out there? [...] There is none.";* - There is basically no vision within the IT, it is more about keeping the daily business running. Since ITG was never a topic at YPSILON, a consciously developed ITG framework does not exist. The few previously described mechanisms do not represent a coherent ITG system, but rather a loose collection of managerial instruments. IT decision rights and accountabilities are in many cases not clearly defined and often the interviewee described a gap between formal guidelines and reality.
IT Relatedness	Low	- *"Eventually, we need to get the business processes harmonised, if that does not happen, we cannot harmonise the supporting IT.", "We have 3 SAP systems [doing the same thing] and wanted to harmonise them, but the business was not positive [...] we would save 2/3 of costs in future, but it is not saved money, it is avoided costs, and they don't want to accept that for the business case.";* - Infrastructure is harmonised to a certain level on the basis of a sourcing solution. However, the application landscape is relatively disparate, not only across locations but as well within the headquarters. Many departments, even in the headquarters, work autonomously with own IT staff on proprietary solutions, even though the central IT department should be in charge of all IT staff.

Construct	Rating	Evidence
Business Process Relatedness	Low	- *"They [production staff] optimised their processes locally over years, here and in COUNTRY2,", "So I try to harmonise the operation control process for PROUCT1, like done here [...]. But in South America we produce PRODUCT1 and PRODUCT2 in the same plant, we can't disconnect them [...]. In Asia the operation control process is further linked to PRODUCT 3, that would be additional 30 million.", "Harmonisation looks easy on slides but it is very hard to be implemented due to our production landscape";* - The interviewee did not provide any examples of business process relatedness across YPSILON's departments. He stated that the IT department supports the idea of shared business processes, but that the complex organisational setting does not offer opportunities for the increase of business process relatedness.
Absorptive Capacity of IT Department	Medium	- *"We had for example three business managers which were very confident that their process is the best. [...] As a pure IT worker you would have no chance, you would not even understand the technical terms [...]. In such cases we staff our people who really understand the processes [...] you have to compare the process bit by bit to find a compromise and solution with them.", "In some cases, the best solution is asking the business.";* - Some challenges where context-specific knowledge is crucial can be met with internal resources or the aggregation of process knowledge. However, the division CIO described situations where the IT is highly dependent on input from business departments.

Construct	Rating	Evidence
Business Performance Impact	Low	- *"We have a lot of variances in our products, but not all products get produced in all sites. The differences [in IT and business processes] rose over time due to different requirements and missing HR capacities [...]. It basically due to the people who are responsible for the processes and pursue some kind of self-fulfilment. The production site in GERMANTOWN2 is broken down into different centres, and every centre has an own director. One of them runs his own, highly specific solution that burns money. [...] There is no objective explanation for that kind of specific solutions.", "It is not so easy with the one best solution. Here we run a highly specific maintenance system. In the course of an SAP rollout we wanted to replace it, because SAP can do that too, but there is now a discussion if and how to get the data from the old system into the SAP. It is hard to find out what the [proprietary] systems delivers in practice.";* - The interviewee reported hardly any business performance impacts of past or ongoing IT projects or business projects that are related to IT. Rather examples were given, for how IT got dismembered, how hard it is to reintegrate it due to technical and cultural reasons. Eventually, various examples were given for how information technology burns cash.

4.6 TAU

Construct	Rating	Evidence
ITG Structures	High	ITG structures are traditionally well developed due to regulatory requirements. The ITG board is supported by several layers of working groups. IT project steering, IT strategy and IT planning committees are in place and reported to be operating efficiently. An IT architecture committee is in place as well, but offers place for improvement.
ITG Processes	Medium	Exceptionally well developed SLAs, charge back arrangements and project prioritisation. Though, effective performance measurement and IT reporting structures are missing. Frameworks like COBIT, ITIL or ISO are seen as too formal according to the interviewee, but some processes are designed according to COBIT recommendations
ITG Relational Mechanisms	Medium	Numerous informal meetings and a generally good internal communication and partnership between business and IT are in place. The interviewee stated that even departments and subsidies that are not bound to the decisions of the central IT mostly follow recommendations in relation to infrastructure and applications. However, weaknesses were reported in relation to the design and optimisation of business processes, since BUs involve the IT in many cases very late.

Construct	Rating	Evidence
ITG Maturity	Medium	- *"We have a clearly documented and agreed on IT governance.", "There is an ongoing and active discussion with our business lines [...] there is consensus which decisions have to be negotiated centrally, decentrally [...].", "We are aiming at enhancing the maturity, it is higher with strategy and planning committees than with the architecture committees.", "There are discrepancies between what is formally decided, and what is really lived.", "Altogether, there are extensive deviations from our ideal conception.";* - While ITG structures are very well developed, ITG processes and ITG relational mechanisms offer space for improvement. Moreover, the corporate structure of TAU is under revision, which often leaves authorities and decision rights relatively uncertain. In consequence, decisions are often made in contradiction to governance guidelines.

Construct	Rating	Evidence
IT Relatedness	Medium	- *"Formerly, many units had their own infrastructure [...] EUCOUNTRY is now as well integrated IT process wise, infrastructure follows.", "Some local business are not integrated yet.", "We have some central applications like consolidation, HR, reporting, intranet and so on, as well as ERP that is used by multiple users [5-digit].", "We have over 1,000 distinct applications running [...] here is huge potential for synergies, but it is hard to reap those due to the decentral structure.";* - Infrastructure is harmonised in large subsidiaries, but not yet in the smaller ones and neither in recently acquired corporations. Harmonisation of infrastructure was reported to be going on. A central SAP system is used for HR, reporting and similar back-office solutions, but besides these systems, over 1,000 distinct applications are running and offer enormous potential for further harmonisation and synergies.
Business Process Relatedness	Low	- *"We would like to integrate the process landscape far more, but there are regulatory obstacles", "We do not roll out processes across the entire corporation.", "The requirements for the processes are too diverse.", "Some processes with relation to the holding get rolled out across the firm.";* - Besides some exceptions, comparable business processes are not rolled out across different departments and subsidiaries at TAU.

Construct	Rating	Evidence
Absorptive Capacity of IT Department	High	- *"The [IT] colleagues were basically running the processes [for the business] over years. [...] Due to rationalisation, people in the business departments with comparable knowledge are gone [...] so you find the process knowledge in the IT.";* - According to the interviewee, IT staff is very familiar with the running business process at TAU and able to provide essential support in the course of process redesign and optimisation to the process owners.
Business Performance Impact	Medium	- *"We can show clear value added in the area of investment planning [...] this is only possible if you are able to force all stakeholders into a certain pattern.", "It is generally hard to show value added [of IT or IT-related projects], but does controlling or HR demonstrate their value added?", "IT hardly takes part in business process optimisation.", "In their output [IT-] projects lead to improved business processes. Example: introduction of a large [harmonised] BACKOFFICE system in EUCOUNTRY. [...] However, IT got involved in this project too late, it would be a great step forwards to involve IT earlier. [...] But sometimes this works, in EUCOUNTRY2 with PROJECTy we got involved earlier.";* - While the harmonisation of IT brought sub-additive costs, TAU reported as well super-additive values in the course of relatedness projects. Among those were unified back office systems in the EUCOUNTRY which enhanced running processes or smart-meter systems that in connection to a harmonised backend offered new business fields. However, such cases represent rather an exception as a corporate-wide integration of IT and business processes is absent.

4.7 SIGMA

Construct	Rating	Evidence
ITG Structures	High	An IT steering committee, a central reporting system and an IT architecture board are installed on a central position. These structures are supported by decentral project steering committees.
ITG Processes	High	Charge back arrangements and numerous SLAs are governed centrally. Project portfolios, budget planning and IT reporting are organised decentrally. ITIL and parts of CMM are rolled out. ISO 9001, ISO 20000 and ISO 27001 are being prepared for certification.
ITG Relational Mechanisms	High	Formal and informal meetings between IT and business managers are scheduled regularly. Key account managers are in place and reported to be well respected. The interviewee stated that in the course of projects a physical allocation of IT staff in business departments proved to be a good basis for the development of a good and constructive relationship.
ITG Maturity	High	- *"We consciously chose a relatively soft ITG in order to be in line with [business strategy].", "Due to changing objectives of the business with rising costs [...], ITG may be adapted.", "We are in a process of reconsidering ITG and I think we may need a more central ITG. The business environment changed due to strong cost pressures.";* - Despite a decentralised ITG structure, SIGMA disposes over a mature IT governance framework involving centrally and decentrally allocated mechanisms that form a homogeneous system. The ITG system was very consciously and purposefully designed to meet the business objectives.

Construct	Rating	Evidence
IT Relatedness	High	- *"Whatever is possible to be done with SAP, we try to do with SAP. The benefit is a high degree of standardisation.", "The[infrastructure of the] five central business units are completely consolidated and running on one data centre.", "Some small firms are not consolidated yet, due to [political reasons].", "IT services are offered for the whole corporation [in the same way].";* - The relatedness of infrastructure and applications is, despite a decentral mode of ITG, high. Data centres are consolidated and applications are provided on the basis of an SAP solution for the utilities industry. A few small and regional subsidiaries are not integrated yet for political reasons, but those represent an exception and a very small fraction of the employee count.
Business Process Relatedness	Low	- *"In many areas, the business units act independently, meaning that in those areas, the business processes are not harmonised. Example: HR. If you ask me, there is not one reason not to harmonise anything what has to do with recruiting, mentoring and development, as those processes are built upon the same logic. Reality is different. Every business unit runs its own HR processes. IT has to do with history. Our competitors have similar problems."* - Despite a shared IT platform, business processes are kept dissimilar among departments and subsidiaries. This is even true for cases in which the logic behind the processes is completely matching, like e.g. for HR processes. However, first pilot projects towards harmonised processes are made, e.g. with employee self services.

Construct	Rating	Evidence
Absorptive Capacity of IT Department	High	- *"The IT staff is sitting often at the customers site. Due to the daily and recurring work with the customers they developed a deep understanding of the business logic. If they let us.", "Some business areas even authorised IT for developing a strategy. However, for others we do only the infrastructure.";* - The absorptive capacity of the IT was described as high in the interview and reasoned primarily with the regular allocation of IT staff in the business departments. However, the head of IT stated that the extent to which the absorbed knowledge can be applied to improve processes is dependent on goodwill of the respective departments. While e.g. the sales unit appreciates ideas from the IT, other departments do not.

Construct	Rating	Evidence
Business Performance Impact	Medium	- *"We see [positive] impacts [of IT], but we still miss the governance that would allow us pursuing our strategic goal of radical cost savings. That is why we are renegotiating ITG at the moment.", "It is hard to measure the impact really. You start with automating a business process, then you keep going and automate it further, and then it is hard to compare the state with the initial situation. However, we aim at improving process efficiencies 2-3% every year.", "The problem is, whenever we want to run an IT harmonisation, we realise that IT is not the problem, but that the supported business process needs to be harmonised. The problem of too high IT costs is seen and the question is posed, why every unit needs its own IT systems and own know-how; then they realise eventually, that it is due to the business processes.", "SUBSIDIARY was exactly such an example. As a consequence, they changed their business processes in the area of accounting, migrated to our harmonised platform and saved a lot of money.";* - The reported performance effects of IT and IT-related projects are primarily sub-additive costs at SIGMA. The heavily disparate business process landscape hinders the firm from reaping synergies in many cases, according to the interviewee. However, some first steps are made towards super-additive synergies with pilot projects like e.g. the employee self services or a recently installed accounting system.

4.8 RHO

Construct	Rating	Evidence
ITG Structures	Low	ITG structures were virtually inexistent and are being redesigned from scratch at the moment.
ITG Processes	Low	Comparable to ITG structures, ITG processes were never consciously enacted at RHO.
ITG Relational Mechanisms	Low	According to the interviewee, various relational mechanisms are currently being enacted, but none of them is running effectively yet.
ITG Maturity	Low	- *"What is known as ITG in other firms was nonexistent at RHO three months ago.", "I got hired due to a lack of leadership and best practices", "My employees asked me after I started here how long I would stay. I had various predecessors in two years, there was no continuity in leadership and guidelines", "We are building ITG from scratch.";* - The interviewee was hired by RHO due to a dismembered IT landscape and a lack of leadership resulting in inefficiencies and various operational difficulties. The whole process of ITG setup is at the very beginning.
IT Relatedness	Low	- *"Basically every store runs its own IT.", "The central IT department was somehow putting the systems together in the back end.", "There was a culture of absolute decentral governance, or let's say no governance at all.";* - The interviewee reported an extreme complexity and disparity of the IT landscape. Every subsidiary runs its own IT, while the central IT department tries to link the systems together.

Construct	Rating	Evidence
Business Process Relatedness	Low	- *"The business processes evolved decentrally over the last 15 years.", "Every department, branch and subsidiary has its own processes.", "There were no incentives given for shared business processes in the past.";* - The company was governed very decentrally and there were no incentives given for shared processes, in a consequence an absolutely dismembered process landscape evolved.
Absorptive Capacity of IT Department	Low	- *"In the course of the ongoing ITG redesign large fractions of the IT staff are spending time at business departments in order to get to know the firm's business processes.", "The goal is to increase the business understanding of the IT department.", "They even have to spend a week near to a checkout counter.";* - Due to the decentralised past, the central IT staff at RHO has no context-specific knowledge and no ability to aggregate such knowledge for upcoming challenges. After realising that fact, the head of IT decided to send the IT staff for two weeks each to RHO's branches and stores in order to provide a basis for an increase in absorptive capacity.
Business Performance Impact	Low	- *"In the past and in the moment it is all about keeping the company running.", "We expect massive cost savings and process improvements after the first harmonisation projects are done";* - The impact of IT and IT related projects is not more than keeping the status quo. The harmonisation of IT is expected to bring massive cost savings in a first step, before super-additive value synergies can be expected as a consequence of a joint redesign of applications and business processes.

4.9 PI

Construct	Rating	Evidence
ITG Structures	High	Due to regulatory requirements, PI disposes over a variety of well developed ITG processes, such as an IT strategy committee, an IT architecture committee or an IT project steering committee.
ITG Processes	Medium	A few well developed ITG processes are in place: charge back arrangements, an efficient project governance and effective IT budget controlling. However, the interviewee reported weaknesses like missing SLAs, unsatisfying TCO calculations or an absent IT performance measurement.
ITG Relational Mechanisms	High	ITG relational mechanisms are according to the interviewee very well developed at PI. Informal meetings, an effective internal communication and a project management office which ensures collaboration between IT and non-IT staff provide the basis for the necessary interaction between the IT and business departments. The interviewee explicated that the relationship between IT and the business side is remarkably cooperative.
ITG Maturity	High	- *"The pressure from industry standards [regulation] gave the first impulses [for ITG introduction].", "After achieving the mandatory maturity related to regulatory demands, we were able to focus on ITG.", "The way ITG is documented and lived is in full correspondence to our objectives. Nevertheless, ITG is never 'finished' and needs to be adopted towards efficiency and effectiveness.";* - ITG maturity at PI can be regarded as high, despite the medium level of ITG processes. The ITG framework as a whole works very efficiently and effectively and is valued by IT and non-IT staff.

Construct	Rating	Evidence
IT Relatedness	High	- *"The list of our harmonised systems is very long.", "IT infrastructure and IT processes are basically harmonised.", "This year we have five new projects where we aim at cost reduction and complexity reduction.", "Another three harmonisation projects are being conducted with our outsourcing partner.";* - The IT harmonisation strategy was developed over a decade ago. Large consolidation projects were implemented between 1998 and 2008. Hardware is sourced completely from one supplier and the application landscape is entirely built around SAP R/3.
Business Process Relatedness	High	- *"IT at PI is comparable to the machinery in the production industry".* - The business processes at PI are to the largest extent harmonised on the basis of the above named SAP solution. However, it is important to note that the most core processes run only once at the headquarters of the firm.
Absorptive Capacity of IT Department	High	- *"IT staff understands the business processes very well and supports the business departments with the formulation of requirements.", "IT staff is very well respected by non-IT managers".* - The business process knowledge is in many cases residing already in the IT department, or comes from technical suppliers or regulators directly to the IT staff. Thus the absorptive capacity of the IT department is seen as inherently high.

Construct	Rating	Evidence
Business Performance Impact	High	- *"As IT is one of the main cost drivers, it [ITG] led to a massive value add through cost reduction.", "Support and facilitation of central processes [...]", "Many [now automated] business processes like contracting de facto correspond to production processes in the production industry.", "A corporation is a socio-technical system and ITG ensures a frictionless process.", "[IT harmonisation] led to flexibility, risk mitigation, precise cost control and [allowed] a focus on core competencies".* - The IT strategy turnaround and the strict harmonisation and outsourcing of the IT a decade ago flooded the company with capital in an essential moment. What is more, a simultaneous increase in business processes relatedness *"based on standard platforms"* led to sub-additive costs and generated super-additive values in the processes of customer acquisition, consulting and contracting. Following relatedness projects, satisfaction ratings for IT and business processes went up throughout the company.

4.10 OMIKRON

Construct	Rating	Evidence
ITG Structures	Medium	The interviewee reported that an IT strategy and steering committee is in place and operating in close collaboration with a project office since 2006.
ITG Processes	High	A large collection of ITG processes is implemented at OMIKRON: detailed charge back arrangements, COBIT-like processes, a structured portfolio management, documented project governance, budget controls and an ex-post benchmarking of IT projects. SLAs are not implemented according to the CIO.
ITG Relational Mechanisms	High	A number of relational mechanisms like formal and informal meetings are in place. Moreover, the CIO emphasised that the role of numerous business/ IT account managers that are in place is of crucial importance for a collaborative and constructive atmosphere.

Construct	Rating	Evidence
ITG Maturity	Medium	- *"Since 2006 we started to redesign things [ITG] very consciously.", "It started with compliance topics; this was generally driven by the industry [regulation]. [...] Then you get into the topics, grow with the discussion and start linking topics.", "Topics are consciously developed and documented, e.g. project management, resource management, security topics [...]. For two years now cooperative development of IT is documented [...] the way of cooperation is defined and documented.", "These things [ITG mechanisms] get systematically written down and documented, its a manifested process.";* - The ITG at OMIKRON is well developed and encompasses a relatively high number of ITG mechanisms. However, the CIO stated that he still can see a lot of potential for further enhancement of the ITG framework, especially in regard to the governance of applications and business processes.
IT Relatedness	Medium	- *"After having many things outsourced, we back-sourced and harmonised many things.", "The new data centre is running here with our own staff and know-how.", "Many things are moving now on SAP.";* - IT infrastructure, including the data centre and telecommunication hardware, was rebuilt in a harmonised fashion from scratch in 2008 and is operated in-house. The application landscape is still dismembered to large parts, which necessitates many interfaces between applications. However, a harmonisation strategy for applications on the basis of SAP is developed and pursued.

Construct	Rating	Evidence
Business Process Relatedness	Medium	- *"A dark highway, meaning that the customer types in his data, and everything happens automated is the ideal. I know that our competitors already run many processes without manual support, [PI is not there yet].";* - Many business processes are being optimised, integrated and harmonised for a few years now. According to the CIO, business process relatedness is closely linked to the degree of the integration of information technology. Especially the high number of interfaces offers still a lot of potential for optimisation. Like at PI, it is important to note that most of the core-processes run only once at the headquarters.
Absorptive Capacity of IT Department	High	- *"What the production plant in an industrial firm is, is represented by the information technology and the IT department at OMIKRON.", "Every IT expert has to deal with business processes, as IT itself is large proportion of the business process.";* - The absorptive capacity of the IT department is, according to the CIO of OMIKRON, high. This is due to the simple fact that the information technology represents the *"insurance factory of the company"*. He further added: The IT staff is hence fully knowledgeable about all aspects of running business processes.

Construct	Rating	Evidence
Business Performance Impact	Medium	- *"Transparency, transparency, transparency! The opportunity to explain what and why IT is doing things is for me of enormous value.", "Compared to the situation before, we save 5-10% on run-costs", "The integration of the IT into the big picture of the organisation, meaning the deduction for goals out of the firm is a real value that I see resulting from a deliberate governance", "We see the positive impacts in the way the firm works now. Previously it was common to say 'not possible'. Today neither IT nor the business units can say that. They need to explain why certain things are not possible.", "It is about time to market, if you need to program code for a while before you can launch a product, that is a catastrophe.", "With the goal to work more cost efficiently as a firm, then I have to think about my business processes, how can I improve those [...] as a consequence IT has to think about how to design the processes in a way, that they do not need any manual input anymore. [...] Our competitors are ahead in these topics, they have self-running systems already, we need to catch up here.";* - The increase in IT relatedness primarily led to sub-additive costs (the CIO reported 5-10%), but involved as well super-additive values, especially in the form of reduced time to market. However, further super-additive values, especially related to business processes, require a further harmonisation of the application landscape and a decrease in interfaces, according to the CIO.

Bibliography

Ahituv, N., Neumann, S., and Zviran, M. 1989. "Factors Affecting the Policy for Distributing Computing Resources", *MIS Quarterly* (13:4), pp. 389-401.

Alavi, M., and Leidner, D. 2001. "Review: Knowledge Management and Knowledge Management Systems: Conceptual Foundations and Research Issues", *MIS Quarterly* (25:1), pp. 107-136.

Allen, B., and Boynton, A. 1991. "Issues and Opinions Information Architecture: In Search of Efficient Flexibility", *MIS Quarterly* (15:4), pp. 435-445.

Amit, R., and Schoemaker, P. 1993. "Strategic Assets and Organizational Rent", *Strategic Management Journal* (14:1), pp. 33-46.

Ammann, M., Oesch, D., and Schmid, M. 2011. "Corporate Governance and Firm Value: International Evidence", *Journal of Empirical Finance* (18:1), pp. 36-55.

Astley, W., and Fombrun, C. 1983. "Collective Strategy: Social Ecology of Organizational Environments", *Academy of management review* (6:4), pp. 576-587.

Avison, D., and Fitzgerald, G. 2003. *Information Systems Development: Methodologies, Techniques and Tools*, (3rd ed.). Maidenhead: McGraw Hill.

Bain, J. 1956. *Barriers to New Competition*. Cambridge: Harvard University Press.

Bain, J. 1968. *Industrial Organization*, (2nd ed.). New York: John Wiley & Sons.

Banker, R., and Johnston, H. 1995. "An Empirical Study of the Business Value of the U.S. Airlines' Computerized Reservation Systems", *Journal of Organizational Computing* (5:3), pp. 255-275.

Banker, R., and Kauffman, R. 1988. "Strategic Contributions of Information Technology: An Empirical Study of ATM Networks", *Proceedings of the Ninth International Conference on Information Systems*, Minneapolis, Minnesota.

Banker, R., and Kauffman, R. 1991. *Quantifying the Business Value of Information Technology: an Illustration of the 'Business Value Linkage' Framework - Working Paper Series, STERN IS-91-21*. New York: Stern School of Business, New York University.

BARefG. 2007. "Berufsaufsichtsreformgesetz." Bonn: Bundesministerium der Justiz, 03.09.2007, BGBl. I, p. 2178.

Barney, J. 1986a. "Strategic Factor Markets: Expectations, Luck, and Business Strategy", *Management Science* (32:10), pp. 1231-1241.

Barney, J. 1986b. "Types of Competition and the Theory of Strategy: Toward an Integrative Framework", *Academy of Management Review* (11:4), pp. 791-800.

Barney, J. 1991. "Firm Resources and Sustained Competitive Advantage", *Journal of Management* (17:1), pp. 99-120.

Baums, T., and Fraune, C. 1995. "Institutionelle Anleger und Publikumsaktiengesellschaft, Eine empirische Untersuchung", *Die Aktiengesellschaft* (3), pp. 97-112.

Behr, K., Kim, G., and Spafford, G. 2004. *The Visible Ops Handbook: Starting ITIL in 4 Practical Steps*. Eugene: Information Technology Process Institute.

Benbasat, I., Dexter, A., Drury, D., and Goldstein, R. 1984. "A Critque of the Stage Hypothesis: Theory and Empirical Evidence", *Communications of the ACM* (27:5), pp. 476-485.

Benbasat, I., Goldstein, D., and Mead, M. 1987. "The Case Research Strategy in Studies of Information Systems", *MIS Quarterly* (11:3), pp. 369-386.

Berle, A., and Means, G. 1932. *The Modern Corporation and Private Property*. New York: Harcourt.

BetrVG. 1952. "Betriebsverfassungsgesetz." Bonn: Bundesministerium der Justiz, 11.10.1952, BGBl. I, p. 681.

Bharadwaj, A. 2000. "A Resource-Based Perspective on Information Technology Capability and Firm Performance: An Empirical Investigation", *MIS Quarterly* (24:1), pp. 169-196.

Bharadwaj, A., Bharadwaj, S., and Konsynski, B. 1999. "Information Technology Effects on Firm Performance as Measured by Tobin's Q", *Management Science* (45:7), pp. 1008-1024.

Black, J., and Boal, K. 1994. "Strategic Resources: Traits, Configurations and Paths to Sustainable Competitive Advantage", *Strategic Management Journal* (15:S2), pp. 131-148.

Black, S., and Lynch, L. 2001. "How to Compete: The Impact of Workplace Practices and Information Technology on Productivity", *Review of Economics and Statistics* (83:3), pp. 434-445.

Blackburn, R., and Rosen, B. 1993. "Total Quality and Human Resources Management: Lessons Learned from Baldrige Award-Winning Companies", *The Academy of Management Executive* (7:3), pp. 49-66.

Blair, M. 1995. *Ownership and Control: Rethinking Corporate Governance for the Twenty-First Century*. Washington, D.C.: Brookings Institution Press.

Borghoff, U., and Pareschi, R. 1998. *Information Technology for Knowledge Management*. Berlin, Heidelberg, New York: Springer.

Bosson, J., Swann, W., and Pennebaker, J. 2000. "Stalking the Perfect Measure of Implicit Self-Esteem: The Blind Men and the Elephant Revisited?", *Journal of Personality and Social Psychology* (79:4), pp. 631-643.

Botzenhardt, A., Meth, H., and Maedche, A. 2011. "Cross-Functional Integration of Product Management and Product Design in Application Software Development: Exploration of Success Factors", *Proceedings of the 32nd International Conference on Information Systems*, Shanghai.

Boynton, A., Jacobs, G., and Zmud, R. 1992. "Whose Responsibility is IT Management", *Sloan Management Review* (33:4), pp. 32-38.

Boynton, A., and Zmud, R. 1987. "Information Technology Planning in the 1990's: Directions for Practice and Research", *MIS Quarterly* (11:1), pp. 59-71.

Broadbent, M. 2002. "CIO futures - Lead with Effective Governance", *Keynote of the ICA 36th Conference*, Singapore.

Broadbent, M., and Weill, P. 1998. *Leveraging the New Infrastructure - How Market Leaders Capitalize on Information Technology*. Cambridge: Harvard Business School Press.

Brown, A., and Grant, G. 2005. "Framing the Frameworks: A Review of IT Governance Research", *Communications of the AIS* (15), pp. 696-712.

Brown, C. 1997. "Examining the Emergence of Hybrid IS Governance Solutions: Evidence from a Single Case Site", *Information Systems Research* (8:1), pp. 69-94.

Brown, C. 1999. "Horizontal Mechanisms under Differing IS Organization Contexts", *MIS Quarterly* (23:3), pp. 421-454.

Brown, C., and Magill, S. 1994. "Alignment of the IS Functions with the Enterprise Toward a Model of Antecedents", *MIS Quarterly* (18:4), pp. 371-403.

Brown, C., and Magill, S. 1998. "Reconceptualizing the Context-Design Issue for the Information Systems Function", *Organization Science* (9:2), pp. 176-194.

Brown, R., Gatian, A., and Hicks Jr, J. 1995. "Strategic Information Systems and Financial Performance", *Journal of Management Information Systems* (11:4), pp. 215-248.

Brynjolfsson, E. 1993. "The productivity Paradox of Information Technology", *Communications of the ACM* (36:12), p. 77.

Brynjolfsson, E., and Hitt, L. 1995. "Information Technology as a Factor of Production: The Role of Differences Among Firms", *Economics of Innovation and New Technology* (3:4), pp. 183-200.

Brynjolfsson, E., and Hitt, L. 1996. "Paradox lost? Firm-Level Evidence on the Returns to Information Systems Spending", *Management Science* (42:4), pp. 541-558.

Brynjolfsson, E., and Hitt, L. 2000. "Beyond Computation: Information Technology, Organizational Transformation and Business Performance", *The Journal of Economic Perspectives* (14:4), pp. 23-48.

Brynjolfsson, E., and Hitt, L. 2003. "Computing Productivity: Firm-Level Evidence", *Review of Economics and Statistics* (85:4), pp. 793-808.

Brynjolfsson, E., Hitt, L., and Yang, S. 2002. "Intangible Assets: Computers and Organizational Capital", *Brookings Papers on Economic Activity* (1), pp. 137-198.

Brynjolfsson, E., Renshaw, A., and Van Alstyne, M. 1997. "The Matrix of Change", *Sloan Management Review* (38:2), pp. 37-54.

Burlingame, J. 1961. "Information Technology & Decentralization", *Harvard Business Review* (39:6), pp. 121-127.

Byrd, T., Sambamurthy, V., and Zmud, R. 1995. "An Examination of IT Planning in a Large, Diversified Public Organization", *Decision Sciences* (26:1), pp. 49-73.

Callahan, J., Bastos, C., and Keyes, D. 2004. "The Evolution of IT Governance at NB Power," in *Strategies for Information Technology Governance,* W. Van Grembergen (ed.). Hershey: Idea Group Publishing, pp. 343-356.

Campbell, A., and Goold, M. 1998. *Synergy: Why Links Between Business Units Often Fail and How to Make them Work.* Mankato: Capstone Publishing.

Capron, L., and Hulland, J. 1999. "Redeployment of Brands, Sales Forces, and General Marketing Management Expertise Following Horizontal Acquisitions: A Resource-Based View", *The Journal of Marketing* (63:2), pp. 41-54.

Carr, N. 2004. "IT Doesn't Matter", *IEEE Engineering Management Review* (32:1), pp. 24-32.

Castanias, R., and Helfat, C. 1991. "Managerial Resources and Rents", *Journal of Management* (17:1), pp. 155-171.

Cavaye, A. 1996. "Case Study Research: a Multi-Faceted Research Approach for IS", *Information Systems Journal* (6:3), pp. 227-242.

Caves, R.E. 1964. *American Industry: Structure, Conduct, Performance*. New Jersey: Prentice-Hall Englewood Cliffs.

Chalmers, A. 1999. *What is this Thing Called Science?* Brisbane: University of Queensland Press.

Chan, Y., and Huff, S. 1993. "Strategic Information Systems Alignment", *Business Quarterly* (58:1), pp. 51-56.

Chan, Y., Huff, S., Barclay, D., and Copeland, D. 1997. "Business Strategic Orientation, Information Systems Strategic Orientation, and Strategic Alignment", *Information Systems Research* (8:2), pp. 125-150.

Chan, Y., and Reich, B. 2007. "IT Alignment: What Have we Learned?", *Journal of Information Technology* (22:4), pp. 297-315.

Chatterjee, S., and Wernerfelt, B. 1991. "The Link Between Resources and Type of Diversification: Theory and Evidence", *Strategic Management Journal* (12:1), pp. 33-48.

Checkland, P., and Holwell, S. 2005. *Information, Systems and Information Systems*. Weinheim: John Wiley & Sons.

Chen, D. 2010. "Information Systems Strategy: Reconceptualization, Measurement, and Implications", *MIS Quarterly* (34:2), pp. 233-259.

Chew, W., Leonard-Barton, D., and Bohn, R. 1991. "Beating Murphy's law", *Sloan Management Review* (32:3), pp. 5-16.

Chmielewicz, K. 1994. *Forschungskonzeptionen der Wirtschaftswissenschaft*, (3rd ed.). Stuttgart: Schäffer-Poeschel.

Choudhury, V., and Sampler, J. 1997. "Information Specificity and Environmental Scanning: an Economic Perspective", *MIS Quarterly* (21:1), pp. 25-53.

Clark Jr, T. 1992. "Corporate Systems Management: An Overview and Research Perspective", *Communications of the ACM* (35:2), pp. 61-75.

Clemons, E., and Row, M. 1988. "McKesson Drug Company: A Case Study of Economost - A Strategic Information System", *Journal of Management Information Systems* (5:1), pp. 36-50.

Clemons, E., and Row, M. 1991. "Information Technology at Rosenbluth Travel: Competitive Advantage in a Rapidly Growing Global Service Company", *Journal of Management Information Systems* (8:2), pp. 53-79.

Coase, R. 1937. "The Nature of the Firm", *Economica* (4:16), pp. 386-405.

Cohen, W., and Levinthal, D. 1990. "Absorptive Capacity: A New Perspective on Learning and Innovation", *Administrative Science Quarterly* (35:1).

Cole, R. 1998. "Introduction", *California Management Review* (45:3), pp. 15-21.

Conner, K. 1991. "A Historical Comparison of Resource-Based Theory and Five Schools of Thought within Industrial Organization Economics: Do We Have a New Theory of the Firm?", *Journal of management* (17:1), pp. 121-154.

Cooper, B., Watson, H., Wixom, B., and Goodhue, D. 2000. "Data Warehousing Supports Corporate Strategy at First American Corporation", *MIS Quarterly* (24:4), pp. 547-567.

Copeland, D., and McKenney, J. 1988. "Airline Reservations Systems: Lessons from History", *MIS Quarterly* (12:3), pp. 353-370.

COSO. 2004. "Enterprise Risk Management: Integrated Framework" Retrieved 04.12.2012, from http://www.coso.org/ERM-IntegratedFramework.htm

Cournot, A. 1838. *Recherches sur les principes mathématiques de la théorie des richesses*. Paris: Hachette.

Creswell, J. 2007. *Qualitative Inquiry & Research Design: Choosing Among Five Approaches*. Thousand Oaks: Sage Publications.

Cronk, M., and Fitzgerald, E. 1999. "Understanding "IS Business Value": Derivation of Dimensions", *Logistics Information Management* (12:1/2), pp. 40-49.

Cross, J., Earl, M., and Sampler, J. 1997. "Transformation of the IT Function at British Petroleum", *MIS Quarterly* (21:4), pp. 401-423.

Crotty, M. 1998. *The Foundations of Social Research: Meaning and Perspective in the Research Process*. Thousand Oaks: Sage Publications.

Csaszar, F., and Clemons, E. 2006. "Governance of the IT Function", *Proceedings of the 39th Hawaii International Conference on System Sciences*, Hawaii.

Daft, R. 2009. *Organization Theory and Design*. Stamford: South-Western College Pub.

Daily, C., Dalton, D., and Cannella Jr, A. 2003. "Corporate Governance: Decades of Dialogue and Data", *The Academy of Management Review* (28:3), pp. 371-382.

Damianides, M. 2005. "Sarbanes-Oxley and IT Governance: New Guidance on IT Control and Compliance", *Information Systems Management* (22:1), pp. 77-85.

Davis, R., and Thomas, L. 1993. "Direct Estimation of Synergy: A New Approach to the Diversity-Performance Debate", *Management Science* (39:11), pp. 1334-1346.

De Haes, S., and Van Grembergen, W. 2004. "IT Governance and its Mechanisms", *Information Systems Control Journal* (1), pp. 27-33.

De Haes, S., and Van Grembergen, W. 2005. "IT Governance Structures, Processes and Relational Mechanisms: Achieving IT/Business Alignment in a Major Belgian Financial Group", *Proceedings of the 38th Hawaii International Conference on System Sciences*, Hawaii.

De Haes, S., and Van Grembergen, W. 2006. "Information Technology Governance Best Practices in Belgian Organisations", *Proceedings of the 39th Hawaii International Conference on System Sciences*.

De Haes, S., and Van Grembergen, W. 2008a. "Analysing the Relationship Between IT Governance and Business/IT Alignment Maturity", *Proceedings of the 41st Hawaii International Conference on System Sciences*, Hawaii.

De Haes, S., and Van Grembergen, W. 2008b. "An Exploratory Study into the Design of an IT Governance Minimum Baseline Through Delphi Research", *Communications of the AIS* (22:24), pp. 443-458.

De Haes, S., and Van Grembergen, W. 2009. "An exploratory study into IT governance implementations and its impact on business/IT alignment", *Information Systems Management* (26:2).

De Vries, H. 1999. *Standardization*. Boston: Kluwer.

Dedrick, J., Gurbaxani, V., and Kraemer, K. 2003. "Information Technology and Economic Performance: A Critical Review of the Empirical Evidence", *ACM Computing Surveys* (35:1), pp. 1-28.

Dehning, B., and Richardson, V. 2002. "Returns on Investments in Information Technology: A Research Synthesis", *Journal of Information Systems* (16:1), pp. 7-30.

DeLone, W., and McLean, E. 1992. "Information Systems Success: The Quest for the Dependent Variable", *Information Systems Research* (3:1), pp. 60-95.

Dess, G., and Robinson Jr, R. 1984. "Measuring Organizational Performance in the Absence of Objective Measures: The Case of the Privately-Held Firm and Conglomerate Business Unit", *Strategic Management Journal* (5:3), pp. 265-273.

Deutsche Bank Research. 2008. "Aktienkultur in Deutschland lässt auf sich warten" Retrieved 04.12.2012, from http://www.dbresearch.de/PROD/DBR_INTERNET_DE-PROD/PROD0000000000222390.PDF

Dewan, S., and Min, C. 1997. "The Substitution of Information Technology for other Factors of Production: A Firm Level Analysis", *Management Science* (43:12), pp. 1660-1675.

Dibbern, J., Winkler, J., and Heinzl, A. 2008. "Explaining Variations in Client Extra Costs Between Software Projects Offshored to India", *MIS Quarterly* (32:2), pp. 333-366.

Dierickx, I., and Cool, K. 1989. "Asset Stock Accumulation and Sustainability of Competitive Advantage", *Management Science* (35:12), pp. 1504-1511.

Dixon, P., and John, D. 1989. "Technology Issues Facing Corporate Management in the 1990s", *MIS Quarterly* (13:3), pp. 247-255.

Dos Santos, B., Peffers, K., and Mauer, D. 1993. "The Impact of Information Technology Investment Announcements on the Market Value of the Firm", *Information Systems Research* (4:1), pp. 1-23.

DrittelbG. 2004. "Drittelbeteiligungsgesetz." Bonn: Bundesministerium der Justiz, 18.05.2004, BGBl. I, p. 974.

Drucker, P. 2005. *The Effective Executive*. New York: Harper Paperbacks.

Drury, D. 1983. "An Empirical Assessment of the Stages of DP Growth", *MIS Quarterly* (7:2), pp. 59-70.

Dubé, L., and Paré, G. 2003. "Rigor in Information Systems Positivist Case Research: Current Practices, Trends, and Recommendations", *MIS Quarterly* (27:4), pp. 597-636.

Duffy, J. 2002. "IT Governance and Business Value Part 2: Who's Responsible for What", *IDC document* (27807).

Duhan, S., Levy, M., and Powell, P. 2001. "Information Systems Strategies in Knowledge-Based SMEs: The Role of Core Competencies", *European Journal of Information Systems* (10:1), pp. 25-40.

Earl, J. 1993. "Experiences in Strategic Information Systems Planning", *MIS Quarterly* (17:1), pp. 1-24.

EC 43. 2006. "Directive 2006/43/EC of the European Parliament and of the Council of 17 May 2006 on statutory audits of annual accounts and consolidated accounts, amending Council Directives 78/660/EEC and 83/349/EEC and repealing Council Directive 84/253/EEC (Text with EEA relevance)." Luxembourg: Publications Office of the European Union. European Parliament, Council.

Ein-Dor, P., and Segev, E. 1978. "Organizational Context and the Success of Management Information Systems", *Management Science* (24:10), pp. 1064-1077.

Ein-Dor, P., and Segev, E. 1982. "Organizational Context and MIS Structure: Some Empirical Evidence", *MIS Quarterly* (6:3), pp. 55-68.

Eisenhardt, K. 1989a. "Agency Theory: An Assessment and Review", *Academy of Management Review* (14:1), pp. 57-74.

Eisenhardt, K. 1989b. "Building Theories From Case Study Research", *The Academy of Management Review* (14:4), pp. 532-550.

Eisenhardt, K., and Graebner, M. 2007. "Theory Building from Cases: Opportunities and Challenges", *Academy of Management Journal* (50:1), pp. 25-32.

Ethiraj, S., Kale, P., Krishnan, M., and Singh, J. 2005. "Where Do Capabilities Come from and How Do They Matter? A Study in the Software Services Industry", *Strategic Management Journal* (26:1), pp. 25-45.

Farjoun, M. 1994. "Beyond Industry Boundaries: Human Expertise, Diversification and Resource-Related Industry Groups", *Organization Science* (5:2), pp. 185-199.

Fiedler, F. 1964. "A Contingency Model of Leadership Effectiveness", *Advances in Experimental Social Psychology* (1), pp. 149-190.

Francalanci, C., and Galal, H. 1998. "Information Technology and Worker Composition: Determinants of Productivity in the Life Insurance Industry", *MIS Quarterly* (22:2), pp. 227-241.

Frick, B., and Bermig, A. 2011. "Mitbestimmung und Unternehmensperformance: Der Einfluss von Arbeitnehmerver-tretern im Aufsichtsrat auf den Unternehmenswert", *Die Betriebswirtschaft* (71:3), pp. 281-304.

Galbraith, J. 1994. *Competing with Flexible Lateral Organizations*. Boston: Addison-Wesley.

Garrity, J. 1963. "Top Management and Computer Profits", *Harvard Business Review* (41:4), pp. 6-12.

Gartner. 2011. "IT Key Metrics Data 2009" Retrieved 20.01.2011, from http://www.gartner.com/technology/consulting/key_metrics_data.jsp#

Gartner. 2012. "Gartner Says Worldwide IT Spending On Pace to Surpass $3.6 Trillion in 2012" Retrieved 04.08.2012, from http://www.gartner.com/it/page.jsp?id=2074815

GCGC. 2010. "German Corporate Governance Code" Retrieved 04.12.2012, from http://www.corporate-governance-code.de/eng/download/kodex_2010/German-Corporate-Governance-Code-2010.pdf

Gerrity, T., and Rockart, J. 1986. "End-User Computing: Are You a Leader or a Laggard", *Sloan Management Review* (27:4), pp. 25-34.

Gill, A. 2008. "Corporate Governance as Social Responsibility: A Research Agenda", *Berkeley Journal of International Law* (26), pp. 452-477.

Golub, H. 1975. "Organizing Information System Resources: Centralization vs. Decentralization," in *The Information Systems Handbook,* F. McFarlan and R. Nolan (eds.). Homewood: Dow-Jones Irwin, pp. 65-91.

Goold, M., and Luchs, K. 1993. "Why Diversify? Four Decades of Management Thinking", *The Academy of Management Executive* (7:3), pp. 7-25.

Grant, R. 1996a. "Prospering in Dynamically-Competitive Environments: Organizational Capability as Knowledge Integration", *Organization Science* (7:4), pp. 375-387.

Grant, R. 1996b. "Toward a Knowledge-Based Theory of the Firm", *Strategic Management Journal* (17:10), pp. 109-122.

Gregor, S. 2006. "The Nature of Theory in Information Systems", *MIS Quarterly* (30:3), pp. 611-652.

Gresov, C. 1989. "Exploring Fit and Misfit with Multiple Contingencies", *Administrative Science Quarterly* (34:3), pp. 431-453.

Guillemette, M., and Paré, G. 2012. "Toward a New Theory of the Contribution of the IT Function in Organizations", *MIS Quarterly* (36:2), pp. 529-551.

Hambrick, D. 1987. "The Top Management Team: Key to Strategic Success", *California Management Review* (30:1), pp. 8-108.

Hambrick, D., Werder, A., and Zajac, E. 2008. "New Directions in Corporate Governance Research", *Organization Science* (19:3), pp. 381-385.

Hammer, M., and Champy, J. 1993. *Business Process Re-Engineering*. London: Nicholas Brealey.

Hannan, M., and Freeman, J. 1977. "The Population Ecology of Organizations", *American Journal of Sociology* (82:5), pp. 929-964.

Harrison, J., Hitt, M., Hoskisson, R., and Ireland, R. 2001. "Resource Complementarity in Business Combinations: Extending the Logic to Organizational Alliances", *Journal of Management* (27:6), pp. 679-690.

Hayek, F. 1945. "The Use of Knowledge in Society", *The American Economic Review* (35:4), pp. 519-530.

Hayes, R., and Wheelwright, S. 1984. *Restoring our Competitive Edge: Competing Through Manufacturing*. New York: John Wiley & Sons.

Heinrich, L., Heinzl, A., and Riedl, R. 2011. *Wirtschaftsinformatik*. Heidelberg, Dordrecht, London, New York: Springer.

Heinrich, L., and Lehner, F. 2005. *Informationsmanagement: Planung, Überwachung und Steuerung der Informationsinfrastruktur*. München: Oldenbourg Wissenschaftsverlag.

Heinzl, A. 1996. *Die Evolution der betrieblichen DV-Abteilung*. Heidelberg: Physica-Verlag.

Henderson, J., and Venkatraman, N. 1993. "Strategic Alignment: Leveraging Information Technology for Transforming Organizations", *IBM Systems Journal* (32:1), pp. 472-484.

Henderson, R., and Mitchell, W. 1997. "The Interactions of Organizational and Competitive Influences on Strategy and Performance", *Strategic Management Journal* (18:1), pp. 5-14.

Hill, C., and Scudder, G. 2002. "The Use of Electronic Data Interchange for Supply Chain Coordination in the Food Industry", *Journal of Operations Management* (20:4), pp. 375-387.

Hirshleifer, J., Glazer, A., and Hirshleifer, D. 2005. *Price Theory and Applications: Decisions, Markets, and Information*, (7th ed.). Cambridge: Cambridge University Press.

Hitt, L., and Brynjolfsson, E. 1994. "The Three Faces of IT Value: Theory and Evidence", *Proceedings of the 15th International Conference on Information Systems*, Vancouver.

Hitt, L., Wu, D., and Zhou, X. 2002. "Investment in Enterprise Resource Planning: Business Impact and Productivity Measures", *Journal of Management Information Systems* (19:1), pp. 71-98.

Hooley, G., Greenley, G., Cadogan, J., and Fahy, J. 2005. "The Performance Impact of Marketing Resources", *Journal of Business Research* (58:1), pp. 18-27.

Hopper, M. 1990. "Rattling SABRE - New Ways to Compete on Information", *Harvard Business Review* (68:3), pp. 118-125.

Horton, F. 1981. *The Information Management Workbook: IRM Made Simple*. Washington, D.C.: Information Management Press.

Howell, W., and Fleishman, E. 1982. *Human Performance and Productivity*. New Jersey: L. Erlbaum Associates.

Ilinitch, A., and Zeithaml, C. 1995. "Operationalizing and Testing Galbraith's Center of Gravity Theory", *Strategic Management Journal* (16:5), pp. 401-410.

ISACA. 2010. "COBIT 5 Design Exposure Draft" Retrieved 01.07.2011, from www.isaca.org/cobit5exposure

ISO. 2008. "IEC 38500 - Corporate Governance of Information Technology" Retrieved 04.12.2012, from http://www.iso.org/iso/catalogue_detail?csnumber=51639

Itami, H., and Roehl, T. 1991. *Mobilizing Invisible Assets*. Cambridge: Harvard Univ Press.

ITGI. 2003. *Board Briefing on IT Governance*, (2nd ed.). Rolling Meadows: IT Governance Institute.

ITGI. 2007. *Cobit 4.1 Executive Summary and Framework*. Rolling Meadows: IT Governance Institute.

ITGI. 2008. *Val IT Framework*. Rolling Meadows: IT Governance Institute.

Jarvenpaa, S., and Leidner, D. 1998. "An Information Company in Mexico: Extending the Resource-Based View of the Firm to a Developing Country Context", *Information Systems Research* (9:4), pp. 342-361.

Jelinek, M. 1977. "Technology, Organizations, and Contingency", *Academy of Management Review* (2:1), pp. 17-26.

Jensen, M., and Meckling, W. 1976a. "Theory of the Firm: Managerial Behavior, Agency Costs and Ownership Structure", *Journal of Financial Economics* (3:4), pp. 305-360.

Jensen, M., and Meckling, W. 1979. "Rights and Production Functions: An Application to Labor-Managed Firms and Codetermination", *Journal of Business* (52:4), pp. 469-506.

Jensen, M., and Meckling, W. 1995. "Specific and General Knowledge, and Organizational Structure", *Journal of Applied Corporate Finance* (8:2), pp. 4-18.

Jensen, M.C., and Meckling, W.H. 1976b. "Theory of the firm: Managerial behavior, agency costs and ownership structure", *Journal of Financial Economics* (3:4), pp. 305-360.

Johannsen, W., and Goeken, M. 2006. "IT-Governance – Neue Aufgaben des IT-Managements", *HMD – Praxis der Wirtschaftsinformatik* (250:43), pp. 7–20.

John, C., and Harrison, J. 1999. "Manufacturing - Based Relatedness, Synergy, and Coordination", *Strategic Management Journal* (20:2), pp. 129-145.

Jones, C., Ramanau, R., Cross, S., and Healing, G. 2010. "Net Generation or Digital Natives: Is There a Distinct New Generation Entering University?", *Computers & Education* (54:3), pp. 722-732.

Jürgens, U., Rupp, J., and Vitols, K. 2000. "Corporate Governance and Shareholder Value in Deutschland" *Diskussionspapier des WZB FS II 00-202* Retrieved 04.12.2012, from http://bibliothek.wz-berlin.de/pdf/2000/ii00-202.pdf

Kast, F., and Rosenzweig, J. 1972. "General Systems Theory: Applications for Organization and Management", *Academy of Management Journal* (15:4), pp. 447-465.

Katz, A. 1993. "Measuring Technology's Business Value", *Information Systems Management* (10:1), pp. 33-39.

Katz, R. 1974. "Skills of an Effective Administrator", *Harvard Business Review* (52:5), pp. 90-102.

Keen, P. 1981. "Communications in the 21st Century: Telecommunications and Business Policy", *Organizational Dynamics* (10:2), pp. 54-67.

Kerlinger, F., and Lee, H. 1999. *Foundations of Behavioral Research*. Stamford: Wadsworth Publishing.

Kettinger, W., Grover, V., Guha, S., and Segars, A. 1994. "Strategic Information Systems Revisited: A Study in Sustainability and Performance", *MIS Quarterly* (18:1), pp. 31-58.

Kieser, A., and Walgenbach, P. 2010. *Organisation*, (6th ed.). Stuttgart: Schäffler-Poeschel.

King, J. 1983. "Centralized Versus Decentralized Computing: Organizational Considerations and Management Options", *ACM Computing Surveys* (15:4), pp. 319-349.

King, J., and Kraemer, K. 1984. "Evolution and Organizational Information Systems: An Assessment of Nolan's Stage Model", *Communications of the ACM* (27:5), pp. 466-475.

Kirsch, L. 2004. "Deploying Common Systems Globally: The Dynamics of Control", *Information Systems Research* (15:4), pp. 374-395.

Klein, B., and Leffler, K. 1981. "The Role of Price in Guaranteeing Quality", *Journal of Political Economy* (89:4), pp. 615-641.

Kohli, R., and Devaraj, S. 2003. "Measuring Information Technology Payoff: A Meta-Analysis of Structural Variables in Firm-Level Empirical Research", *Information Systems Research* (14:2), pp. 127-145.

KonTraG. 1998. "Gesetz zur Kontrolle und Transparenz im Unternehmensbereich." Bonn: Bundesministerium der Justiz, 27.04.1998, BGBl. I, p. 786.

Korac-Kakabadse, N., and Kakabadse, A. 2001. "IS/IT Governance: Need for an Integrated Model", *Corporate Governance* (1:4), pp. 9-11.

Kraemer, K., Dedrick, J., and Yamashiro, S. 2000. "Refining and Extending the Business Model with Information Technology: Dell Computer Corporation", *Information Society* (16:1), pp. 5-21.

Krcmar, H. 2005. *Informationsmanagement*. Berlin, Heidelberg: Springer.

Kude, T., Dibbern, J., and Heinzl, A. 2012. "Why Do Complementors Participate? An Analysis of Partnership Networks in the Enterprise Software Industry", *IEEE Transactions on Engineering Management* (59:2), pp. 250-265.

Kumar, N., Stern, L., and Anderson, J. 1993. "Conducting Interorganizational Research Using Key Informants", *Academy of Management Journal* (36:6), pp. 1633-1651.

Küpper, H. 2008. *Controlling: Konzeption, Aufgaben und Instrumente*. Stuttgart: Schäffer-Poeschel.

La Belle, A., and Nyce, H. 1987. "Whither the IT Organization", *Sloan Management Review* (28:4), pp. 75-86.

Lazic, M., Groth, M., Schillinger, C., and Heinzl, A. 2011a. "The Impact of IT Governance on Business Performance," in: *Proceedings of the 17th Americas Conference on Information Systems*. Detroit.

Lazic, M., Heinzl, A., and Neff, A. 2011b. "IT Governance Impact Model: How Mature IT Governance Affects Business Performance", *Proceedings of JAIS Theory Development Workshop*, Shanghai.

Lee, A. 1989. "A Scientific Methodology for MIS Case Studies", *MIS Quarterly* (13:1), pp. 33-50.

Lee, J., Juhn, S., and Hwang, K. 2009. "New Development of Advanced ITG Framework", *Proceedings of the 42nd Hawaii International Conference on System Sciences*, Hawaii.

Lee, J., and Kim, Y. 1999. "Effect of Partnership Quality on IS Outsourcing Success: Conceptual Framework and Empirical Validation", *Journal of Management Information Systems* (15:4), pp. 29-61.

Lehr, B., and Lichtenberg, F. 1999. "Information Technology and its Impact on Productivity: Firm-Level Evidence from Government and Private Data Sources", *Canadian Journal of Economics* (32:2), pp. 335-362.

Lentz, C., Gogan, J., and Henderson, J. 2002. "A Comprehensive and Cohesive IT Value Management Capability: Case Studies in the North Amercian Life Insurance Industry", *Proceedings of the 35th Hawaii International Conference on System Sciences*, Hawaii.

Lewis, E., and Millar, G. 2009. "The Viable Governance Model - A Theoretical Model for the Governance of IT", *Proceedings of th 42nd Hawaii International Conference on System Sciences*, Hawaii.

Liang, T., Chiu, Y., Wu, S., and Straub, D. 2011. "The Impact of IT Governance on Organizational Performance," in: *Proceedings of the 17th Americas Conference on Information Systems*. Detroit.

Lichtenberg, F. 1995. "The Output Contributions of Computer Equipment and Personnel: A Firm-Level Analysis", *Economics of Innovation and New Technology* (3:3-4), pp. 201-217.

Liebowitz, S., and Margolis, S. 1995. "Path Dependence, Lock-In, and History", *Journal of Law, Economics, and Organization* (11:1), p. 205.

Lindsey, D., Cheney, P., Kasper, G., and Ives, B. 1990. "TELCOT: An Application of Information Technology for Competitive Advantage in the Cotton Industry", *MIS Quarterly* (14:4), pp. 347-357.

Lippman, S., and Rumelt, R. 1982. "Uncertain Imitability: An Analysis of Interfirm Differences in Efficiency Under Competition", *The Bell Journal of Economics* (13:2), pp. 418-438.

Loh, L., and Venkatraman, N. 1992. "Diffusion of Information Technology Outsourcing: Influence Sources and the Kodak Effect", *Information Systems Research* (3:4), pp. 334-358.

Luftman, J. 1996. *Competing in the Information Age: Strategic Alignment in Practice*. Oxford, New York: Oxford University Press.

Luftman, J. 2000. " Assessing Business - IT Alignment Maturity", *Communications of AIS* (4:14), pp. 1-50.

Luftman, J., and Brier, T. 1999. "Achieving and Sustaining Business - IT Alignment", *California Management Review* (42:1), pp. 109-122.

Luftman, J., Dorociak, J., Kempaiah, R., and Rigoni, E. 2008. "Strategic Alignment Maturity: A Structural Equation Model Validation", *Proceedings of the 14th Americas Conference on Information Systems*, Toronto.

Luftman, J., and Kempaiah, R. 2007. "An Update on Business - IT Alignment: "A Line" Has Been Drawn", *MIS Quarterly Executive* (6:3), pp. 165-177.

Madill, A., Jordan, A., and Shirley, C. 2000. "Objectivity and Reliability in Qualitative Analysis: Realist, Contextualist and Radical Constructionist Epistemologies", *British Journal of Psychology* (91:1), pp. 1-20.

Mallin, C. 2011. *Corporate Governance*, (3rd ed.). Oxford, New York: Oxford University Press.

Mankiw, N.G. 2011. *Principles of Economics*, (6th ed.). Mason: South-Western.

Manrodt, K., and Vitasek, K. 2004. "Global Process Standardization: A Case Study", *Journal of Business Logistics* (25:1), pp. 1-24.

Mason, E. 1939. "Price and Production Policies of Large-Scale Enterprise", *The American Economic Review* (29:1), pp. 61-74.

Mata, F., Fuerst, W., and Barney, J. 1995. "Information Technology and Sustained Competitive Advantage: A Resource-Based Analysis", *MIS Quarterly* (19:4), pp. 487-505.

McAfee, A. 2002. "The Impact of Enterprise Information Technology Adoption on Operational Performance: An Empirical Investigation", *Production and Operations Management* (11:1), pp. 33-53.

Melville, N., Kraemer, K., and Gurbaxani, V. 2004. "Review: Information Technology and Organizational Performance: An Integrative Model of IT Business Value", *MIS Quarterly* (28:2), pp. 283-322.

Merton, R. 1968. *Social Theory and Social Structure*. New York: The Free Press.

Meyer, M., Zarnekow, R., and Kolbe, L. 2003. "IT-Governance - Begriff, Status Quo und Bedeutung", *Wirtschaftsinformatik* (45:4), pp. 445-448.

Miles, M., and Huberman, A. 1994. *Qualitative Data Analysis: An Expanded Sourcebook*. Thousand Oaks: Sage publications.

Milgrom, P., and Roberts, J. 1995. "Complementarities and Fit Strategy, Structure, and Organizational Change in Manufacturing", *Journal of Accounting and Economics* (19:2-3), pp. 179-208.

Mingers, J., Mutch, A., and Willcocks, L. 2011. "Call for Papers, MIS Quarterly Special Issue on Critical Realism in Information Systems Research" Retrieved

09.07.2012, from http://misq.org/skin/frontend/default/misq/pdf/CurrentCalls/CriticalRealism.pdf

MitbestG. 1976. "Gesetz über die Mitbestimmung der Arbeitnehmer." Bonn: Bundesministerium der Justiz, 04.05.1976, BGBl. I, p. 1153.

Monnoyer, E., and Willmott, P. 2005. "What IT Leaders Do: Companies That Rely on IT Governance Systems Alone Will Come Up Short", *McKinsey Quarterly* (August).

MontanMitbestG. 1951. "Montan-Mitbestimmungsgesetz." Bonn: Bundesministerium der Justiz, 21.05.1951, BGBl. I, p. 347.

Mooney, J., Gurbaxani, V., and Kraemer, K. 1996. "A Process Oriented Framework for Assessing the Business Value of Information Technology", *Proceedings of the 16th International Conference on Information Systems*, Amsterdam.

Morrison, C. 1997. "Assessing the Productivity of Information Technology Equipment in U.S. Manufacturing Industries", *Review of Economics and Statistics* (79:3), pp. 471-481.

Mukhopadhyay, T., Kekre, S., and Kalathur, S. 1995. "Business Value of Information Technology: A Study of Electronic Data Interchange", *MIS Quarterly* (19:2), pp. 137-156.

Myers, M., and Avison, D. 1997. "Qualitative Research in Information Systems, MISQ Discovery" Retrieved 04.12.2012, from http://www.qual.auckland.ac.nz/

Nelson, R., and Winter, S. 1982. *An Evolutionary Theory of Economic Change*. Cambridge: Belknap Press.

Newman, J., and Kozar, K. 1994. "A Multimedia Solution to Productivity Gridlock: A Re-Engineered Jewelry Appraisal System at Zale Corporation", *MIS Quarterly* (18:1), pp. 21-30.

Nolan, R., and McFarlan, F. 2005. "Information Technology and the Board of Directors", *Harvard Business Review* (83:10), pp. 96-105.

Nonaka, I. 1994. "A Dynamic Theory of Organizational Knowledge Creation", *Organization Science* (5:1), pp. 14-37.

Nonaka, I., and Takeuchi, H. 1995. *The Knowledge-Creating Company: How Japanese Companies Create the Dynamics of Innovation*. New York, Oxford: Oxford University Press.

Norton, D. 1973. "Information Systems Centralization: The Issues," in *Information Systems Administration,* F. McFarlan, R. Nolan and D. Norton (eds.). New York: Holt Rinehart and Winston, pp. 485-498.

O'Neill, P., and Sohal, A. 1999. "Business Process Reengineering A Review of Recent Literature", *Technovation* (19:9), pp. 571-581.

OECD. 1995. *OECD Economic Surveys: Germany 1995*. Paris: OECD Publishing.

Oechsler, W. 2006. *Personal und Arbeit*. München: Oldenbourg Wissenschaftsverlag.

Oh, W., and Kim, J. 2001. "The Effects of Firm Characteristics on Investor Reaction to IT Investment Announcements", *Proceedings of the 22nd International Conference on Information Systems*, New Orleans.

Olson, M., and Chervany, N. 1980. "The Relationship Between Organizational Characteristics and the Structure of the Information Services Function", *MIS Quarterly* (4:2), pp. 57-68.

Orlikowski, W., and Baroudi, J. 1991. "Studying information technology in Organizations: Research Approaches and Assumptions", *Information Systems Research* (2:1), pp. 1-28.

Österle, H. 1987. "Erfolgsfaktor Informatik - Umsetzung der Informationstechnik in der Unternehmensführung", *Information Management* (2:3), pp. 24-31.

Oxford Dictionaries. 2012a. "governance" Retrieved 17.01.2012, from http://oxford dictionaries.com/definition/governenace

Oxford Dictionaries. 2012b. "inform" Retrieved 17.01.2012, from http://oxford dictionaries.com/definition/inform

Oxford Dictionaries. 2012c. "information" Retrieved 17.01.2012, from http://oxford dictionaries.com/definition/information

Oxford Dictionaries. 2012d. "technology" Retrieved 17.01.2012, from http://oxford dictionaries.com/definition/technology

Oxford Dictionaries. 2012e. "value" Retrieved 17.01.2012, from http://oxford dictionaries.com/definition/value

Palfrey, J., and Gasser, U. 2010. *Born Digital: Understanding the First Generation of Digital Natives*. New York: Basic Books.

Parker, M., Benson, R., and Trainor, H. 1988. *Information Economics: Linking Business Performance to Information Technology*. Englewood Cliffs: Prentice Hall.

Patton, M. 2002. *Qualitative Research and Evaluation Methods*. Thousand Oaks: Sage Publications.

Penrose, E. 1959. *The Theory of the Growth of the Firm*. New York: John Wiley & Sons.

Peppard, J., and Ward, J. 2004. "Beyond Strategic Information Systems: Towards an IS Capability", *Journal of Strategic Information Systems* (13:2), pp. 167-194.

Peteraf, M. 1993. "The Cornerstones of Competitive Advantage: A Resource-Based View," in *Resources, Firms, and Strategies: A Reader in the Resource-Based Perspective,* F. Nicolai (ed.). New York: Oxford University Press, pp. 187-203.

Peterson, R. 2004a. "Crafting Information Technology Governance", *The EDP Audit, Control, and Security Newsletter* (32:6), pp. 1–24.

Peterson, R. 2004b. "Information Strategies and Tactics for Information Technology Governance," in *Strategies for Information Technology Governance,* W. Van Grembergen (ed.). Hershey: Idea Group Publishing, pp. 37-80.

Peterson, R., O'Callaghan, R., and Ribbers, P. 2000. "Information Technology Governance by Design: Investigating Hybrid Configurations and Integration Mechanisms", *Proceedings of the 21st International Conference on Information Systems*, Brisbane.

Porter, M. 1980. *Competitive Strategy*. New York: The Free Press.

Porter, M. 1985. *Competitive Advantage*. New York: Free Press.

Porter, M. 1990. *The Competitive Advantage of Nations*. New York: Free Press.

Porter, M. 1991. "Towards a Dynamic Theory of Strategy", *Strategic Management Journal* (12:S2), pp. 95-117.

Porter, M., and Millar, V. 1985. "How Information Gives You Competitive Advantage", *Harvard Business Review* (63:4), pp. 149-160.

Powell, T., and Dent-Micallef, A. 1997. "Information Technology as Competitive Advantage: The Role of Human, Business, and Technology", *Strategic Management Journal* (18:5), pp. 375-405.

Prahalad, C., and Bettis, R. 1986. "The Dominant Logic: A New Linkage Between Diversity and Performance", *Strategic Management Journal* (7:6), pp. 485-501.

Prensky, M. 2006. "Listen to the Natives", *Educational Leadership* (63:4), pp. 8-13.

Ravichandran, T., and Lertwongsatien, C. 2005. "Effect of Information Systems Resources and Capabilities on Firm Performance: A Resource-Based Perspective", *Journal of Management Information Systems* (21:4), pp. 237-276.

Ravishankar, M., Pan, S., and Leidner, D. 2011. "Examining the Strategic Alignment and Implementation Success of a KMS: A Subculture-Based Multilevel Analysis", *Information Systems Research* (22:1), pp. 39-59.

Ray, G., Barney, J., and Muhanna, W. 2004. "Capabilities, Business Processes, and Competitive Advantage: Choosing the Dependent Variable in Empirical Tests of the Resource-Based View", *Strategic Management Journal* (25:1), pp. 23-37.

Reed, R., and DeFillippi, R. 1990. "Causal Ambiguity, Barriers to Imitation, and Sustainable Competitive Advantage", *Academy of Management Review* (15:1), pp. 88-102.

Reich, B., and Benbasat, I. 1996. "Measuring the Linkage Between Business and Information Technology Objectives", *MIS Quarterly* (20:1), pp. 55-81.

Remenyi, D., Bannister, F., and Money, A. 2007. *The Effective Measurement and Management of ICT Costs and Benefits*, (3rd ed.). Oxford, Burlington: CIMA Publishing, Elsevier.

Rivard, S., Raymond, L., and Verreault, D. 2006. "Resource-Based View and Competitive Strategy: An Integrated Model of the Contribution of Information Technology to Firm Performance", *The Journal of Strategic Information Systems* (15:1), pp. 29-50.

Robins, J., and Wiersema, M. 1995. "A Resource Based Approach to the Multibusiness Firm: Empirical Analysis of Portfolio Interrelationships and Corporate Financial Performance", *Strategic Management Journal* (16:4), pp. 277-299.

Rockart, J. 1988. "The Line Takes the Leadership: IS Management in a Wired Society", *Sloan Management Review* (29:4), pp. 57-64.

Rockart, J., Bullen, C., and Kogan, J. 1979. *The Management of Distributed Processing*. Cambridge: CISR Report 39, Massachusetts Institute of Technology, Sloan School of Managment.

Rockart, J., Earl, M., and Ross, J. 1996. "Eight Imperatives for the New IT Organization", *Sloan Management Review* (38:1), pp. 43-55.

Romano, R. 2005. "The Sarbanes-Oxley Act and the Making of Quack Corporate Governance", *Yale ICF Working Paper No. 05-23, Yale Law Journal* (June 2005).

Ross, J., and Beath, C. 2001. "Beyond the Business Case: New Approaches to IT Investment", *MIT Sloan Management Review* (43:2), pp. 51-59.

Rumelt, R. 1974. *Strategy, Structure and Economic Performance*. Cambridge: Harvard University Press.

Rumelt, R. 1984. "Towards a Strategic Theory of the Firm," in *Competitive Strategic Management,* R. Lamb (ed.). Englewood Cliffs: Prentice Hall, pp. 556 - 570.

Sabherwal, R., and Becerra-Fernandez, I. 2005. "Integrating Specific Knowledge: Insights from the Kennedy Space Center", *IEEE Transactions on Engineering Management* (52:3), pp. 301-315.

Sabherwal, R., and Chan, Y. 2001. "Alignment Between Business and IS Strategies: A Study of Prospectors, Analyzers, and Defenders", *Information Systems Research* (12:1), pp. 11-31.

Sambamurthy, V., and Zmud, R. 1999. "Arrangements for Information Technology Governance: A Theory of Multiple Contingencies", *MIS Quarterly* (23:2), pp. 261-290.

Sambamurthy, V., and Zmud, R. 2000. "Research Commentary: The Organizing Logic for an Enterprise's IT Activities in the Digital Era - A Prognosis of Practice and a Call for Research", *Information Systems Research* (11:2), pp. 105-114.

Sanchez, R. 2004. "Understanding Competence-Based Management: Identifying and Managing Five Modes of Competence", *Journal of Business research* (57:5), pp. 518-532.

Santhanam, R., and Hartono, E. 2003. "Issues in Linking Information Technology Capability to Firm Performance", *MIS Quarterly* (27:1), pp. 125-153.

Sauer, C., and Burn, J. 1997. "The Pathology of Strategic Management," in *Steps to the Future,* C. Sauer and P. Yetton (eds.). San Francisco: Jossey-Bass, pp. 99-112.

Scheer, A. 1988. *Wirtschaftsinformatik*. Heidelberg: Springer.

Scherer, F. 1980. *Industrial Market Structure and Economic Performance*. Boston: Houghton Mifflin.

Schmidt, R. 2003. *Corporate Governance in Germany: An Economic Perspective, CFS Working Paper No. 2003/36*. Frankfurt: Center for Financial Studies an der Johann Wolfgang Goethe-Universität.

Schwarz, A., and Hirschheim, R. 2003. "An Extended Platform Logic Perspective of IT Governance: Managing Perceptions and Activities of IT", *The Journal of Strategic Information Systems* (12:2), pp. 129-166.

Seddon, P. 1997. "A Respecification and Extension of the DeLone and McLean Model of IS Success", *Information Systems Research* (8:3), pp. 240-253.

Sherer, S. 2004. "IS Project Selection: The Role of Strategic Vision and IT Governance", *Proceedings of the 37th Hawaii International Conference on System Sciences*, Hawaii.

Shleifer, A., and Vishny, R. 1997. "A Survey of Corporate Governance", *Journal of Finance* (52:2), pp. 737-783.

Siegel, D. 1997. "The Impact of Computers on Manufacturing Productivity Growth: A Multiple-Indicators, Multiple-Causes Approach", *Review of Economics and Statistics* (79:1), pp. 68-77.

Silva, E., and Chaix, Y. 2008. "Business and IT Governance Alignment Simulation Essay on a Business Process and IT Service Model", *Proceedings of the 41st Hawaii International Conference on System Sciences*, Hawaii.

Silverman, B. 1999. "Technological Resources and the Direction of Corporate Diversification: Toward an Integration of the Resource-Based View and Transaction Cost Economics", *Management Science* (45:8), pp. 1109-1124.

Silvius, A. 2006. "Does ROI Matter? Insights Into the True Business Value of IT", *The Electronic Journal Information Systems Evaluation* (9:2), pp. 93–104.

Simonsson, M., and Johnson, P. 2006. *Defining IT Governance - A Consolidation of Literature - EARP Working Paper MS103*. Stockholm: Department of Industrial Information and Control Systems, Royal Insitute of Technology.

Smith, A. 1776. *An Inquiry Into the Nature and Causes of the Wealth of Nations*. London: W. Strahan and T. Cadell.

Smith, G. 2006. *Straight to the Top: Becoming a World-class CIO*. Hoboken: John Wiley & Sons.

Soh, C., and Markus, M. 1995. "How IT Creates Business Value: A Process Theory Synthesis", *Proceedings of the 16th International Conference on Information Systems*, Amsterdam.

Solow, R. 1987. "We'd Better Watch Out", *New York Times Book Review* (12th of July, 1987), p. 36.

SOX. 2002. "PUBLIC LAW 107 - 204 - SARBANES-OXLEY ACT OF 2002." Washington: U.S. Government Printing Office.

Spanos, Y., and Lioukas, S. 2001. "An Examination Into the Causal Logic of Rent Generation: Contrasting Porter's Competitive Strategy Framework and the Resource Based Perspective", *Strategic Management Journal* (22:10), pp. 907-934.

Spender, J. 1996a. "Making Knowledge the Basis of a Dynamic Theory of the Firm", *Strategic Management Journal* (17:S2), pp. 45-62.

Spender, J. 1996b. "Organizational Knowledge, Learning and Memory: Three Concepts in Search of a Theory", *Journal of Organizational Change Management* (9:1), pp. 63-78.

Stone, E. 1978. *Research Methods in Organizational Behavior*. Pacific Palisades: Goodyear Pub. Co.

Strassmann, P. 1990. *The Business Value of Computers*. New Canaan: The Information Economic Press.

Straub, D., Boudreau, M., and Gefen, D. 2004. "Validation Guidelines for IS Positivist Research", *Communications of the Association for Information Systems* (13:24), pp. 380-427.

Streeck, W., and Hoepner, M. 2003. *Alle Macht dem Markt? Fallstudien zur Abwicklung der Deutschland AG*. Frankfurt, New York: Campus.

Szilagyi, A., Wallace, M., and Ivancevich, J. 1980. *Organizational Behavior and Performance*. Pacific Palisades: Goodyear Pub. Co.

Szyperski, N., and Eschenröder, G. 1983. "Information-Resource-Management," in *Management Betrieblicher Informationsverarbeitung,* R. Kay (ed.). München: Oldenburg.

Tanriverdi, H. 2005. "Information Technology Relatedness, Knowledge Management Capability, and Performance of Multibusiness Firms", *MIS Quarterly* (29:2), pp. 311-334.

Tanriverdi, H. 2006. "Performance Effects of Information Technology Synergies in Multibusiness Firms", *MIS Quarterly* (30:1), pp. 57-77.

Tanriverdi, H., and Venkatraman, N. 2005. "Knowledge Relatedness and the Performance of Multibusiness Firms", *Strategic Management Journal* (26:2), pp. 97-119.

Tatsiopoulos, I., Ponis, S., Hadzilias, E., and Panayiotou, N. 2002. "Realization of the Virtual Enterprise Paradigm in the Clothing Industry Through e-Business Technology", *Production and Operations Management* (11:4), pp. 516-530.

Tavakolian, H. 1987. *A study of the Relationship Between the Degree of User Control Over Information Systems Functions and the Overall Strategies of Organizations*. Atlanta: Georgia State University, Ph. D. Thesis.

Tavakolian, H. 1989. "Linking the Information Technology Structure with Organizational Competitive Strategy: A Survey", *MIS Quarterly* (13:3), pp. 309-317.

Teece, D. 1982. "Towards an Economic Theory of the Multiproduct Firm", *Journal of Economic Behavior & Organization* (3:1), pp. 39-63.

Teece, D., Pisano, G., and Shuen, A. 1997. "Dynamic Capabilities and Strategic Management", *Strategic Management Journal* (18:7), pp. 509-533.

Teubner, A., and Feller, T. 2008. "Informationstechnologie, Governance und Compliance", *Wirtschaftsinformatik* (50:5), pp. 400-407.

Thompson, J., and Bates, F. 1957. "Technology, Organization, and Administration", *Administrative Science Quarterly* (2:3), pp. 325-343.

Tirole. 2000. *Corporate Governance - Center for Economic Institutions - Working Paper Series 2000-1*. Tokyo: Institute of Economic Research, Hitotsubashi University.

Turban, E., and Volonino, L. 2008. *Information Technology for Management: Advancing Sustainable, Profitable Business Growth*, (6th ed.). New York: John Wiley & Sons.

Turnbull, S. 1997. "Corporate governance: its scope, concerns and theories", *Corporate Governance* (5:4), pp. 180-205.

Van Grembergen, W. 2000. "The balanced scorecard and IT governance", *Information Systems Control Journal* (2:1).

Van Grembergen, W. 2001. *Information technology evaluation methods & management*. Idea Group Pub.

Van Grembergen, W. 2002. "Introduction to the Minitrack IT Governance and Its Mechanisms", *Proceedings of the 35th Hawaii International Conference on System Sciences*, Hawaii.

Van Grembergen, W. 2004. *Strategies for Information Technology Governance*. Hershey, London: IgI Global.

Van Grembergen, W., and De Haes, S. 2005. "Measuring and Improving IT Governance Through the Balanced Scorecard", *Information Systems Control Journal* (2).

Van Grembergen, W., De Haes, S., and Guldentops, E. 2004. *Structures, processes and relational mechanisms for IT governance*. Hershey: IGI Global.

Van Grembergen, W., De Haes, S., and Van Brempt, H. 2007. "Prioritising and Linking Business and IT Goals in the Financial Sector").

Venkatraman, N. 1989. "Strategic orientation of business enterprises: The construct, dimensionality, and measurement", *Management Science* (35:8), pp. 942-962.

Venkatraman, N. 1997. "Beyond outsourcing: managing IT resources as a value center", *Sloan Management Review* (38:3), pp. 51-64.

Venkatraman, N., and Ramanujam, V. 1986. "Measurement of business performance in strategy research: A comparison of approaches", *Academy of management review* (11:4), pp. 801-814.

Von Simson, E. 1995. "The recentralization of IT", *Computerworld* (29:51), pp. 1–5.

Von Simson, E.M. 1990. "The centrally decentralized IS organization", *Harvard Business Review* (68:4), pp. 158-162.

Wade, M., and Hulland, J. 2004. "Review: The resource-based view and information systems research: Review, extension, and suggestions for future research", *MIS Quarterly* (28:1), pp. 107-142.

Ward, J., and Peppard, J. 2002. *Strategic planning for information systems*. Wiley.

Wastell, D.G., White, P., and Kawalek, P. 1994. "A methodology for business process redesign: experiences and issues", *The Journal of Strategic Information Systems* (3:1), pp. 23-40.

Webb, P., Pollard, C., and Ridley, G. 2006. "Attempting to Define IT Governance: Wisdom or Folly?": IEEE, p. 194a.

Weber, R. 2004. "Editor's comments: the rhetoric of positivism versus interpretivism: a personal view", *MIS Quarterly* (28:1), pp. iii-xii.

Weill, P. 1992. "The relationship between investment in information technology and firm performance: A study of the valve manufacturing sector", *Information Systems Research* (3:4), pp. 307-333.

Weill, P. 2004. "Don't just lead, govern: How top-performing firms govern IT", *MISQ Executive* (3:1).

Weill, P., Broadbent, M., and Subramani, M. 2002. "IT Infrastructure for Strategic Agility", *MIT Sloan Management Review* (44:1), pp. 57-65.

Weill, P., and Olson, M. 1989. "An assessment of the contingency theory of management information systems", *Journal of Management Information Systems*), pp. 59-85.

Weill, P., and Ross, J.W. 2004. *IT Governance: How Top Performers Manage IT Decision Rights for Superior Results*. Boston, MA: Harvard Business School Press.

Weill, P., and Woodham, R. 2002. *Don't Just Lead, Govern: Implementing Effective IT Governance - MIT Sloan Working Paper No. 4237-02*. Cambridge: Massachusetts Institute of Technology, Sloan School of Management.

Wenger, E., and Kaserer, C. 1998. "German banks and corporate governance: A critical view", *Comparative Corporate Governance - The State of the Art and Emerging Research*), pp. 499-536.

Wentges, P. 2002. *Corporate Governance und Stakeholder-Ansatz: Implikationen für die betriebliche Finanzwirtschaft*. Duv.

Wernerfelt, B. 1984. "A resource-based view of the firm", *Strategic Management Journal* (5:2), pp. 171-180.

Wetherbe, J. 1988. "The MIS Conundrum—Centralization or Decentralization", *Chief Financial Officer USA*).

Wheelock, A.R. 1982. "Service Center or Profit Center?", *Datamation* (28:5), pp. 167-176.

Wiggers, P., Kok, H., and De Boer-de Wit, M. 2004. *IT performance management*. Butterworth-Heinemann.

Wiggins, R.R., and Ruefli, T.W. 2002. "Sustained competitive advantage: Temporal dynamics and the incidence and persistence of superior economic performance", *Organization science*), pp. 82-105.

Williams, M.L., and Frolick, M.N. 2001. "The evolution of EDI for competitive advantage: The FedEx case", *Information Systems Management* (18:2), pp. 47-53.

Williamson, O.E. 1975. *Markets and hierarchies: analysis and antitrust implications: a study in the economics of internal organization*. Free Press New York.

Windolf, P., and Beyer, J. 1995. "Kooperativer Kapitalismus. Unternehmensverflechtungen im internationalen Vergleich", *Kölner Zeitschrift für Soziologie und Sozialpsychologie* (47:1), pp. 1-36.

Winter, R., and Fischer, R. 2007. "Essential layers, artifacts, and dependencies of enterprise architecture", *Journal of Enterprise Architecture* (3:2), pp. 7-18.

Wollnik, M. 1988. "Ein Referenzmodell des Informationsmanagements", *Information Management* (3:3), pp. 34-43.

Worthen, B. 2007. "The IT Factor: Tech Staff's Bigger Role", *Wall Street Journal*).

Wüllenweber, K., Beimborn, D., Weitzel, T., and König, W. 2008. "The impact of process standardization on business process outsourcing success", *Information Systems Frontiers* (10:2), pp. 211-224.

Yin, R. 2009. *Case study research: Design and methods*. Thousand Oaks: Sage Publications.

Zachman, J.A. 1987. "A framework for information systems architecture", *IBM systems Journal* (26:3), pp. 276-292.

Zmud, R., Boynton, A., and Jacobs, G. 1986. "The information economy: A new perspective for effective information systems management", *ACM SIGMIS Database* (18:1), pp. 17-23.

ENTSCHEIDUNGSUNTERSTÜTZUNG FÜR ÖKONOMISCHE PROBLEME

Herausgegeben von Christian Becker, Wolfgang Gaul, Armin Heinzl, Alexander Mädche und Martin Schader

Band 1 Ingo Böckenholt: Mehrdimensionale Skalierung qualitativer Daten. Ein Instrument zur Unterstützung von Marketingentscheidungen. 1989.

Band 2 Jürgen Joseph: Arbeitswissenschaftliche Aspekte der betrieblichen Einführung neuer Technologien am Beispiel von Computer Aided Design (CAD). Felduntersuchung zur Ermittlung arbeitswissenschaftlicher Empfehlungen für die Einführung neuer Technologien. 1990.

Band 3 Eva Schönfelder: Entwicklung eines Verfahrens zur Bewertung von Schichtsystemen nach arbeitswissenschaftlichen Kriterien. 1992.

Band 4 Michael Bargl: Akzeptanz und Effizienz computergestützter Dispositionssysteme in der Transportwirtschaft. Empirische Studien zur Implementierungsforschung von Entscheidungsunterstützungssystemen am Beispiel computergestützter Tourenplanungssysteme. 1994.

Band 5 Reinhold Decker: Analyse und Simulation des Kaufverhaltens auf Konsumgütermärkten. Konzeption eines modell- und wissensorientierten Systems zur Auswertung von Paneldaten. 1994.

Band 6 Wolfgang Gaul / Martin Schader (Hrsg.): Wissensbasierte Marketing-Datenanalyse. Das WIMDAS-Projekt. 1994.

Band 7 Daniel Baier: Konzipierung und Realisierung einer Unterstützung des kombinierten Einsatzes von Methoden bei der Positionierungsanalyse. 1994.

Band 8 Ulrich Lutz: Preispolitik im internationalen Marketing und westeuropäische Integration. 1994.

Band 9 Kirsten Petersen: Design eines Courseware-Entwicklungssystems für den computerunterstützten universitären Unterricht. CULLIS-Teilprojekt I. 1996.

Band 10 Stefan Neumann: Einsatz von Interactive Video im computerunterstützten universitären Unterricht. CULLIS Teilprojekt II. 1996.

Band 11 Eberhard Aust: Simultane Conjointanalyse, Benefitsegmentierung, Produktlinien- und Preisgestaltung. 1996.

Band 12 Peter Heydebreck: Technologische Verflechtung. Ein Instrument zum Erreichen von Produkt- und Prozeßinnovationserfolg. 1996.

Band 13 Michael Pesch: Effiziente Verkaufsplanung im Investitionsgütermarketing. 1997.

Band 14 Frank Wartenberg: Entscheidungsunterstützung im persönlichen Verkauf. 1997.

Band 15 Thomas Lechler: Erfolgsfaktoren des Projektmanagements. 1997.

Band 16 Alexandre Saad: Anbahnung und Erfolg von europäischen kooperativen F&E-Projekten. Eine empirische Analyse anhand von ESPRIT-Projekten. 1998.

Band 17 Michael Löffler: Integrierte Preisoptimierung. 1999.

Band 18 Frank Säuberlich: KDD und Data Mining als Hilfsmittel zur Entscheidungsunterstützung. 2000.

INFORMATIONSTECHNOLOGIE UND ÖKONOMIE

(Neuer Reihentitel ab Band 19)

Band 19 Rainer Kiel: Dialog-gesteuerte Regelsysteme. Definition, Eigenschaften und Anwendungen. 2001.

Band 20 Axel Korthaus: Komponentenbasierte Entwicklung computergestützter betrieblicher Informationssysteme. 2001.

Band 21 Markus Aleksy: Entwicklung einer komponentenbasierten Architektur zur Implementierung paralleler Anwendungen mittels CORBA. Mit Beispielen aus den Wirtschaftswissenschaften. 2003.

Band 22 Michael Zapf: Flexible Kundeninteraktionsprozesse im Communication Center. 2003.

Band 23 Yvonne Staack: Kundenbindung im eBusiness. Eine kausalanalytische Untersuchung der Determinanten, Dimensionen und Verhaltenskonsequenzen der Kundenbindung im Online-Shopping und Online-Brokerage. 2004.

Band 24 Lars Schmidt-Thieme: Assoziationsregel-Algorithmen für Daten mit komplexer Strutkur. Mit Anwendungen im Web Mining. 2003.

Band 25 Stefan Hocke: Flexibilitätsmanagement in der Logistik. Systemtheoretische Fundierung und Simulation logistischer Gestaltungsparameter. 2004.

Band 26 Viktor Jung: Markteintrittsgestaltung neugegründeter Unternehmen. Situationsspezifische und erfolgsbezogene Analyse. 2004.

Band 27 Lars Brehm: Postimplementierungsphase von ERP-Systemen in Unternehmen. Organisatorische Gestaltung und kritische Erfolgsfaktoren. 2004.

Band 28 Ralf Gitzel: Model-Driven Software Development Using a Metamodel-Based Extension Mechanism for UML. 2006.

Band 29 Bernd Stauß: Optimale Gestaltung von Auswahlmenüs und deren Verwendung im Variantenmanagement. 2006.

Band 30 Nils Schumacher: EDI via XML. Potentiale und Strategien für global orientierte kleine und mittlere Unternehmen. 2007.

Band 31 Christian Cuske: Quantifizierung operationeller Technologierisiken bei Kreditinstituten. Eine Ontologie-zentrierte Vorgehensweise im Spannungsfeld bankinterner und aufsichtsrechtlicher Sichtweise. 2007.

Band 32 Matthias Merz: Konzeptioneller Entwurf und prototypische Implementierung einer Sicherheitsarchitektur für die Java Data Objects-Spezifikation. 2008.

Band 33 Tobias Hildenbrand: Improving Traceability in Distributed Collaborative Software Development. A Design Science Approach. 2008.

Band 34 Karen H. L. Tso-Sutter: Towards Metadata-Aware Algorithms for Recommender Systems. 2010.

Band 35 Thomas Schoberth: Eine Längsschnittstudie der Kommunikationsaktivität in virtuellen Gemeinschaften. 2010.

Band 36 Nima Mazloumi: Entwurf eines Refernzmodells und Frameworks zur Erstellung hybrider Lehr- und Lernszenarien. Mit Fallbeispielen aus der Betriebswirtschaftslehre und der Wirtschaftsinformatik. 2010.

Band 37 Anja Zöller: Effizienzanalyse grundlegender Gestaltungsgrößen der OP-Organisation. 2010.

Band 38 Jessica Katharina Winkler: International Entry Mode Choices of Software Firms. An Analysis of Product-Specific Determinants. 2009.

Band 39 Martin J. Lafleur: *Loyalty Profiling*. Erfolgsdimensionen und Modellansätze eines effizienten und effektiven Customer Relationship Management. 2010.

Band 40 Ingo Ott: Effizientes Prozessmanagement im öffentlichen Dienst. 2010.

Band 41 Stefan Seedorf: Ontologie-gestützte Entwicklung komponentenbasierter Anwendungssysteme. Ein wissensbasiertes Informationssystem zur Unterstützung der Entwicklung und Wartung von Geschäftskomponenten (KompIS). 2010.

Band 42 Dominic Gastes: Erhebungsprozesse und Konsistenzanforderungen im Analytic Hierarchy Process (AHP). 2011.

Band 43 *erscheint in Kürze*

Band 44 Olaf Thiele: Informationsvisualisierungen auf mobilen Endgeräten zur Unterstützung des betrieblichen Datenmanagements. 2011.

Band 45 Krisztian Antal Buza: Fusion Methods for Time-Series Classification. 2011.

Band 46 Thomas Kude: The Coordination of Inter-Organizational Networks in the Enterprise Software Industry. The Perspective of Complementors. 2012.

Band 47 Alexandra Rebecca Klages: Clusteranalyse für Netzwerke. 2012.

Band 48 Christian Thum: Enabling Lightweight Real-time Collaboration. 2012.

Band 49 Miroslav Lazic: The Impact of Information Technology Governance on Business Performance. 2013.

www.peterlang.de

FSC
www.fsc.org
MIX
Papier | Fördert gute Waldnutzung
FSC® C083411

Kolibri 360 GmbH
Ferdinand-Jühlke-Straße 7
99095 Erfurt, Deutschland
produktsicherheit@kolibri360.de